SELECTED WRITINGS OF ALFRED H. MENDES

Selected Writings of

ALFRED H. MENDES

Edited by Michèle Levy

THE UNIVERSITY OF THE WEST INDIES PRESS

Jamaica • Barbados • Trinidad and Tobago

The University of the West Indies Press
7A Gibraltar Hall Road, Mona
Kingston 7, Jamaica
www.uwipress.com

A catalogue record of this book is available from the
National Library of Jamaica.

ISBN: 978-976-640-322-5

Cover illustration: Boscoe Holder, *Straw Hat* (1943).
Courtesy of 101 Art Gallery, Port of Spain, Trinidad and Tobago.

Book and cover design by Robert Harris

Set in Scala 10/14 x 27

Printed in the United States of America.

For my grandchildren
Justine and Cameron Anderson
Sebastian and Tobias Levy

and

In memory of Frank Schirmacher

CONTENTS

2. SHORT STORIES

3. JOURNALISM

4. LETTERS

FOREWORD

THIS IS THE FOURTH COLLECTION of the writings of the Trinidadian author Alfred H. Mendes that I have edited. The previous books include two anthologies of his short stories, dating mainly from the 1920s and 1930s, and his autobiography, which was written in the mid- to late 1970s.

Though fragmented and unfinished, Mendes's autobiography does cover considerable ground in filling out the successive stages of his life. It also shares some of his most private thoughts and formative experiences with the reader. In this latest selection of his work, which includes some of his early excursions into poetry, the significant period of his fiction and the journalism, especially of the 1940s, I am attempting to support Mendes's memories by supplying evidence of his creative development and further insights into his character as they are manifested in the trends and preoccupations of his earlier writing.

This does not mean that a reader of *Selected Writings* need rush off to read Mendes's autobiography beforehand. The pieces selected here are certainly fine enough to stand on their own, with the support of the notes for historical references and the occasional obscurity. Rather, the slant I have identified reflects my own increasing perception of the life and work of Alfred Mendes as an integrated whole. So I apologize in advance if frequent referrals to pertinent chapters in the autobiography should cause distraction to the reader.

I became interested in researching Mendes's life and work purely as a result of serendipity: my son, then a student in London, met Mendes's granddaughter there, and began to go out with her. A chance enquiry from me turned up the information that boxes of her grandfather's stories and correspondence were waiting patiently to be discovered by the right person. I subsequently met other members of the family, who were all incredibly helpful, and supportive of my suggestion that we try to publish a collection of the short stories initially, followed by the autobiography. Like me, they felt that it was time that Mendes was recognized properly for his writing, rather than being relegated to a brief mention or a footnote in history books.

One of my greatest pleasures in working on Mendes has been getting to know members of his lively and gifted family socially over the years. The friendships which developed have been further enhanced by the marriage of my son Bruce and Bianca Mendes in April 2000. Their sons, my grandsons Sebastian and Tobias, are also Alfred H. Mendes's great-grandchildren. Their place in the dedication of this book both connects our families permanently and symbolizes the completion of more than one metaphorical journey.

I had previously read Mendes's two published – and surviving – novels, *Pitch Lake* and *Black Fauns*, and his stories in the *Beacon*, and had been impressed by the tremendous energy which I detected behind the words. A growing feeling of familiarity with his subject-matter crystallized when I acquired editorial control of his "boxes" and was able to read more deeply among his huge output of short stories. As a small child, born in the United Kingdom but growing up in colonial Jamaica, I had encountered situations and attitudes which at the time I was too young to understand, but which made me uneasy and often unhappy. In Mendes's stories about life in colonial Trinidad I have found mirror-reflections of much of my own experience, and with the wry wisdom of hindsight, explanations for those early discomforts. So, in addition to a scholar's appreciation of his work, I owe my author a deeply personal debt of gratitude.

This subjective aspect in my response has almost certainly determined my approach in presenting Mendes's work. My interest is in the historical perspective, the window opening onto the life of colonial Trinidad, both intellectual and everyday. I would like to think that showing Mendes's importance as a recorder and interpreter of former times could assist today's West Indian students, born two or three decades after their countries acquired political independence in the 1960s, to make better informed sense of their past. In Derek Walcott's haunting phrase, Alfred Mendes is "witness to the early morning".

Another of the rewards of my research has been to locate "lost" stories, and occasionally to stumble upon pieces of writing that Mendes himself had forgotten, in "little" magazines published in the 1920s and 1930s. Every researcher dreams of discovering the ultimate cache of unknown, unpublished writing. I continue to hope that copies of the seven novels which Mendes burned in New York City during an emotional crisis before returning to Trinidad in 1940, may surface at some point in someone's attic. The quality and very different concerns of *Pitch Lake* and *Black Fauns* suggest that he would have been highly influential in the development of the West Indian novel had those manuscripts survived.

Fortunately, however, enough of his literary output exists for his readers to obtain a vivid sense of Mendes's surroundings and of the fierce anti-colonialism which drove his writing. There is more than enough material for contemporary scholars to sink their teeth into, Mendes's early use of Trinidadian Creole being only one such area, and his subtle exploration of gender another. The extent and variety of his interests and the accessibility of his writing should attract a permanent general readership among West Indians curious about their shared past, and how it connects with their present, however that may differ from island to island.

In a letter to Mendes and his wife Ellen, thanking them for hospitality in their Barbados home, George Lamming wrote affectionately:

> My Dear Alfy,
>
> I would like very much to let you know what a great joy it was for me to see you again, and to find you in such exuberance of spirit. Entertaining as ever, you have carried the joys and adversities of a long life with grace and courage. I wish you continuing delight in your eightieth year and hope you will be with us forever. In an important sense your work will make this so.
>
> (9 November 1977)

It is my own modest hope that this collection of Alfred H. Mendes's writings will help to ensure that Lamming's prediction proves true.

ACKNOWLEDGEMENTS

GRATEFUL THANKS TO MARK PEREIRA and Ilka Hilton-Clarke of 101 Art Gallery, Port of Spain, Trinidad, for all of their help to me when I was researching paintings by Trinidadian artists of the 1940s.

As ever, thanks to the highly professional team at the University of the West Indies Press for guiding this collection of Alfred H. Mendes's writings into its final form.

And as ever, thanks to Jennifer Thompson, my invaluable typist, for her efficiency and the patient care which she took with a challenging manuscript.

Without the support of Mendes's family there would have been no publications. I shall always be grateful to them for taking a chance on me all those years ago, when I told them that I thought I could find a publisher for Mendes's writings, with a great deal more confidence than market evidence to that date could justify. Loads of love for Pennie Mendes, Jason and Gill Mendes, Bianca and Bruce Levy, and Zoe and Christophe Defert for contributions which make them truly a part of this book's publication.

Finally, for my own dear family, all of whom have encouraged and believed in me over the years, my fondest love always.

INTRODUCTION

ALFRED HUBERT MENDES (1897–1991) was born in Port of Spain, Trinidad, the eldest child of Portuguese Creole parents. His father, Alfred senior, was a provision merchant who later became a successful businessman, with interests that stretched from the traditional selling of onions and potatoes to the acquisition of cocoa, citrus, sugar and tonka bean estates and an alpargata factory in Trinidad, and a coconut estate in Tobago. As Mendes senior's business ventures prospered, the family moved from the working-class area of Belmont to middle-class neighbourhoods in Port of Spain, and settled eventually in a large house on Stanmore Avenue near the Queen's Park Savannah.

Alfred Mendes senior and his wife Isabella Jardine had four sons and a daughter. Isabella Mendes died of consumption in 1911, and a year later her husband remarried and had a fifth son with his second wife. This second marriage seems to have been difficult for his eldest son to deal with,[1] and in 1912 Mendes senior took the decision to send him to school in England.

In Trinidad, Alfred H. Mendes was educated at the prestigious Queen's Royal College in Port of Spain, where they still have a record of his later wartime service. In England he was sent to Hitchin Grammar School near Letchworth in Hertfordshire, and settled down to make friends and discover in himself a passion for reading and writing. Had the Great War not broken out in 1914, Mendes would have completed his education at Hitchin and almost certainly gone on to university, and perhaps his writing career would have taken a completely different track. But his father, panicking over the hostilities in Europe, brought him back to Trinidad in 1915.[2]

A trip to France with his tutor just as war broke out may have encouraged a desire in Mendes to play an active part in the conflict. Once back home, he promptly enlisted in the Merchants' and Planters' Contingents of Trinidad, and sailed back to Britain. From there he was sent to the Belgian Front, where he fought as an infantryman with the King's Royal Rifles. He distinguished himself in battle, while enduring all the horrors of trench warfare, and was only sent back to Britain before the war ended because, while snatching a quick nap in a foxhole, he had inhaled the poisonous mustard gas used as a weapon by the enemy. He spent several months in hospital, and before returning to Trinidad in 1919, he was awarded the Military Medal for bravery in the field by the British government.

An autobiographical story, "Over the Top",[3] included in this collection, describes in harrowing detail the attack by British forces on a German position. There is no indication as to when it was actually written, but the urgency in the prose and use of the present tense lend it an immediacy which the war chapters in his autobiography,[4] written in the mid-1970s as part of a contemplative retrospect of his life, do not possess. Both pieces of writing, however, emphasize a point that is important for understanding the turn that his writing would later take: the camaraderie he experienced with working-class British soldiers or "Tommies" and the respect which he felt for their sturdy independence were ultimately to influence him in his choice of predominantly working-class or peasant characters for his novels and short fiction.

In 1919, after his return to Trinidad, Mendes met and married his first wife, Jessie Rodriguez. They had a son, Alfred John, a year later, but Jessie died tragically of pneumonia in 1921, while pregnant with their second child. A second marriage, to Juanita Gouveia, "Nita", in 1922, proved to be an error of judgement on both sides, and within a few years the couple separated.

In Trinidad, while working in his father's many businesses, Mendes poured all his spare time and energy into the intellectual life of the colony. Somewhere in the early 1920s he met C.L.R. James, who was then a master at the Queen's Royal College, and later, Ralph de Boissière and Albert Gomes, and a vibrant group of artists, writers and intellectuals developed. They met regularly to exchange ideas, especially at Mendes's house on Richmond Street. He had amassed a large collection of books and gramophone records, which all were at liberty to borrow. The letters of James to Mendes during this period reflect something of the ferment of their interaction. In their old age, each writer was to testify to the importance of the other in establishing a Trinidad-based literature.[5]

A number of small magazines and journals were published during the 1920s, including the *Trinidad Presbyterian*, which Mendes published in and helped edit; the *Quarterly Magazine of the Richmond Street Literary and Debating Association*, edited by W.H. Dolly; and the *Quarterly Magazine*, edited by Austin M. Nolte. Together, James and Mendes edited *Trinidad* 1, no. 1 (1929), and *Trinidad* 1, no. 2 (1930), in an attempt to raise some money for James.[6] *Trinidad* 1, no. 1, which published James's barrack-yard story "Triumph", caused considerable controversy among its readers because of the shift of interest to poor Trinidadian women living in a tenement, coupled with the use of Creole as the medium for expression.[7] *Trinidad* 1, no. 2, was less disturbing, but is noteworthy today for Mendes's "Commentary", in which he works out for himself the kind of writing which he intends to pursue. "Commentary" is included in the journalism section of this book because it was written at a strategic point in Mendes's development.

The two issues of *Trinidad* were literary in focus. The *Beacon*, edited by Albert Gomes and published every month from 1931 to 1933, offered greater scope to its contributors, while cementing the artistic and literary side of the movement. It was a radical, left-leaning publication, and its writers united in centring on Trinidad's working and peasant classes as the subjects of their fiction.

Mendes himself identified the Russian Revolution of 1917, and his wartime combat experiences shared with working-class soldiers from the north of England (see above) as formative influences in his creative development. It was a short step to apply these sympathies to colonial Trinidad, where he perceived a society in urgent need of transforming, based as it was on social injustice and hypocrisy, and administered by a foreign power.

While working in his father's businesses, Mendes travelled frequently to rural areas, where he encountered a different form of social structuring in the organization of the cocoa, sugar, citrus, coconut and tonka bean plantations owned by his father, which was tied to the agricultural year. In Port of Spain the provision store at 52 South Quay brought him in contact with porters, cartermen, small commission agents, and clerks, all of whom were incorporated into the stories which he was writing nightly, after he returned from work. His father also owned a factory which made alpargatas, a type of cloth sandal, and there Mendes met an attractive but feckless young man named Septimus Louhar, whom he used as a model for his story "Sweetman",[8] even giving his protagonist the name "Seppy". Louhar sued him for libel in October

1932 and won his case. Mendes's father, who had to pay the costs, was furious, and Mendes himself emerged from the experience badly shaken, and with a lifelong dread of courts of law. For subsequent publications he changed his character's name to "Maxie", and thereafter studiously avoided offering any potentially libellous material for publication.[9]

During the same period the colonial administration proposed a bill to allow divorce to be made legal in Trinidad, thereby provoking a storm of reaction from Trinidad's Catholic community. The ensuing debate, both in and outside of the council chamber, polarized the island into factions for and against, from 1931 until the passing of the bill on 1 January 1933. Mendes, whose estranged wife Nita was a Catholic, had been raised as a Presbyterian despite having a Catholic mother, and with a vested interest in seeing it passed, enthusiastically supported the bill. Ironically, despite his anti-colonial sentiments, he ranged himself firmly on the side of the administration, obviously as the lesser of two evils. He wrote letters to the newspapers,[10] made early morning sorties to put up posters in the streets of Port of Spain, and delivered himself of a blistering diatribe against the Catholic Church in the shape of an article published in the *Guardian*. The article, "Revolt", is included in this collection. Trinidad's Catholics were outraged, and the controversy became so bitter that the governor, Sir Alfred Claud Hollis, suggested to Mendes senior that he might be wise to ship his son out of the island for a time until things cooled down, as the Catholic faction was considering a lawsuit for blasphemy. Mendes took the advice and went to Grenada, where he stayed for about six weeks until the bill was passed.[11]

Although James and Mendes had had some short stories published abroad – James's story "La Divina Pastora" had been published in the English *Saturday Review* in 1927, the first foreign publication for the group, and Mendes's and Algernon "Pope" Wharton's joint effort "Lai John" in the *London Mercury* in 1929 – both writers appear to have decided at roughly the same time that if they wished to make a career out of their writing, they needed to find a climate more sympathetic to intellectual goals. James migrated to England in February 1932, and Mendes moved to New York in October 1933, at the same time that the *Beacon* folded from chronic lack of funding.

Mendes remained a committed West Indian throughout his long life, but his experiences of school in England and fighting on the Belgian front gave him a sense of the world outside of Trinidad, with its great metropolitan centres. He understood that sometimes a writer needed to be away from his roots, the better to translate them into his work; and that the pain of that separation could be the price one had to pay for clarity of vision. In this respect he and his friends and colleagues C.L.R. James and Ralph de Boissière, who later migrated to Australia, were forerunners of the waves of writers from the former British West Indies who moved to Europe and the United States in the succeeding decades of the twentieth century.

Alfred Mendes stayed in New York City for seven years, intending to hone his craft as a writer, and hopeful of finding new outlets for publishing his work. Possessed of enormous energy and gregarious by nature, he moved in all of the literary and intellectual circles that flourished in New York City at the time.[12] Among his particular friends were the writers Malcolm Lowry, William Saroyan, Benjamin Appel and Dorothy McLeary, and among the writers of the Harlem Renaissance, Harold Jackman, Countee Cullen, Dorothy West, and the Jamaican Claude McKay. His novels *Pitch Lake* and *Black Fauns* were published in Britain in 1934 and 1935 respectively, and he also published several short stories in American magazines and journals. America, however, was then in the grip of a recession, and although Mendes worked for a time in the US government's Federal Writers' Project, part of the Works Progress Administration, and indeed turned his hand to whatever came his way (including selling vacuum cleaners from door to door), his financial position became increasingly precarious. Marriage to his third wife, Ellen Perachini, in 1938, and the birth of their son Peter in 1939, eventually drove him to ask his father for financial assistance in moving his young family to Trinidad.

This period in Mendes's life was traumatic for a number of reasons. He had been forced to go on welfare; his application to become an American citizen had been rejected on "moral" grounds (the federal government did not recognize his Mexican divorce from Nita); he was unable to make a decent living from his writing; and the responsibilities involved in caring for his wife and son, combined to bring about a nervous breakdown, during the course of which he burned the manuscripts of seven unpublished novels as an apparent farewell to his art.[13] The quality of the two published novels and the short stories suggests that these lost works would have made an incalculably valuable contribution to his known *oeuvre*.

Back in Trinidad, Mendes threw himself once more into every aspect of life there. He was once again working in his father's businesses, but far from giving up literary and intellectual pursuits, he became a member of the Public Library Committee, and began writing on a steady basis for the *Guardian*. He published, and republished, a few of his stories in the *Sunday Guardian*, but the decade of the 1940s is particularly associated with the articles which he wrote as arts critic for the *Guardian*. He wrote about Trinidad's artists and sculptors, the theatre, Beryl McBurnie and the "Little Carib", and pieces on Trinidad's annual Carnival, for which he and his wife Ellen acted as judges for many years.

Mendes also briefly associated himself with politics as a founding member of Jack Kelshall's left-wing United Front party.[14] As a dogged anti-colonialist, he found himself in a conflict of loyalties when he went to work for the colonial government in 1946 as accountant, Harbour and Wharves. He did well in the job, however, and in 1949 was appointed deputy general manager of the Port Services Department. In 1955 he became general manager of the Port Services Department, but was not suited by nature to the political manoeuvring which accompanied the more prominent position. He retired from the post in 1957, and once more worked with his father until 1966, when he joined the Singer Sewing Machine Company as personnel and industrial relations manager. He worked very happily with Singer, travelling extensively on business throughout the West Indies, and editing the in-house publication *Trinidad Singer*, for which he also wrote editorials, stories and the occasional bit of verse. He retired from Singer in 1972.

In the same year the University of the West Indies conferred the honorary degree of doctor of letters upon Alfred Mendes, for his contribution to the development of West Indian Literature. At this time, he and Ellen retired to Barbados, where in 1975 Mendes embarked upon his final piece of writing, his autobiography. He was already elderly, and lacked the energy to complete the project. Despite the gaps, however, it is a remarkable record of the life of an extraordinary West Indian, who wrote always from the perspective of an informed and enlightened insider.

For their remaining years, Mendes and Ellen lived contentedly in Barbados, welcoming family and friends, and visitors like John La Rose and George Lamming to their home. Unhappily, Mendes, like his father, became senile for the last four years of his life. He died on 21 August 1991, six months after his wife, and is buried with her in Christ Church Cemetery, Christ Church, Barbados.

Writing

Alfred Mendes was an incredibly driven and prolific writer. In all, he wrote nine novels and at least ninety, possibly as many as a hundred short stories, many of which he reworked two or three times.[15] He wrote volumes of letters to family and friends, other writers, the *Port of Spain Gazette*, and especially the *Trinidad Guardian*, and, invaluable for a future researcher, kept many of his drafts as well as the recipients' responses. This has enabled the publication of the early letters of C.L.R. James to Mendes, which cast a fascinating light on the interaction of the two writers, and bear out much that both have said in interviews about that early period.

A quick survey of publication dates suggests that Mendes's early writing interests fall into roughly three categories in three successive periods: poetry in the early 1920s; fiction in the mid-1920s until 1940; and journalism in the decade 1940–1950. The distinction is useful as a starting-point for a discussion of his development as a writer, but needs qualification. Mendes wrote stories as well as poems in the early 1920s. By the time the *Beacon* appeared in March 1931, his interest was clearly in fiction: his first novel, *Pitch Lake*, had been completed, in addition to a great number of short stories, which he apparently wrote often on a nightly basis. Despite his obvious confidence in prose as medium, though, he continued to write poems. By 1931 their focus had shifted from personal concerns and responses to the natural beauty of Trinidad's landscape to an outward-looking awareness of social injustices suffered by its peoples, which manifested itself in sometimes strident poems of protest. He never lost his love of the natural world, however. Alongside the protest poems in the *Beacon* are love poems which use the land or seascape as their frame of reference. And some of his finest short stories: "Boodhoo", "Malvina's Nennen" and "Colour" (*The Man Who Ran Away*), which set out to expose social and sexual hypocrisies, draw heavily on the beauties of nature, whether simply to establish a setting, or for structural purposes of irony and contrast.

At the same time that Mendes was feeling his way in poetry and prose fiction in the mid-1920s, he was writing a series of critical and biographical pieces for the *Trinidad Presbyterian*, a monthly magazine put out by the Presbyterian Church in Trinidad. His choice of poets reveals the poetic influences which he drew upon for his early poems: great writers of the past like Dante and Milton, the Romantics, W.B. Yeats, and poets of the late nineteenth and early twentieth centuries. His early rhymed poems are steeped in romantic imagery, florid language, and reverence for things medieval, and in fact show many of the traits of the worn-out Victorianism which he castigates and rejects in his "Commentary" (April 1930). Comparison of "A Commentary" with the piece which he wrote for the *Trinidad Presbyterian*, "Contemporary Poetry and Poets" (May 1926) is instructive in that it shows how far he has progressed from the preoccupations of his first three anthologies: *Three Poems* (1924), *Spare Moments* (1924) and *The Wages of Sin and Other Poems* (1925), with titles such as "The Ballade of Love and Life", "Ode to My Native Land" and "The Faithfulness of Sir Christamond" (the last named written when he was fifteen years old), titles which speak to his early allegiances. The disdain he shows for the work of the great modernist T.S. Eliot in "Contemporary Poetry and Poets" – "From the dung-heap a croaking blackbird tunes its throat" – and for others who employ free verse in place of rhyme has disappeared by the time he is writing the anti-colonialist "Government House", "Social Worker", "Wedding" and "Last Night I Saw Arthur". His anti-war poems "Warmonger", "Boy Scout" and "Cadet Corps", fuelled by his own revulsion against the carnage of the trenches, are better suited to free verse than to the ballads, sonnets and rigid stanzas of his early poems. The adoption of free verse, with its closeness to everyday prose and consequently a more naturalistic effect, as his preferred vehicle signals the point at which Mendes's poetry catches up with his present.

THE POEMS

In selecting poems for this anthology I have tried to include those with which I think Mendes would have been comfortable. He came to despise his early verse as pretentious and derivative, and he made it his business to buy all copies of his published collections from Trinidad's bookshops and to burn them, so that he would not be embarrassed by their being read. While it has to be said that the juvenilia suffer from forced and clumsy rhymes and faded subject-matter, the long poem *The Poet's Quest* (1927) points to a shift in interest and concentration, its quest theme reflecting Mendes's own intellectual journey to find his subject-matter as well as his poetic voice.

Between 1926 and 1927 Mendes published several short poems and sonnets in the *Trinidad Guardian*. These are largely descriptive: "New Year's Eve, 1925", "March – Evening in My Garden", "August Song", "September Butterflies", "October Savannah", "Gold". He also published in the *Trinidad Presbyterian* a few of the poems which he had anthologized in *Three Poems*, *Spare Moments* and *The Wages of Sin*. Some titles are: "The Coming of Christ", "The Mystic Tale of Gwendoline", "The Misanthropist", "Rasselas", "Love Betrayed" and "Satan's Boasts". Most of them are of the longer narrative type. Long poems would probably not have been welcomed by the *Guardian*'s editor, but Mendes was free to write whatever he chose for these three little books because he published them himself. His liking for long narratives is evident in *The Poet's Quest*, published by Heath Cranton, London, which runs to eighty-eight pages. The poem describes a voyage undertaken by a poet to escape a decaying old world (Europe) and to find a new, uncontaminated world with a resident "goddess of the isle" (Trinidad). There is one copy of *The Poet's Quest* in the British Library, which has been microfilmed and is available to researchers for copying. The other three books, because of Mendes's bonfire, are extremely difficult to find.

Mendes does not seem to have written verse during his New York period 1933–1940, nor in the ensuing decade after his return to Trinidad. While working with Singer from 1966 to 1972 he wrote occasional whimsical verses about needles and sewing-machines and Singer salesmen, which he published in *Trinidad Singer*. His final serious use of the medium was in the nine sonnets which he wrote for Rowena Scott in 1970.[16] These took the form of a poetic exercise in the Shakespearian manner with Rowena, then nineteen, as the inspiration. Though deeply personal, they involve great public themes such as youth and age, love and time, art and death, and taken together they constitute a writer's meditation on the ageing self. And they lead inevitably into his last great prose work, the autobiography.

Readers interested in Mendes's poetry may wish to read more of his work in the *Beacon*. Most of the original issues have probably disappeared or disintegrated with the years, but the Kraus Reprint of the *Beacon* (1977) may be accessed through libraries. It has proved an invaluable source for my own research, and I hope that the editors of the Kraus Reprint will forgive my pointing out an error in their very helpful listing of Mendes's writings. A short poem "The Spanish Galleon" (I. 12. 11) credited to Mendes was in fact written by his son Alfred J. (John) Mendes, who was then aged eleven. The mistake is easily made. Mendes's father, Alfred Mendes senior, established the tradition of naming the eldest Mendes son Alfred. Although the tradition does not go beyond Alfred John's son, two of Alfred H. Mendes's grandsons have given their sons the name as a second name. So the continuity has been re-established.

A number of themes in Mendes's poems find fuller treatment in his stories. "Malvina's Nennen" treats the idea in "Cadet Corps" and "Boy Scout", that "responsible" authorities carry a huge burden of blame for encouraging young men to go to war and death; "Over the Top" describes the experience of battle in bloody detail; "Bert and Betty Briggs – English" (*Pablo's Fandango*) examines the situations outlined in "Government House Book"; "Boodhoo" and "Malvina's Nennen" treat sexual hypocrisy as dealt with in "Wedding", "Last Night I Saw Arthur" and "Governor's Gardens". The constraints of time and space imposed by poetry that he did not self-publish disappear with his prose fiction. In his short stories he was able to develop the ideas outlined in his poems at a more leisurely pace, and to show their effects through rounded human characters.

FICTION

Alfred Mendes consistently maintained in interviews and letters to friends that the short story was his real love. In the absence of the seven novels in manuscript that he burned in New York, his reputation as a creative writer rests heavily on his short fiction, with his two published novels, *Pitch Lake* and *Black Fauns*, as indicators of the influential novelist which he might have been. Since the greatest volume of his surviving work is in his short stories, an anthology of his writings must always include a proportionate number of these. However, there are connections to be made between some of the short stories and the "lost" novels as he described them.

Mendes stated that of the seven novels which he destroyed, one was the sequel to *Black Fauns*, a real loss as the latter ends on a note of high drama, but with the fate of tragic Martha, who murders her rival Mamitz, left suspended. It represented an experiment in writing for the author, a deliberate attempt to move away from the linear approach of *Pitch Lake* to a cyclical movement of the narrative, and the loss of its sequel, which might have completed the experiment as well as tying up the loose ends in the plot, is particularly distressing.

Correspondence from Mendes's New York period shows that he was thinking about this sequel at the time that *Black Fauns* was in production. A letter of 12 July 1935 from the writer Millen Brand asks Mendes how his novel is going, and Mendes himself wrote to Ellen c. 1936, while still living in Baldwin, Long Island, to say that his London publisher Duckworth wanted to publish his "new novel" in the spring. "But that's completely out of the question. If I am to have it ready for the fall of 1937 I must get started on it right away. *I must*, I MUST!"

Mendes published three extracts from *Black Fauns* in the *West Indian Review*: "Miriam", "Ethelrida and Some Others" and "White Man's Magic".[17] They are chapters in the novel, lifted as complete episodes in themselves with only a little tinkering, and published as short stories. He seems to have done the same with some of the burnt novels. "Beti" (*The Man Who Ran Away*) was published first in the *Trinidad Singer* as "An Ironic Sales Story", but seems to have been a fragment of one of the novels entitled *Beti*, which Mendes said was "a love story set in the East Indian community".[18] "In a Restaurant", with its abrupt ending, may have been lifted from another novel which Mendes claimed was based on a love affair which he had had with a young girl of eighteen from one of Trinidad's "best" families.[19] It is reproduced in this collection along with another apparent fragment of a novel: "A Day of Sorrow".

"A Day of Sorrow" had been written by June 1928.[20] It is mentioned by Mendes's close friend, the Trinidadian artist Hugh Stollmeyer, in a letter to the former unfortunately dated only "Monday Night". Since it mentions stories published in the *Beacon* and especially "Colour", which was published over a period of four months in 1933, it is safe to assume that the letter was written late in 1933. Mendes had sent a number of his stories and a novel to Stollmeyer for his opinion, and the letter details Stollmeyer's responses. He mentions "A Day of Sorrow", but says that the effect is lessened for him by his having read the novel, of which it seems to be a fragment.

The remaining novels Mendes stated had been about his family, one of them about his grandfather opening the provision shop on what was then known as the Almond Walk.[21] The novel which Hugh Stollmeyer had read is almost certainly one of these, though whether it is a fictionalized account of his own mother's death or that of another family member will probably never be known. I think it worthwhile to reproduce a shortened version of Stollmeyer's long critique, not only for his deeply subjective response to the novel, but for what it implies about the quality of the friendship between artist and writer.

> As to the novel . . . it upset me terribly. I wept! . . . In my opinion it is a splendid piece of writing. The emotion is delicate without being the least bit sentimental . . . and parts of it struck me as being quite lovely poetry in prose. I also liked the

> mourning-poem in it. It moved me like hell . . . That poem and the little passage
> about "The Flamboyante tree that grew in our yard" I took the liberty of copying
> . . . to me it is a short "Ave Maria" as a symbol and prelude to the longer "Ave
> Maria" that was to come of the mother's death and the mourning . . . your book
> is a very emotional work . . . it is very splendid, and it will be highly surprising
> should it not get the praise from foreign (and more worthy critics than I) which I
> feel is due to it.

Mendes mentions sending a collection of his short stories to Duckworth
while living in New York,[22] but nothing more has ever been heard about it. I
myself made some enquiries from the publisher, but was told that Duckworth
had had a fire in its warehouse that had destroyed all manuscripts and records
from that early period, so there is no means of verifying Mendes's assertion.
After his return to Trinidad in 1940 he published odd stories in the *Trinidad
Guardian*, in the Barbadian journal *Bim*, and in anthologies of Caribbean writing in the 1970s, but despite his earnest desire to have a collection of his stories
printed, nothing happened until 1983 when, at the request of John La Rose of
New Beacon Books, Mendes put together a selection of short stories. It was
never published, possibly because of controversy over who should write the
introduction, possibly because La Rose was overstretched and felt that the market at the time would not be receptive to a collection of short stories. Mendes
himself had been prevailed upon to write an introduction, but he was by then
eighty-six, and his memories of people, dates and events were beginning to be
confused. Although there are some useful insights in his handwritten introduction to his manuscript, which he called *A Pattern of People*, there are too
many inaccuracies for it to be published in complete form.

I did not feel, at the time when I was thinking about publishing Mendes's
writings, that his selection was the best one for the market in 1998, when
Pablo's Fandango and Other Stories came out. In both *Pablo's Fandango* and *The
Man Who Ran Away and Other Stories* I have mixed previously published with
unpublished stories, of which there are still a great many. With the publication
of this selection, most of the stories in *A Pattern of People* will have been
published.

Mendes listed the following stories for *A Pattern of People*: "Sweetman", "On
the Seventh Day", "My Mother was Left Alone", "A Little Cargo", "Afternoon
in Trinidad", "Pablo's Fandango", "A Life", "Lulu Gets Married", "Torrid
Zone", "The Larsons at Home", "Snapshots", "Malvina's Nennen", "Marie and

Rampatia", "And Then the Hurricane Came", "Her Chinaman's Way", "Colour" and "Five Dollars' Worth of Flesh". He had originally tried to narrow the list down to fourteen, but these are the stories in the manuscript of *A Pattern of People*. He seems also to have considered "The Hen" for his collection, as the typescript is numbered within the sequence he used for the title above.

With the publication of this anthology, the only stories which remain on Mendes's list are "On the Seventh Day", which had been published earlier,[23] and two unpublished stories, "The Larsons at Home" and "My Mother Was Left Alone". "On the Seventh Day" is a reworking of the plot of "The Good Sloop Grenville Lass" (*Pablo's Fandango*). "The Larsons at Home" is a story about an American family with whom Mendes boarded for a time in New York.[24] And "My Mother Was Left Alone" is a story about a widow with a teenaged daughter who resents her mother's entertaining an admirer. The story is set in Trinidad and may be a re-imagining of thirteen-year-old Alfred Mendes's own resentment over his father's remarriage fifteen months after the death of his mother Isabella.

When picking the stories for this anthology I have followed my earlier rules and mixed published with unpublished. I have also tried for as varied a selection of interests as possible. So there is a war story ("Over the Top"); a cricketing story ("News"); a courtroom story ("The Hen"); a story of childhood ("Scapular"); two stories believed to be fragments of lost novels ("A Day of Sorrow" and "In a Restaurant"); two stories about middle-class aspirations and follies ("At the Ball" and "Snapshots"); two autobiographical stories ("Introspection" and "Torrid Zone"), into which category also fall "Gold Beans" and possibly "A Day of Sorrow"; two stories about the struggles to exist of poor working-class women ("A Life" and "Five Dollars' Worth of Flesh"); a story of working-class characters set partly in a dance hall and partly at sea, with the illegal opium trade as background ("A Little Cargo"); a very short story set in Trinidad's commercial district about an embarrassing blunder ("Faux Pas"); and finally, a story which is not really a story at all, though it contains several stories within its framework, but is more of an autobiographical, journalistic piece like "Orinoco Interlude" (*Pablo's Fandango*): "Gold Beans", about, among other things, cocoa.

JOURNALISM

Although Mendes's most fruitful period of journalism was the 1940s, when he was writing for the *Trinidad Guardian* on at least a weekly basis, he did write a number of articles and reviews for local journals as well as the *Guardian* before he left for New York City in October 1933. In 1926 he was commissioned by the editor of the *Trinidad Presbyterian*, the Reverend Gilbert Earle, to write a series of *Pen Portraits* for the publication, and later to assist in editing the magazine. He edited *Trinidad* 1, no. 1 (December 1929), and *Trinidad* 1, no. 2 (April 1930), with C.L.R. James, contributing his own "A Commentary" to the second issue, and wrote some of the editorials for the *Beacon* when Albert Gomes launched the monthly journal in March 1931. For the *Guardian* he wrote letters and articles on topical issues, and the occasional review.

It is interesting to compare the earlier pieces with those that Mendes wrote after his New York period, upon his return to Trinidad. The nature of the writing for which he was paid while working with the Works Progress Administration: a guide to Long Island, to which he contributed along with other writers in the project, and the brochure for the New York State Exhibition Building at the World's Fair of 1939, for which he was solely responsible, helped to broaden his scope and discipline his style, which can be diffuse. The constant interaction and discussions with other writers, often by letter, and the competition for publication forced him to think more carefully about what he had written, with the result that his style post New York, though still inclined to be discursive, is noticeably crisper and more focused. His concerns remain the same, however, and the enthusiasm and vigour with which he tackles his subjects are unabated.

Mendes's journalism – and public speaking – made him a byword in his own time. Everyone in Trinidad knew him, and he knew everyone, and took a profound interest in their lives and problems. His journalism afforded him an outlet for his own philosophy of life. He was able to formulate his ideas about culture, the arts, and what made a man a human being, and in the process, reveal himself with honesty, clarity and generosity. Anson Gonzales wrote in reference to Mendes's *Autobiography*: "A passionate, creative, talented, energetic and romantic creature was he – in life and death."[25] I hope that my selection of Mendes's writings will bring an extra dimension to the man depicted in the autobiography, and encourage the appreciation which both the man and his work deserve.

NOTES

1. Alfred H. Mendes, *The Autobiography of Alfred H. Mendes*, ed. Michèle Levy (Kingston: University of the West Indies Press, 2002), 27.
2. Ibid., 41–42.
3. *Beacon* 1, no. 2 (1931).
4. Mendes, *Autobiography*, 41–65.
5. James in an interview with Daryl Cumber Dance, in *New World Adams. Conversations with Contemporary West Indian Writers*, ed. Daryl Cumber Dance (Leeds: Peepal Tree, 1992), 110–19. Mendes, *Autobiography* 72.
6. Mendes, *Autobiography*, 76. See also Letters, this volume.
7. *Trinidad Sunday Guardian*, 22 December 1929, published a highly critical review of *Trinidad* 1, no. 1, on its front page. The writer, James Belmont, seems to have objected primarily to the "recurring vulgarities" in the stories.
8. *Beacon* 1, no. 7 (1931). Also published in *This Quarter* (Paris) 5, no. 2 (December 1932), ed. Edward Titus; *Story* (New York) 5, no. 2 (October 1934), ed. W. Burnett and M. Foley; Reinhard W. Sander with Peter Ayers, eds., *From Trinidad with Love: An Anthology of Early West Indian Writing* (London: Hodder and Stoughton; New York: Holmes and Meier, 1978); Michèle Levy, ed., *Pablo's Fandango and Other Stories* (London: Addison, Wesley and Longman, 1997).
9. Mendes, *Autobiography*, 78–79.
10. One such letter, "What Is All the Din About? Divorce Is Not a Tax", is included in the journalism section of this book The furore over the divorce legislation is described in Mendes, *Autobiography*, 77, 79–80.
11. The long story "Colour", published in *Beacon* 2, no. 12; 3, no. 1; 3, no. 2; 3, no. 3; and 3, no. 4 (1933), was most probably written during this period. It is set in Grenada.
12. Mendes, *Autobiography*, chapters 8, 9 and 10.
13. Ibid., 130–31.
14. Ibid., 132–33
15. For a list of Mendes's short fiction, see ibid., 181–87.
16. Mendes, *Autobiography*, 159–63.
17. "Miriam" appeared in *West Indian Review* 3, no. 6 (February 1937); "White Man's Magic" in 3, no. 7 (March 1937); "Ethelrida and Some Others" in 3, no. 9 (May 1937).
18. In a videotaped interview with Bruce Paddington, c. 1983.
19. Mendes, *Autobiography*, 82.
20. See the letter from Hulbert Footner to Mendes in this volume.

21. Interview with Bruce Paddington. See also Mendes, *Autobiography*, xxvii–xxviii.

22. *Trinidadian* (October–November 1934): 31.

23. In *Manchester Guardian*, 29 November 1932; *Trinidadian* 3, no. 4 (August–September 1935), ed. Ronald John Williams (Port of Spain: Caribbean Publishing Co.); and *Challenge* 1, no. 4 (January 1936), ed. Dorothy West (New York).

24. Mendes, *Autobiography*, 112–16.

25. *Generation Lion* 1, no. 2, *The Legacy Issue* (2006–7), ed. Rubadiri Victor (Port of Spain: Passionfruit Publishing), 63.

PUBLICATION DETAILS

The first ten poems reproduced here have never, as far as I have been able to discover, been published. The first four were probably written earlier than the other six, when Mendes was still experimenting with rhyme, and looking to the flora and fauna of Trinidad for his inspiration. The following six, in free verse and all with a strong anti-colonial thrust, seem to me to be contemporary with the poems which he published in the *Beacon* (edited by Albert Gomes, Port of Spain).

The eight published poems came out in successive issues of the *Beacon* as follows: "Stars", 1, no. 3 (1931); "Governor's Gardens", 1, no. 5 (1931); "Tropic Night", 1, no. 10 (1932); "Nostalgia", "Lines" and "Lines Written at Sea for Monica", 2, no. 9 (1933); "The Moon Laughs" and "Cadet Corps", 2, no. 11 (1933).

The fifteen stories in this collection have been arranged in roughly chronological sequence. The four unpublished stories, "A Day of Sorrow", "In a Restaurant", "A Little Cargo" and "Gold Beans", have been grouped where internal dating or content suggests that they fit into the corpus of Mendes's writing (discussed in the introduction).

Of the eleven published stories, "Introspection" came out in the *Trinidad Presbyterian Magazine* 24, no. 6 (June 1927) (edited by Reverend Gilbert Earle, Port of Spain); "The Hen", "Torrid Zone" and "At the Ball" (by "Hubert Alfred") were published in the *Quarterly Magazine* (edited by Austin M. Nolte, Port of Spain) in issues for December 1927, December 1928 and December 1932 respectively. "Torrid Zone" was also published in *Bim* 3, no. 11 (1949) (edited by John Wickham, Barbados). And "At the Ball" was also published in *Forum Quarterly*, September 1933 (edited by Frank Mitchell, Barbados). "Faux

Pas" and "News" were published in *Trinidad* 1, no. 1 (December 1929) (edited by Alfred H. Mendes and C.L.R. James, Port of Spain) and *Trinidad* 1, no. 2 (April 1930) (edited by Alfred H. Mendes, Port of Spain) respectively. "Faux Pas" was republished, with slight alterations, as "In Port of Spain" in the *Manchester Guardian* (3 July 1931) and in the *Little Magazine*, September–October 1934 (edited by Philip Lahr, New York). And "News" was republished as "Cricket News", again with slight alterations, in *Trinidad Guardian Weekly*, 12 October 1947 (Port of Spain). "A Life" was published in *New English Weekly* 2, no. 26 (13 April 1933) (edited by A.R. Orage, London).

The remaining four stories were published in the *Beacon* (edited by Albert Gomes, Port of Spain): "Over the Top" in 1, no. 2 (1931); "Five Dollars' Worth of Flesh" in 1, no. 6 (1931); "Scapular" in 2, no. 5 (1932); and "Snapshots" in 2, no. 7 (1932). "Scapular" has been reprinted in *The Book of Trinidad*, edited by G. Besson and B. Brereton (Port of Spain, 1992).

The two "Pen Portraits of the Poets", on "Contemporary Poetry and Poets" and "Countee Cullen", were published in *Trinidad Presbyterian* 23, no. 5 (May 1926) and no. 7 (July 1926) respectively (edited by Reverend Gilbert Earle, Port of Spain). "Countee Cullen" was also published in *Quarterly Magazine of the Richmond Street Literary and Debating Association* 3, no. 2 (June 1928), second quarter (edited by W.H. Dolly, Port of Spain), in "Three Contemporary Poets".

"A Commentary" was originally published in *Trinidad* 1, no. 2 (April 1930) (edited by A.H. Mendes, Port of Spain). It was reprinted in *From Trinidad, with Love: An Anthology of Early West Indian Writing*, edited by Reinhard W. Sander (London, 1978). The remaining items, apart from the three final articles, were published in the *Trinidad Guardian*. Dates of publication follow each piece.

I have not been able to uncover any information about "On the Pre-Atomic Gentleman". Mendes refers to his "readers", but the tone of the piece suggests that it was delivered as a talk, possibly on radio, or at the public library. The reference to Henry Wallace, vice president of the United States (1941–45), dates it in the mid- to late 1940s.

"The Man, His Land, and His Culture" was apparently Mendes's contribution to a panel discussion of the topic at the Little Carib Theatre. The Little Carib opened on 25 November 1948, so this piece probably belongs, like the following talk, to the period 1948–50.

"All My Sons" is referred to by Mendes as a "talk". It may be dated roughly between 1948 and 1950, based on the publication of the *Kinsey Report* (1948) and the first productions of Arthur Miller's play *All My Sons* (in the United

States on 29 January 1947, in the United Kingdom on 11 May 1948, and a film in 1948), which Mendes mentions in the course of the article.

The year 1950 may be a cut-off point for Mendes's journalism. In March of that year he was sent on a course by his employer, the Port Services Department, to observe port systems in the United States and Europe. He was away for nine months, and on his return the challenging nature of his duties may have left him with little time for writing until his retirement in 1957.

Section 1

~ POEMS ~

THE POEMS I HAVE CHOSEN FOR this selection are ones I both like and consider representative of Mendes's development in the genre. "In the Cocoa", though it contains Keatsian echoes, describes a typical Trinidadian agricultural landscape, one very familiar to Mendes from working in his father's businesses, with immortelle trees shading the cocoa and morbleu butterfly seeking the darkness of the cocoa grove. As he was later to explain in his journalism, Mendes considered it essential for the writer or artist to incorporate the sensuous feel of the island in his or her work. The persona's dreamy appreciation of the natural setting is brought up sharply against the reality of the black workers who "chatter and harangue" and wish him "good marnin', baas".[1]

"Addressed to a Porter" is set in Mendes's father's provision store at 52 South Quay. It establishes an opposition between the heat and dust of the city's business quarter and the reviving countryside. The fellow-feeling that the persona expresses for the porter struggling to nurture two palm plants set in tins is typical of Mendes's ability to empathize with Trinidad's working classes. As in the previous poem and the two that follow, his rhyme scheme is careful and unobtrusive, sounding the note of prose which is later developed in the free verse experiments.

"Heat" and "World's End" show Mendes in descriptive vein, both poems encompassing the idea of rebirth and renewal through nature. The language, though figurative, and with the traditional allusion to the sun god in "World's End", has moved from the consciously poetic and occasionally derivative effects of "In the Cocoa" to a more natural-seeming expression, as in "Addressed to a Porter".

The next four poems, all written in free verse, treat some of Mendes's favourite anti-colonial themes: the short-sightedness and sycophancy of Trinidad's creoles who strive to climb the social ladder through invitations to Government House; the disparity between rich white and poor black, and the half-hearted attempts by the former to bridge the gap, in "Social Worker"; and sexual infidelity, with the hypocrisy which the cult of respectability promotes. The poetic voice here is ironical and detached, that of one who observes and reports. The anger simmering beneath is controlled and managed, and thus far more effective than the rant which mars some of the anti-war poems in the *Beacon*.

"Warmonger" and "Boy Scout" both treat favourite themes: the waste of young lives in the battlefields of Northern France and Belgium, and the responsibility of those in authority for the slaughter. Whether for recruiter or scout leader, the message is the same. These poems, because of the similarity of theme, were probably written around the same time as "Cadet Corps", which appeared in the *Beacon*, and which embodies memories of Mendes's own wartime experiences. "Cadet Corps" is an overtly angry poem. Its language is stronger and its images repellent, though not as repellent as those of its companion poem "Poppy Day", where the images of disgust are so overdone as to mitigate the effect.

The *Beacon* poems in this selection are a mixed bag. "Stars", a catalogue poem like "September Butterflies" (*Trinidad Guardian*, 19 September 1927), and the splendidly apocalyptic "Tropic Night" hark back to earlier nature poems in subject-matter, but with bolder and stronger imagery. The message of renewal which nature holds for Mendes is seen again in "Stars": "life, bone-robust- / has surely not been sent / to end in dust".

"Governor's Gardens" is related by style and subject to the free verse poems discussed above. Its lightly satirical tone thinly veils the contempt of the persona for the parade of social climbers dressed in their Sunday best. "Poor Eileen", pregnant and abandoned, represents for them merely an opportunity for juicy gossip. Again, the uncomplicated purity of the natural world caught in the soaring birdsong, forms an ironical contrast to the artificial social scene with its grating superficial chatter.

The three poems "Lines", "Nostalgia" and "Lines Written at Sea, for Monica" were published on a single page in the *Beacon*, and were evidently meant to be read together, with the third named as climax. The first two poems establish the now familiar contrast between the soul-destroying worlds of commerce and society and the restorative power of the natural world, in this case the cleansing, "invigorating" sea. "Lines Written at Sea, for Monica" is a love poem which likens the beloved to the sea in all its manifestations. It has a lyrical, almost incantatory sweep, which echoes the movement of the sea, and as in "Stars", envisages the natural world as both timed and timeless. Through the beautiful children at the end of "Lines" and the naked woman at the end of "Nostalgia", we arrive at the final image of the pregnant woman in "Monica", thus establishing the seascape as life-giving alternative to the barren worlds of commerce and society.

"The Moon Laughs" is another poem of protest against what man has made of man, a stronger variation on the rich-poor divide examined in "Social Worker". Excess and waste are countered by hunger and nakedness, images of disgust (gorged bellies, swollen bladders) by images of pathos (empty bags, plantain-leaves and tattered rags). The moon's imagined monologue and the cosmic laughter at human folly lend detachment to Mendes's condemnation, but the anger is not far beneath the surface. The final address to the reader, or to a putative second person with whom the persona is having a discussion: "Comrade, how can we blame the moon and the stars?" introduces the idea that perhaps the communists have got it right in trying for a more equitable distribution of wealth, or perhaps that such injustice is enough to turn one into a communist. Mendes always maintained that the 1917 Russian Revolution was one of the formative influences both on his thought and on his creative development.

The final poem selected, "Cadet Corps", articulates Mendes's revulsion against not just the horrors of war and waste of promising young lives, but also the responsibility of the authorities for programming schoolboys for the slaughter through institutions such as the Cadet Corps. Mendes had lived through the trenches and knew at first-hand the horrors which he outlines. It is in retrospect that the experience turned sour for him, twelve or thirteen years after the Armistice, when he was no longer a part of the conflict, and able to count the cost. The final lines, with their grim pun "cadet-corpsed", are an over-statement in what is otherwise a poem of great emotional power.

On a note of interest, Mendes's eldest son Alfred John, whom he refers to in "Cadet Corps", followed in his footsteps and fought in the Second World War of 1939–45 as a commando. Mendes later conceded that this was a war against evil that needed to be fought.[2]

NOTES

1. This is one of the very few uses of Creole in Mendes's poems. He evidently pre-ferred standard or Trinidadian English for his poetry and journalism.
2. Mendes, *Autobiography*, 42.

IN THE COCOA

I stray alone beneath the cocoa trees,
where purple sunlessness sleeps quietly,
save when the leaves are stirred by a bright breeze
into soft words of a forgotten speech.
I cannot see what clouds in heaven reach
their pearly arms to clasp and hide the sun,
nor what blue-haunting bird has just begun
its skyey song. Above me a green roof
spreads everywhere, and woven into its woof
are pods of cocoa, yellow brown and red,
and these are stars that light a loveless bed
of fallen leaves. The mouldering ferny musk
wordlessly calls the morbleu[1] as she flaps
ungainly solemn wings through boskey gaps.
A scurring[2] bat, dipping in freakish flight,
thinks that the night has come when his sharp sight[3]
must trace a whirring passage through the dusk.
The tall immortelles, blossoming above
the stunted tops of cocoa, drop for love
of the cool earth their flowers one by one,
dipped in the golden beams of the gold sun.
No insect tunes his reed: the grasshopper
for once is still and does not dare to stir,
but clings to the bark of that old tree
like a green parasite, waiting to see
the open sky with the sun burning there.

The weeds are riotous, coiléd to ensnare
the careless step, and intersecting drains
are yet damp from the copious April rains.
And suddenly I come upon a gang
of negro-labourers who chatter and harangue
each other while they prune disorderly trees;
and eyeing me, they say: "good marnin', baas,"
and double the energy of their work to please
me standing by before I onwards pass.

NOTES

1. Mendes writes of the morbleu in "March – Evening in My Garden" (*Trinidad Sunday Guardian*, 10 March 1926):

    > Slow and forlorn
    > The morbleu, butterfly of night, in dreams
    > Of purple wandering moves on
    > As lazily as laziness in flight.

    and in "September Butterflies": "Morbleus with ungainly wings" (*Trinidad Sunday Guardian*, 19 September 1926).

2. "Scurr", more usually "skirr": to move, run, fly, sail, etc., rapidly or with great impetus. Sometimes implies a whirring sound accompanying the movement.

3. Poetic licence. Bats do not possess keen eyesight.

ADDRESSED TO A PORTER

First, you've tinned those two dwarf-palms,
and next you bring them here into this store
that stocks a dozen vegetables or more;
and every evening, after the day's alarms
with bartering Chinamen and Indians, you,
before washing your feet and getting ready
for going home, sprinkle some water on them to
revive them from the day's dust-heat.
                             But steady, steady:
both you and I know what this place is;
and palms and human spirits, though not related,
need virgin air and songs of birds and the buzz
of bees in flowers if they must know
fulfillment; and if death, or what is just as hated,
conscious despair, then here, by all means, bring them.

Because here, you and I are what we are, and so
Why not two palms? and more, they let me sing them.

HEAT

The sky is an inverted bowl
with no cloud-dregs.
The desiccated land, like coal
burning, steams and the glare
quivers everywhere.
The frightened trees on dry legs
huddle together in fright,
the sun's rays seeping
into every dry brown leaf
hidden from the sight.
The birds' songs are brief
notes that, in leaping
from dust-mote to dust-mote,
frog-like croak. Two crickets gloat,
screeching across the heat
that rests sultrily on the brain;
and the beat
of long rods of sun-rain
on the savannah sends the cows
cowering in the hot shade.
Nothing is alive but life.
The island's womb is being made
ready for parturition
at the touch of the evening's cool midwife.

WORLD'S END

Light spouted up the purple east
in two and three and four jets; then
these merged together and increased
to a rising tide of light that ran
about the heaven's Atlantic floor:
another flood flowing with ore.
It rose into the zenith and
filled up the earth to its green brim.
While men slept on in a dream-land
the heaving water sang a hymn
of light about the windows, there
surging and swaying glare on glare.
But all slept on and did not know
the world's end: how drowned they were
in this Phoebean[1] overflow.
And when the flood ebbed back, the earth was once again
from a new birth.

NOTE

1.   From Phoebus Apollo, the sun god of the ancient Greek pantheon.

GOVERNMENT HOUSE BOOK

To put your name in government house book
helps you a great deal socially
you will sooner or later get an invitation
to dinner
or to a dance
or to a garden party
and you may meet there all the bigwigs.

If you can say that you've been
to a dinner
or a dance
or a garden party
at government house
it means that you have arrived;
and if you can get the Humming Bird[1]
to mention you in her Talk of Trinidad
as having attended a government house function
then everybody will think you a deuce of a fellow.

Of course, I'm just now speaking only to creoles.

English people who come out to the island
don't have to strive after government house
because they're obviously white
and educated
and cultured
and clever

and full of a sense of the responsibility of carrying the
                              white man's burden.
English people who come out to the island,
everyone of them,
are all these things.

Well, you really shouldn't wonder
when you remember that they belong to *the* superior race.

NOTE

1.   "The Talk of Trinidad" was a long-running social column in the *Trinidad
     Guardian* started in 1929. The first "Humming Bird" was Jerry Lynch.

SOCIAL WORKER

I can't blame her for wanting something to do.
All day long she sits at home doing nothing
she has maids to count the clothes for her
and dust and sweep and make up the room
and she has her cook to make the food for her:
Occasionally she does a little darning
and a little sewing
but as her husband can afford to buy new socks
and have her clothes made for her
it isn't often that she does these things.
Going to town to shop
and going to the theatre
and to dances
and to cocktail parties
are her main activities.

She often tells you how lazy her servants are.

But now and again her conscience pricks her
and she indulges in a little social work.
She likes to hold in her arms for a while
little black screaming babies:
it makes her think how truly humble she is
and how much she is ready to sacrifice
in the cause of the poor
and it makes her feel that God is extra pleased with her.

After such an experience
she goes home and tells her husband all about it.

Her own whiteskinned baby,
having had its bottle of milk,
is warmly expensively tucked away in a white linened bed.

WEDDING

The wedding was a grand one.
Because they were rich they had three priests
to perform the ceremony
and the bells were rung, loudly and jubilantly,
to proclaim to all the island
how important it is when rich people marry.
Across the sumptuously spread table
happy speeches were made
by the priests
and the bride's father
and the bridegroom's father
and the bestman.
The burden of all the speeches was:
fifty-fifty,
each must give and take,
fifty-fifty.
Toasts were drunk in *Moet et Chandon*
and the bride's face beamed
and the bridegroom's face beamed.
There were hundreds of presents
and everybody congratulated the happy pair,
even the young girls who were on the marriage market
and envious of the bride.
The bride's going away dress was lovely
the papers said the next day
and the papers said lots of other nice things.

But
"You're late for dinner" she said to him two months later.
"Office" he said,
but there was something in his face that told her he was lying.

"I'm off to the country for the weekend," he said a year later.
"Business" he explained.
She told him to his face then
she knew that he was lying
and they quarrelled loudly and bitterly.
They quarrelled several times after that
and at last she discovered that he had a mistress.

But in the presence of their friends
they continued to "dear" and "darling" each other.

LAST NIGHT I SAW ARTHUR

Last night I saw Arthur in the theatre
he came in with his wife and a few others.

I also saw Emily there.
Emily, a beautiful East Indian girl,
is Arthur's mistress.

I hear that he's very fond of her,
visits her regularly.
I hear that she gets much more of him than his wife.

Arthur glanced at Emily through the corner of his eye.
Emily looked boldly at Arthur,
but neither spoke.

For all the others knew,
Emily and Arthur might have been complete strangers.

You see, Arthur is a very nice and respectable fellow.

WARMONGER

We have our cadet corps officers
and our volunteer corps officers
and our boyscout masters
and our girlguide officers:
we have our warmongers
and we have our whoremongers.

I should prefer to be a whoremonger
than to be a warmonger.

The whoremonger might inject his poison into two or three women in
  a lifetime:
the warmonger injects his poison into hundreds of school children
and then proceeds to follow them up as they leave school
until he sees them all mutilated on a battlefield.

BOY SCOUT

The boy scout has to do his good deed every day
if he's to be a good and true scout.
(A good deed a day
keeps the devil away
Baden-Powell[1] seems to say)

He's disciplined to do his good deed every day
and he's taught to drill and to click his heels and to salute smartly
because he's a military christian before anything else,
he's a Christ-plus-Mars[2] combination.

Gentle Jesus meek and mild
rat-tat-tat
boom-boom
look upon a little child.

He's taught to love his country so much
that he must take up arms for her "in her hour of need"
and the minute after he's done his good deed
he's drilled
and taught how to click his heels
and how to salute smartly.

It's only when his young body is punctured by a bullet
that he sees what scouting has helped to do for him.

Even battle is so arranged
that he might perform his good deed while engaged in it.

His wounded comrade is in nomansland
and while the bullets fly swiftly past
swiftly past
and the shells fall thick and fast
thick and fast
but he goes into the open and brings his comrade in.

Gentle Jesus meek and mild
rat-tat-tat
crash-crash
look upon a little child.

NOTES

1.   Robert Stephenson Smyth Baden-Powell, later Lord Baden-Powell of Gilwell
     (1857–1941), founder of the Boy Scout Movement.
2.   The Roman god of war.

STARS

Against my window-sill
I lean and see
heaven's dark bowl spill
stars over me:
Antares, green Sirius,
baleful Altair,
Betelgeuse, Arcturus
and white Archernar;
Southern Cross, Charioteer,
winking Pleiades,
Cassiopeia's high chair
and cameled Hyades.[1]
So far they seem beyond,
yet bound, I know,
by some mysterious bond
with me below.
For this august event –
life, bone-robust –
has surely not been sent
to end in dust.
Against my window-sill
I lean and see
the quiet sky distil
one star for me.

NOTE

1.   Antares, Sirius, Altair, Betelgeuse, Arcturus and Archernar are especially bright stars. The Southern Cross, Charioteer (constellation Auriga) and Cassiopeia are constellations. The Pleiades, "winking" because not readily visible all at the same time, are a cluster of stars in the constellation of Taurus. The "cameled Hyades", also a cluster, appear in Taurus, not in the Camel (constellation Camelopardalis).

GOVERNOR'S GARDENS

It is amusing of a Sunday afternoon to sit
on a bench by the Governor's Gardens and watch the cars parked
along the road.
Well-dressed women and men
sit in them ostensibly for the purpose of listening
to the military band as it tries its weak forces
with Beethoven, Bach or Brahms.
The eyes of all these well-dressed women and men
watch eagerly for acquaintances to whom they might wave or bow
and so show to the world that they know the Attorney-General
or the Solicitor-General
or the Chief-of-Police
or the Chief Justice, *Sir* Albert Monkerton,[1]
or the Governor[2] himself (whisper it)
or the most popular social figure in the city,
jovial Promise Cuity,
about whom there is such a delightful scandal, my dear.
    "Yes, not a word, this is only between you and I
    and the door-post;
    in the family-way, poor Eileen, and he won't even marry her.
    It's the least he can do for a girl from such good family."
Meanwhile, Beethoven, Bach or Brahms sings to the air,
and the birds in the trees vie with the women in the cars:
only, the birds' colours are natural
and the birds' lyrics soar from their hearts.

NOTES

1. The chief justice for Trinidad from 1930 to 1937 was Sir Charles Frederic Belcher, Kt. "Sir Albert Monkerton" may be a composite made up from names in "The Talk of Trinidad", or he may have been a real person in quite another walk of life.
2. The governor of Trinidad from 1930 to 1936 was Sir Alfred Claud Hollis.

TROPIC NIGHT

Over this city from the outside
crawls the tarantula of night:
long hairy legs and two bright eyes
and no light, no light.
Not even a star in the black sky
and the moon has her backside to earth,
the tarantula of night is huge and hairy:
monster of an ancient mud-birth.
All the lights in this place have been switched off
by accident, or I know not what.
Through the once bright streets the tarantula
of night crawls, huge and hot.
The houses flank the streets like shadows
of aboriginal Indians returning
on the back of the huge tarantula
Night, in wrath burning.

NOSTALGIA

The dust and heat are enervating
and the mind's peace is disturbed by the
            raucous voices
of bartering Chinese and Indian shopkeepers.
I don't like heat and dust,
I don't like bartering people.
Now there is a nostalgia in my heart for
        white beach
            blue sea
                houses with red roofs
and pink and blue and green fronts
and I want to hear again the happy surf-shouts
and I want again to watch my friend Jim[1]
putting onto canvas all the island's beauty
while two lovely children sit on my knees
chattering like early morning keskidees.

NOTE

1. Jim Patton, the artist friend with whom Mendes lived for a while in New York
    City (Mendes, *Autobiography*, 91).

LINES

The dusty haunts of men make my belly sick.
Men and women in commerce and society
are all stupid and hypocritical.
The way they dress is a lie:
       their weddings and their funerals,
          their church-parades, their love-making
            their money-making
all these things are lies.
I like people to be natural
even if they are bad.
It is more despicable to be good and unnatural
than to be bad and natural.
It is easiest to be natural away from crowds.
I have begun to think that beachcombing
is better than being in business.
There are always fish in the sea
and the white sand of the beach is beautiful
and the sea is clean and invigorating
and a woman naked on the beach is more lovely
than naked anywhere else.
I have really begun to hate the dusty haunts
      of men.

LINES WRITTEN AT SEA FOR MONICA

The sea is young and old.
It is young in its rhythm,
the pulse and beat of its procreative movement,
    backwards and forwards,
      ceaselessly,
        night and day,
          from the beginning of time
it has been young in its procreative rhythm.
And it is old because it has seen
the dawn of time and the midday of time
    (and we don't know what it will see in the night
      of time).
It is young again because it gives to the land
rain that will strike the root downward
and throw the seed up and the fruit at last
it will drop into man's belly
and man will live, on and on to the end of the
    world and time.
And you, too, my love, are young and old.
You are young because you stand
at the door of earthtime and everything.
And there's beauty in the world for you,
    beauty and truth
      in the white beach, blue sea
        and multicoloured housefronts.
The very procreative rhythm of the sea

within your body is your age.

It is the life of you and me
        and Neanderthal man:
it will be the life of the infant in your womb.
And you are as old as Neanderthal man
and as young as your earthtime.

THE MOON LAUGHS

I saw the moon to-night looking on the earth
with a very queer expression on its face.
It seemed to say:
"Well, well, you're a strange race of monkeys.
Just a few of you are dressed up to the nines
and housed in palaces, two and three to a palace,
gorging your bellies with the best of foods
swelling your bladders with the best of wines
while millions of you are crouching in hovels
and wearing plantain-leaves and tattered rags,
crawling around like empty bags
and food is being burnt and dumped into the sea
and warehouses are stocked to choking both with food and clothes.

"While food is being dumped into the sea and burnt
and warehouses are overstocked with clothes and food
you crawl around in millions, hungry and hollow-faced
and hollow-eyed and debased.
Well, well, believe me, you're a queer race of monkeys
queerer than those I see leaping from branch to branch
of the forest-trees."

I'm sure I heard the moon laugh out aloud,
aloud and long
and all the stars, hearing the moon laugh,
looked at the earth and laughed too
loud and long.

Comrade, how can we blame the moon and stars?

CADET CORPS

When I see schoolboys being drilled at school
uniformed into cadet corps,
when I hear the officers shouting out commands
rapping out commands
and see the squares of young uniformed bodies
click into movement with a machine precision:
then the bowels in my belly growl in anger
and my mind is a bright hot flame
and my heart is sick unto vomiting
for I know that these boys are being disciplined
        for war.

And I remember the months I spent in the
trenches with lice playing hide-and-seek about
my body in the midst of mud and the stench
        of decomposed bodies.

and I remember the futility
and the wickedness
and the beastliness of it all.

Comrade, rather than see my son cadet-corpsed
        at school
I should prefer to see his young virile body
stretched out stiffly in a stark coffin.

Section 2

~SHORT STORIES~

OF ALL THE STORIES ANTHOLOGIZED HERE, "Introspection" is, as its title suggests, the most inward-looking. Dialogue chiefly takes the form of the persona Tom's argument with himself as he tries to balance the expectations of his marriage with his own ambitions of becoming a writer, examining his feelings for his wife and his own insecurities and frustrations. His wife, Alice, comes alive quite as much through this internal debate as through physical description, though obviously we are getting a skewed perception here.

When questioned about this story Alfred Mendes's son Peter immediately identified Tom and Alice as Mendes and his second wife Nita. Nita was Catholic, and may never have read this story, as it was first published in *Trinidad Presbyterian* in 1927, five years after their marriage. Unlike Mendes's first wife Jessie, she was not tolerant of his writing ambitions.

The story touches also on writer's block, feared by all authors, as the persona finds himself haunted by the whiteness of the paper before him. The pain and self-doubt evident here give "Introspection" a poignancy far beyond the perceived mutual incompatibility in the marriage. The tone of lyrical sadness is very different from the angry vigour of "Torrid Zone", published a year later in *Quarterly Magazine*, which Mendes stated was based on an actual incident during his courtship of Nita.[1] The latter is a fine study of sexual jealousy with strong themes of racism and class differences woven through it. Unlike "Introspection", it focuses on the reactions and behaviour of the persona Malcolm in a manner that is paradoxically both involved and detached. There is humour in Malcolm's considering of the moon as arbiter of his conduct, and in his furious puffing away at a pipe that has long since gone cold. But these are part of a steady psychological build-up of impotent resentment and rage, which climaxes in shocking violence as he hurls the gramophone at his rival's head.

In this story and "The Hen", which rely heavily on verbal interaction to move their plots, fury and dislike are on occasion expressed in the unlovely "n-word". The latter is also employed matter-of-factly by the mixed-race Mari in "A Little Cargo" and in "Gold Beans" by the "brown" Renwick, who is himself married to a black woman, with no animus, as a means of identifying the African segment of Trinidad's working class. It is worth noting that it is the unattractive Dutchman Van Druten who hurls this abuse at Malcolm, who has bettered him in their argument, and that this is the final insult which spurs Malcolm into an act of physical revolt. In "The Hen" the two women accused of fighting over the hen trade the insult each in derision of the other, but importantly, the presiding magistrate bans the use of the term in his court.

Even in the second decade of the twenty-first century this particular insult retains the power to shock and upset, and I have considered replacing it with a less offensive term. I have decided not to meddle. The stories are of their time, and the language employed, whether Trinidadian English or Creole, is of its time also, and used by Mendes in specific contexts to draw attention to differences in his characters' backgrounds and personalities. To bowdlerize would be not only to mitigate effects in the stories, but also to interfere with the writer's attempts to render his subjects faithfully, in voice as well as appearance.

Mendes's court story "The Hen" was published in *Quarterly Magazine* in 1927, five years before the "Sweetman" case landed him in court himself, accused of libel. It is a sparkling vignette of a resident magistrate's court, with a hilarious ending. The use of the present tense gives the slender plot immediacy, and the extensive use of Creole, with active participation by the court's audience, both humour and vitality. Like many of Mendes's stories which rely heavily on dialogue, it would lend itself particularly well to dramatization.

"A Day of Sorrow" and "In a Restaurant" are stories of Trinidad's middle class, both with strong autobiographical content. "A Day of Sorrow", which deals with death and a funeral among Mendes's own Portuguese community, is, as noted by Hugh Stollmeyer, above, a fragment or offshoot of one of Mendes's destroyed novels. It is one of the stories read and liked by Hulbert Footner (see the Letters section of this volume). The prevailing mood of sorrow maintained by the almost constant weeping of the bereaved family and the persistent accompanying rain, provides a backcloth for a developing attraction between the married older man Roberto and the eldest daughter of the house, Adelina. The influence of the English writer D.H. Lawrence may be traced here, in the countering of death and loss with the life-affirming possibilities of love and sex.

"In a Restaurant" takes its title directly from an early poem by T.S. Eliot, "Dans un Restaurant". Mendes, despite his early reservations about Eliot's poetry, seems to have had another look at his work. As in the poem,[2] very little happens in this story, which relies heavily on dialogue. It details the start of a love affair between Peter, a married writer, and Helen, a younger woman, and relies for its effect on the sexual tension between the two. The story ends abruptly in bathos, though with sexual innuendo, and I think must be seen as a detached fragment, possibly a chapter, from the novel described by Mendes about his affair with an eighteen-year-old girl while still living with Nita.

The restaurant in the story is a soda fountain on Frederick Street in Port of Spain. Mendes moves his characters all around the capital, as well as other areas of Trinidad, and he is very careful to plot their paths, giving each road and district its name. A Trinidadian reader of the time, and today as well, would have quickly registered the social gulf between working-class Belmont and predominantly East Indian St James and upper-class residential areas like Cascade. Where Mendes's characters lived would have said quite as much about them as their manner of speaking.

"Faux Pas" sets out to shock. A very short story (editors of the English journals which published some of Mendes's work called those of similar length "short shorts"), it is set in South Quay, the business area of Port of Spain, in front of a provision store like the one owned by Mendes's father. It takes the form of a conversation between the store's head clerk and two commission agents. The talk is desultory and bored. They speak of crop failure and hardship, and as an example of the poverty on the streets around them, a ragged urchin rushes ahead of a crowd of his fellows to grab a pigeon that has been wounded by a passing cart. The pigeon is obviously destined for the pot, but this is the only aspect of the incident which seems to strike the men. Similarly, the comment by the white commission agent that "the coolies round Penal must be smelling hell" elicits agreement from the others, but no sense that this is something that matters, apart from a decline in their trade. The men are unattractive: one picks his nose for most of the story. The conversation is shallow and unedifying, and the only spark of genuine interest shown is in a passing sexily dressed woman who provokes leers, winks and lewd remarks, especially from the white man. He is hoist with his own petard when the clerk follows suit with the beginnings of a remark about the white commission agent's own wife and daughter who happen to pass, and both conversation and story come to an abrupt ending. The reader is left with a sense of the same stifling boredom and paralysis which Mendes identifies in the poem "Addressed to a Porter". This was one of the stories in *Trinidad* 1, no. 1, that aroused the ire of the *Trinidad Guardian*'s critic James Belmont.[3] Belmont described it as "revolting". It is certainly depressing, showing traits of character that are even less attractive than the physical appearances of the men. But it is true to Mendes's intention to make his fellow islanders central to his writing, whatever their class, colour or creed, and however unattractive morally and physically they might be.

Mendes claimed that he was not really a cricket enthusiast,[4] but he certainly had an eye to its unifying potential, and he knew enough about the game and its history as it affected the West Indies to be able to produce this light-hearted story. Perhaps something rubbed off in his association with C.L.R. James. At any rate, he acknowledges James's part in the cricketing scene in Trinidad at the time with a teasing reference: Anzora's son, for whom he dreams of a brilliant cricketing future, is named "Nello", James's nickname among his intimates.

The story combines the excitement of a small knot of cricket enthusiasts over a West Indian tour of England with a very West Indian phenomenon: the rapidity with which a rumour may spread and be totally corrupted from the original information before it has gone beyond two or three people. The news of a crushing defeat for the West Indian team arrives just as they are celebrating its famous victory with expensive champagne. To compound their humiliation, it is brought by the very Englishman over whom in their triumph they had expected to crow.

This story was reprinted as "Cricket News" in the *Trinidad Guardian Weekly* of 12 October 1947, with some minor but significant alterations (as distinct from poor editing). The story was first published in *Trinidad* 1, no. 2 (1930), before the "Sweetman" trial. After the trial Mendes was careful not to use names in his stories that could be traced to real people and possibly give rise to other legal actions. In the 1947 version Anzora is changed to Marcelle, Halliday to Carabache, and Zorana to Beaufort. Interestingly, Mendes is much more sensitive here in the matter of racial distinctions. McPherson, the commission agent, is no longer described as "coloured". The clerk Sankeralli's East Indian origins are omitted and his Chinese customer is no longer described as "mean". The Union Club becomes the "Commercial Club", and its porter James is no longer described as "black".[5]

The war story "Over the Top" was first published in the *Beacon* (1931), though it may have been written earlier. It is a poetic evocation written in the present tense of an attack by Allied forces on a German position in the Ypres Salient in Belgium, in which Mendes took part. The figurative language in no way detracts from the immediacy and the horror of trench warfare, with its nightmarish landscape pitted with foxholes filled with dead or dying soldiers. The camaraderie with working-class British soldiers which Mendes spoke of is very evident in their teasing of him over the rum ration and the cheerful irreverence which they show for the "Far-flung British Hempire". Mendes's ear for their northern speech is as sharp as for the Creole of his native island.

Their brief huddle in the rain and darkness before the battle is a small refuge of kindness and humour from the hell around. A brilliant, poignant touch is added when someone says that the rum they are drinking is from Jamaica: "Jamaica, and the sun shines for an infinitesimal second."

Mendes's fast-paced and gritty account carries the reader along with him to the tautly achieved climax. However, there is still a place in his story for him to remember a German friend from his schooldays whom he had liked, and to wonder whether Uhlandt is now the enemy, and whether the Germans really are the enemy. In the anti-war poems of the *Beacon* and in "Malvina's Nennen" he places the blame squarely on the shoulders of warmongering authorities and unscrupulous businessmen who make capital out of the waste of young lives. His focus in this story differs in that he clearly wishes to recreate the apocalyptic sights, sounds and smells of battle, together with the fear and the grim hardships which ordinary soldiers endured. He has read the war poet Siegfried Sassoon.[6] He may have also read the poems of Sassoon's friend Wilfred Owen, who set out in his poetry to tell the stories of common soldiers in the Great War. Certainly, he is here feeling his way towards the epiphany which climaxes Owen's poem "Strange Meeting": "I am the enemy you killed, my friend."

"Five Dollars' Worth of Flesh" and "A Life" illustrate Mendes's compassion for and understanding of the plight of impoverished women. "A Life", spare and shorter than "Five Dollars", reads like a story by Guy de Maupassant. The writing is unsentimental, almost clinical, but the back-breaking labour and misfortunes endured by Camachee, and the indifferent cruelty of the neighbours who ignore her suffering, are no less affecting for the matter-of-fact descriptions. The story is full of ironies: the fathers of Camachee's two daughters, though "buckras" and a source of pride, take no responsibility for their support,[7] and in fact contribute to her East Indian neighbours' resentment of her. But the supreme irony occurs after her death, when the neighbours "relent", club together, and give her "as fine a funeral as had been seen in St. James for many a year".

"Five Dollars' Worth of Flesh" takes place over a single day.[8] As in "A Day of Sorrow" the mood is established by the weather, in this case a thick blanket of fog which masks the city of Port of Spain from view. Against this inauspicious start to the day unfolds the story of Isadora Guerra, who struggles to feed her two children with no money coming into the house and an abusive layabout for a husband, who urges her to sell herself to obtain the money they need. All of her efforts to find work are met with cold refusals because of her outstanding beauty, except from the Portuguese Texeira, who offers to pay her for sexual favours. She reacts furiously at first, but is forced to humble her pride and accept his offer, in order to buy food for her starving children. Isadora is a strong woman who makes an independent decision, but it is the only one that she can make. Unlike Sé-sé in the eponymous story (*The Man Who Ran Away*), who comes under similar pressure from her own mother, Isadora is not saved. And there is no doubt that the life of a prostitute will be all that she can look forward to.

Like Camachee, Isadora lives in St James. She is of mixed race and feels at a disadvantage in the predominantly East Indian community. The general indifference which surrounds her, though, is offset by the loving kindness of her black neighbours, who send food over for her and her children out of their own modest store, and mind the children while she tries to find work. Their warm humanity is the only alleviation in this bleak tale.

A completely different note is sounded in "Scapular", a story of remembered boyhood and growing up. Although it concerns one of Mendes's favourite hobby-horses, the control exerted by the Catholic religion over the minds of its adherents, and the ironic dénouement is directly related to this, the overall impression left by "Scapular" is of mischievous but idyllic boyhood. There is a wonderful evocation of the Cunapo River, with its wooded banks and overhanging trees, creaking bamboos and birdsong, bubbling water, and even a shy deer making a brief appearance, as the boys balance skilfully on the forbidden logs and are wafted downstream. The inevitable disaster occurs when the unpractised "St Anthony" falls off his log and narrowly escapes drowning as his hand becomes entangled with the scapular hanging around his neck. However, this is a tale about growing up, and he saves himself at the expense of the scapular and with the assistance of the now sobered Auguste. Anthony is not the only lad to learn a hard lesson here.

Auguste's recognition of Anthony's hand sticking out of the water "like the hand that gripped Excalibur" is typical of Mendes's style. The observation is a very boyish one: tales of King Arthur and his Knights of the Round Table were favourite reading for children in the early twentieth century, and certainly for Mendes himself, whose early narrative poems were strongly influenced by the legends. But the imaginative leap that makes this association at a moment of genuine peril, and the mind that endows the river setting with a paradisal quality, belong to the artist in the making.

"Snapshots" and "At the Ball" are stories about Trinidad's middle and upper classes, which examine the ills imposed by an artificial social structure. "Snapshots" shares preoccupations in subject-matter and treatment with other *Beacon* stories "Boodhoo", "Colour", and the related "Malvina's Nennen". Nothing is what it seems to be on the surface. However, the wilful blindness and smug complacency of Mr Levitt and others in his social circle (apart from the quicker-witted Mrs Marsden), and the racism and anti-semitism which flavour the conversation at cocktail party and dinner, render all characters unsympathetic. Their shock and humiliation when their favourite Rose's sexual proclivities become known after his sudden death, seem only just deserts. Mr Levitt's reaction at finding snapshots of his young son Richard, whom he had pushed into friendship with Rose, among Rose's trove of erotic photographs, is left to the reader's imagination. But the ridicule which he will certainly incur is bound to be as mortifying for him as that experienced by the social climber Jean de la Roche in "At the Ball".

The action of "Snapshots" takes place over a protracted period of time, and ranges from places of business in downtown Port of Spain to social functions at private houses and clubs. "At the Ball" is a very much shorter story which takes place entirely at the society ball attended by de la Roche and his wife. The racism examined here is subtle. De La Roche is of mixed race, but could "pass for white", and he makes a point of snubbing people of darker complexions, especially his former schoolfellow, the clever barrister St Hill. His lack of judgement is made evident when he seeks out the unconventional but popular "Mac" and makes much of him, even cancelling one of the dances he had booked to lead Mac's partner onto the floor. Basic commonsense should have informed him that a man widely known to be impatient of convention might well have selected a young lady of similar persuasions to be his partner. Fittingly, the news that she has shared her favours with every young man in town, with the unspoken corollary that by even acknowledging her de la Roche has brought social ruin on himself, is delivered with delighted malice by St Hill.

"A Little Cargo" is one of several stories which Mendes wrote about opium-trafficking in Trinidad. Some are very short, like "Bête Rouge", "Profit on Opium" and "Opium-Smugglers",9 which confine their attention to the mechanics of the trade: the running of the drug by smugglers from Venezuela and its purchase by members of Trinidad's Chinese community. "A Little Cargo" is longer and finely developed, with a plot that is very similar to Mendes's highly praised "Her Chinaman's Way" (*Pablo's Fandango*). Each of these stories involves a voluptuous woman of mixed race who lives with a Chinese shopkeeper. In the latter story Maria has a baby for her keeper Hong Wing, which she loves devotedly. She is bored with Hong Wing and would like to leave him for a handsome carterman. But she is also afraid of him.

Mari in "A Little Cargo" is in love with a handsome calypsonian who has migrated to New York. Her liaison with Sing Hop is entirely mercenary. She extracts as much money from him as she can, and puts it into a savings account against the day when she can join her lover in New York. Ironically, Sing Hop is also secretly saving money against his return one day to China. When the affluent and aptly named Fats becomes infatuated with her, Mari plots to use him to rid herself of the parsimonious Sing Hop, and provide her with even more money for her secret fund.

Maria, and Mari indirectly, arrange to have the police pick up their Chinese keepers while the latter are at sea obtaining supplies of opium. In either case, the shopkeeper gets the better of those who are trying to sell him out. "A Little Cargo" begins in the dance hall where Mari meets Fats, moves to the home behind the shop which she shares with Sing Hop, and details the actual putting to sea to obtain the cargo and subsequent chase by the police. It ends with Sing Hop the lone survivor of the gun battle, cautiously wading in the sea parallel with the beach, a can of opium in either hand. There is no sense in this story that he realizes that Mari has betrayed him.

"Her Chinaman's Way" takes the plot further. The scene moves from the house, which Maria shares with Hong Wing and the baby, to his shop, where she works, and which she leaves briefly to arrange his arrest, and it returns to the house for the dénouement. The action at sea is not described, but Hong Wing survives with his opium, and the realization that only Maria could have betrayed him to the police. When her back is turned he takes ferocious revenge by swiftly strangling their baby.

The possibilities of a relationship between a working-class Chinese shopkeeper and a beautiful woman of mixed blood seem to have fascinated Alfred Mendes. In "One Day for John Small" (*The Man Who Ran Away*) the philandering Small briefly visits the shopkeeper Lee Sing and his woman Felicia to sell his cocoa. Small has fantasized about making advances to Felicia, who like Maria has a baby for her keeper, but refrains for fear of arousing Lee Sing's suspicions.

"A Little Cargo" is important for its sexual politics, the machinations of Mari, a kept woman who bargains for what she wants with the only assets she possesses, her beauty and her body. It is also important for its examination of the interracial relationships which develop within Trinidad's working class. The Chinese shopkeeper was well known to Mendes through his father's businesses as a purchaser of cocoa, just as he would have been well known to commission agents like John Small. He is featured in "Pablo's Fandango" (*Pablo's Fandango*) as Sing Lee, who buys Pablo's cocoa, and in "Gold Beans", as Chin Lee.

The final story in this selection, "Gold Beans", is also the latest chronologically. Mendes claims at the conclusion that he is looking back on one particular boom year, 1929, on his father's cocoa plantation Santa Carlotta, from the year 1938, but in fact the typescript for this story is dated 1934, with his New York address. It is not a short story as the form is usually known, but a hybrid: somewhere between autobiography, travel writing and fiction. It describes the growing, harvesting, and preparation of the cocoa pods from the tree right to the finished product, which is then bagged, weighed, and sent to the warehouse. But it also describes the people involved in the cocoa trade: the Chinese shopkeeper, the East Indian labourers, the mixed-race Grenadian overseer with his black wife and their seventeen children. It explains commission agents like John Small. And it contains the germs of stories like "Beti" and the story-within-the-story in "Boodhoo" of an unfaithful East Indian wife (*The Man Who Ran Away*), and of "And Then the Hurricane Came" (*Pablo's Fandango*). So in more ways than one it is retrospective, including many of the issues, plots and characters which are found in Mendes's fiction. At the same time, its quality of reportage links it with the journalism which in the 1940s was to be Mendes's main area of interest.

NOTES

1. Videotaped interview with Bruce Paddington c. 1983.
2. Eliot's poem, written in French, contains a brief dialogue between a bored and unsavoury-looking waiter and a hapless diner who is forced to listen to the waiter's lascivious memories of a childhood tryst.
3. James Belmont, the *Trinidad Guardian*'s critic, wrote on the front page (22 December 1929): "Read what Mr. Mendes writes . . . about the three men conversing in front of the provision store in South Quay. It is one of the most revolting things I have ever come across. Its truth is no excuse for its utter nastiness. Mr. Mendes knows as well or better than many of us what idle men in South

Quay (or anywhere else) talk and think about. But he might have spared us the disgusting chronicle."

4.   Mendes, *Autobiography*, 34.

5.   This may have been brought about by Mendes's political activities in the mid-1940s (*Autobiography*, 132, 133). It may also reflect his sensitivity to a growing spirit of nationalism in the decade and a half before Trinidad achieved independence from Great Britain in 1962.

6.   See "Contemporary Poetry and Poets", this volume.

7.   Unlike Henry Lawrence in "Boodhoo", who gives his illegitimate son food and shelter, although his sense of obligation does not extend to an education.

8.   An earlier version of its plot exists in "Poverty" (*Quarterly Magazine*, September 1927 [edited by Austin M. Nolte, Port of Spain]), a short, plangent piece in which a poor family, including a virtuous and loving husband, is the victim of circumstance. Like Isadora, the mother Carmen is forced into prostitution to save her family from starvation.

9.   "Opium Smugglers" was not published. "Bête Rouge" came out in the *Quarterly Magazine*, Christmas 1930 [edited by Austin M. Nolte, Port of Spain]; in *Clarion* 4, no. 1 (4 January 1932) [London: London Caledonian Press]; and in *Trinidad Guardian Weekly*, 22 February 1948 [Port of Spain]. "Profit on Opium" was published in the *Manchester Guardian*, 10 March 1931; in the *Quarterly Magazine*, September 1931 [by "Hubert Alfred"; edited by Austin M. Nolte, Port of Spain]; and in the *Trinidad Guardian Weekly*, 23 November 1947 [Port of Spain].

INTROSPECTION

Mr. and Mrs. Parkins lived in a quiet part of the town. They had chosen the particular spot even before they were married because it had seemed so quiet. And what was more, there were green trees in its near neighbourhood that added to its peacefulness the verisimilitude of countryside homeliness. Of course, they were young then, very young indeed, and they liked to think that life for them would mean living for each other alone. That appeared to their yet inexperienced minds the ideal sort of marriage. Alice had visualised it all in the days of their engagement: how Tom and she would breakfast together, for she didn't believe that a wife should be too tired to rise with her husband and cheer with her presence the first meal of the day; how she would kiss him off to his office; how he would return in the evening full of business worry which she would soothe down with loving caresses; how, sometimes, they might go for walks after supper and then – most thrilling picture of all – how they would sit near each other in the parlour chatting before they retired to their white-sheeted, comfortable bed. For Alice loved chatting. She could think of nothing so consoling as going over in aimless conversation the happenings of the day. And she had always told Tom that that was to be an essential of their connubial bliss. He, – poor fellow – in the ease of that dreamy courtship-state that succumbs to any suggestion from the loved one, had been only too glad to dilate upon Alice's plans for their happiness. Not that he liked chatting. He had never been accustomed to it; for the passion of his life had always been reading and writing. It is true that he had been so far unsuccessful in getting anything of his into print; but that urge which prompts and often forces one into composition could not be subdued by rejection slips. He had that "infinite capacity for taking pains" which the Scotch philosopher called genius.[1] He had felt in himself some power which editors had so far not recognised, and methodically, perseveringly, hopefully he had plodded on with the conviction that one day he would "arrive".

When Alice had greeted him one evening all in a tremble of excitement with the information that she had seen just the little home that would make them cosy and comfortable as a married couple he had gone off the following day after business to view the house. In regarding it for the first time he had thought how wonderful it was for his hours of reading and writing. The setting was so romantic, so poetic. The green trees, the green grass, the scurrying clouds, the singing birds – what more could a writer of short stories and poems want? Going through the house he had even tentatively chosen the room where he would keep his little library and place his mahogany desk that had for so many years felt the light pressure of his pen. Yes; just the thing he had been longing for, and it was Alice's glorious privilege to have discovered it for him. Dear little Alice!

As Tom sat before his desk this evening there was a puzzled expression on his face. He was thinking of the three years of his marriage, three years that should have conjured up for him pleasant and inspiring memories. But that was not so. They were years that had brought bitter disappointment to his dreams of marital peace and joy. Why? The cause was so simple and yet so ineradicable! He reviewed the qualities that he possessed which were vital to a successful union. Homeliness, fidelity, affection on occasion – he had all these. Still, his marriage had been a failure. He was bound to make the admission – a failure. The thought came to him with something of a shock. He had never before considered his marriage seriously. His three years of it had been so engrossed by the care of his library and his writing and reading in every one of his spare moments that he had lived through them in a world of his own. As he sat there now, gazing vacantly before him, the blank foolscap sheet on his desk was forgotten for the moment, his forehead contracted into tiny wrinkles and his thin lips pressed tightly together. He could not imagine how any woman could be so blind to his purpose in life as to want him to forsake it for the small matter of "keeping her company". That was what Alice had been saying to him from the week after they were married: "Please keep me company, Tom. Do you love your books more than you love me?" Really, this was beyond reason and so exasperatingly selfish! Why should his great purpose in life be sacrificed to the silly whim of his wife – the whim of wanting him to talk to her from the minute of his arrival at home after office hours?

He knew he loved her. When the day of recognition came for him, how proud he would be for Alice! Yes; he knew he loved her in an undemonstrative sort of way, for he didn't believe in overdone affection. Such he called affectation, and was wont to add: "still waters run deep". What a pity, he thought, that Alice was not a literary woman! How he would delight, then, in reading his effusions to her! What silent, cunning joy he would find in watching the wondering look in her eyes as he came to the dénouement of any one of his short stories! Only last night he had said to her: "My dear, why don't you read?"

"Read!" she had hotly replied. "Why read when we can live, actually live for ourselves what some fool is trying to tell us about in a cold book!"

That had been too much for him, and he had sat quietly listening to her tirade against the selfishness and cruelty of man.

He tried to write, but could not. It came to him how extraordinary it was that he should be thinking her selfish when she was in the habit, the nightly habit, of accusing him of selfishness. It was either that he was wrong or that she was wrong. At this moment no amount of summoned sympathy for her apparent loneliness could outweigh the balance in his favour. His ambition was a great thing; if realized, greater in its consequences than all else in his life. The crest of its wave could take him anywhere, landing him on strange shores of glory where the light would never die. And Alice was of him, his "better half" as they say colloquially. His reverence for the sacrament of marriage had awed him with the indivisibility of those taking its oath. Should he go down into the dale of misfortune, as surely must his wife go down with him; should he ascend the slopes of success, as surely must Alice be with him. The thought thrilled him, and his face was suffused with an ecstatic smile . . .

Again his eyes wandered over the white sheet before him. It looked so naked in its intense whiteness that he could almost have thought that it called to him for the clothing of his neat words. For a long time he stared at it, unwinking. Following the course of such protracted gazes, it grew smaller and smaller until it assumed the proportions of a large eye which he saw pearled with tears. Violently he roused himself, rose, knocking the chair over with his rapid movement, and began pacing the floor. Could it be possible that his marriage had been a failure? And if so, how is it he had not before realized it? And why should such a silly idiosyncrasy of his wife have been pitted against the grave seriousness of their marriage with such shattering effect? What a fool Alice had been all along! And, after all, there were big mercies she had to be thankful for – his faithfulness, his homeliness. These should have been sufficient in themselves to have made her supremely happy. But the biggest mercy of all was yet to come – and the circumambient air fashioned itself into a pedestal upon which Alice and he stood, receiving the homage of an admiring nation!

Once more he returned to his desk, silently adjusting the fallen chair. His window looked out on the night, a night filled with stars that shone like so many eyes regarding him. He turned off the switch of his desk-lamp and the darkness came over him like a balm. Immediately he saw the outlines of massive trees in the field beyond; great, spreading patches of foliage that harboured a deeper darkness. There was no wind so that everything seemed composed in slumberous immobility. Just such another night as this came to his memory; the first night of his marriage when he had sat at this very window with his bride on his lap and his hopes and dreams before him. He had told her many things in that long-ago time. (How long ago it seemed!) He had told her that she had brought into his lonely life a new conception that had lined with a rosy tinge the solitary cloud of his spirit. And he had seen then nothing but a calm comfort for the future, a comfort in which his wife would share. How was he to know that differences of temperament, varying their ideals, could bring disaster to their assurances?

An owl hooted far off several times before he heard it. Its mate replied from a nearby tree. The antiphon of "tu-whit, tu-whoo" was very lulling to his fevered introspection. The calls were mellow and full of feeling, so that he knew there was harmonious love in these birds this night; the kind of love which he had never known and which the owls could tell him about with their tranquillizing calls. How strange the whole scheme of things was!

The darkness was becoming oppressive, stifling. Fumblingly his fingers rested on the switch and the darkness went out by the window. He looked around. His gilt-lettered books shone to his sight. These which had served him in all exigencies now looked like so many sentinels mocking his helplessness. Though they were friends indeed, they did not, this time, prove to be friends in need. How well he knew them! How often he had read many of them! But now they were distant because of the nearness of a concern which they had helped to create.

Poor Alice! Too well he remembered how she had reproached him for his heavy expenditure in books at a time when the foundation stones on which might rest their welfare in the dim future should have been laid. He had been very harsh with her then and yet she had meant well. He had told her many callous things, which like boomerangs, were now coming back upon him with dull pain. She of course, had retaliated with cruel words, words which she knew would hurt him because of their appropriateness.

"You will never succeed, you fool! You will never succeed with the rubbish you have been writing all these years!"

How that remark, uttered in a vexed, high-pitched tone, had gone to his heart! It echoed all around him now! . . .

"Poor Alice! She was like some dear little animal at bay."

His voice startled him in the stillness. It sounded deep, like the echo of a heavy gong. His head rested on his hands and the white sheet before him was like a large eye, pearled with tears.

There was a low tick, the sound that a drop of dew makes when falling on a dead leaf. Hastily he rose and dried his eyes; he, who had always prided himself on his strength!

"You will never succeed, you fool! Rubbish. . . . years!" Distinctly he heard the horrible words from every corner of the room and every nook of his mind. "You will never succeed, you fool! You will never succeed!" banged on his brain like hammer-blows. Still he paced the room, his eyes frightened into wideness, his lips tightened into a grim determination.

Eight long years he had been writing! He was only sixteen when his first MS. had gone out on its hopeless pilgrimage. Eight years ago, and still he had found no favour in the eyes of editors! "You will never succeed! You will never succeed! Rubbish. . . . years!"

He flung himself on his chair and stared through the window, his legs fully extended, his head drooping forward, his hands crossed over his stomach. The night met his gaze like the curtain of doom. There was nothing on it, nothing beyond it but the blurred patches of deeper darkness lurking in clusters of trees . . .

A distant clock struck nine, slowly, as though reluctant to allow time to travel his impatient way. The soft strumming of a piano reached his ears. It was his wife, playing her favourite Schubert's "Serenade." The music was very sweet and very sad . . .

Why should he be a failure in literature and love? Why should Alice suffer for his blind determination to conquer what was for him unconquerable? . . .

He raised his head and saw the stars twinkling. The curtain of doom had fallen below his field of vision and now he looked on the infinite depths of heaven, blue by day and brimmed with stars by night.

NOTE

1.   David Hume (1711–76).

THE HEN

The Court is packed to suffocation. There are more women than men. The faces vary through all the shades of brown and black, with here and there a blotch of white. It is the last case of the day. A tired-faced magistrate sits on the bench. He is a little red man with a very long nose, which appears to be longer still because of a pimple on its tip.

"Miriam Rebecca Martha Caracciolo!" shouts a constable in a stentorian voice. The name is taken up elsewhere and loses itself in the bowels of the witness rooms. Presently a large black woman shambles in.

"Hurry up there," the constable admonishes.

"Isn't Oi hurryin'?" the woman demands in a shrill voice. The constable takes her by the arm and stands her before the magistrate. The clerk begins to read the charge.

"You are charged with fighting . . ."

"Me foightin'? Oi never . . ."

"Shut up," the constable growls sharply. She looks daggers-drawn at him.

"You are charged with fighting . . ."

"Whoa with, ner?" the accused retorts, her gaze fixed on the clerk.

"Shut up, woman!" the magistrate shouts at her.

". . . with fighting on the morning of the 10th inst. at the bus- stand at Marine Square." The clerk raises his eyes. "Guilty or not guilty?"

"Sah, Oi . . ."

"Guilty or not guilty?" the magistrate interposes, angrily.

"Not guilty, sah."

"Your honour," whispers the constable by her side. She casts a contemptuous look at him.

The magistrate commands the woman to be placed in the witness-box. She is duly sworn in. The prosecuting Inspector of police rises. He is a medium-sized man with a chest thrown out like a turkey's in its most dignified mood. He fixes his pince-nez on his aquiline nose and asks: "Your name?"

"Miriam Rebecca Martha Caracciolo."

"Do you live in this Island?"

"Oi were born in Barbados."

"Answer my question: do you live in this Island?

"Yaas sah, but Oi were born in Barbados."

"Do you remember the morning of the 10th inst.?"

"Froiday las' week, sah?"

The Inspector looks inquiringly at the clerk. The clerk nods, with the suspicion of a smile on his brown face.

"Will you tell us what happened?"

The woman raises the hem of her petticoat and blows her nose loudly in it. A titter runs through the court. The Magistrate calls for silence. The court waits to hear the woman's story. She says nothing.

"Speak woman!" The Inspector's voice is severe.

"Wah is dis, ner? One tell me speak, de oder silence."

Raucous laughter breaks from the court. The Magistrate glares. Two or three policemen call harshly for silence.

"We are waiting," the Inspector says.

"All de trouble start in Toco. Abaht twelve month ago . . ."

"What?" The Inspector regards the woman hopelessly. "Tell us what happened on the morning of the 10th. We have nothing to do with twelve months ago."

"What happen twelve month ago is why what happen on Froiday las' week. If dat nasty nigger-woman didn't meddle wit dat fowl Oi raise wid me own two hand . . . Dat fowl born in me own yard. Jimmy – dat is me husban' – look him dere." The accused raises her ponderous arm and points vaguely at the dark sea of faces. One of the faces is suddenly seen to elevate itself.

"Dat's me, my honour," proclaims a bass voice, aspirating the "h" as though he would wreak vengeance on it.

"Put that man out of the court," the Magistrate orders. Two or three policemen converge on the conspicuous man. A noisy confusion follows. It subsides and order is again restored.

"Proceed." The Inspector wears an exasperated expression. The Magistrate's face is expressionless. All gaze at the accused, who stands with her arms akimbo, breathing stertorously.

"Yaas, my honour" – a giggle exposes innumerable rows of teeth – "dat man, Jimmy Napoleon Caracciolo is me husban'. You 'ave put me asunder from him. 'Ow can a woife speak widout her husban'? A woife is cockroach widout her husban'."

A long drawn-out "ah" surges from the dark sea of faces like a breaking wave. The clerk looks at the Inspector. The Inspector looks at the Magistrate. The Magistrate is looking at no one.

A dead silence follows as when a wave has broken and another is preparing to advance.

"Give your statement, woman," the Inspector thunders.

"Dat fowl, my honour, Oi raise in me own yard. Oi buy de egg from Louisa Rowbottom foo tree cent. Oi set de . . ."

"The woman is talking nonsense. Stand her down." The Magistrate's patience is being sorely tried. The woman is drawn firmly from the box by the delighted constable.

"Agatha St Louise Walcott!" The name is repeated by several voices, eventually dying outside of the court-room.

A tall lean black woman enters. She enters as a bull enters the arena: with flashing eyes. The Magistrate looks at her interestedly. The clerk reads the charge without interruption. A plea of not guilty is entered.

The accused is sworn in, the woman glowering at the Magistrate and her fat opponent the while.

"Your name?" the Inspector asks, pompously.

"Agatha Walcott St Louise." The Inspector consults the clerk's charge-sheet.

"You mean Agatha St Louise Walcott."

"You gwine teach me me own name now?"

"You were arrested as Agatha St Louise Walcott," the Inspector replies heatedly, adding: "and I caution you against rudeness." The Inspector clears his throat. "Do you remember the morning of the 10th?"

"Yaas and no."

The court rumbles with suppressed laughter.

"Silence!" shouts a policeman.

"What do you mean?" asks the inspector.

"Yaas, I remember the tent' because I beat dat nigger-woman dere. No, because I aint finished wid her yet."

The court roars. The Magistrate is beside himself with rage and threatens to clear the court.

"Will you give your statement, woman?" snorts the Magistrate.

"Wha-at, yer honour?"

"Your statement. Tell us what you know, what actually happened."

The Magistrate leans back in his chair with an exhausted irritability.

"On the mornin' of de tent', yer honour, I take de bus at Sangre Grande. I have tree fowl in me tray. When I get into de bus dat nigger woman dere . . ."

"Woman, woman; there's no necessity for the nigger in this court."

"Aint she black, yer honour? And aint black people niggers?"

The Magistrate leans forward irately. "This is the last caution you get against rudeness, woman."

An ominous two minutes of stillness follows. The tall lean woman continues: "When I get into de bus, dat nig . . . dat woman dere, yer honour, make no room foo me. I tell her: 'gi' me room.' She say: 'make it.' I give her a chuck. She chuck me back. Den we fight."

The Inspector rises. "Oh, you fought in Sangre Grande too, eh?" he says triumphantly.

"And I beat her," the lean woman remarks, maliciously.

"You lie, you son of . . ."

"Hold your tongue!" the Magistrate thunders at the fat woman. "Constable, indict her on a charge of hindering the procedure of the court."

The constable grips the woman by the arm, striking an authoritative attitude.

"When we reach Port of Spain, yer honour, dat woman dere, yaas, dat woman dere hold on to me hen and make a rumpus."

"Why did she hold on to your hen?" the Inspector asks.

"Why? Yaas, dat is de question. Why you hold on to me hen, eh?" the lean accused bellows at the fat accused.

"Because Oi knows me hen when Oi sees it. De hen dat Oi raise wid me own two . . ."

The constable tugs violently at the woman's arm. She turns on him wrathfully and strikes him a blow on the stomach. The constable doubles up with the pain. The court grows excited. There is a low murmur of voices, as of bees in swarm.

"Woman, you're charged a second time, for assaulting a constable while in the execution of his duty." The Magistrate's face is red with anger. The clerk titters. The Inspector's fingers are twitching, as though they would like to grip something. The lean accused proceeds: "Den yer honour, she say de fowl hers. When we reach Port of Spain she snatch de fowl outer de tray and I beat her. Can't I beat her foo me own property?"

"Any witnesses?"

"Yaas, yer honour."

A constable's voice is heard calling for Mary Williams Encinas. The Magistrate inquires if the fowl is in court. On learning that it is, he orders it to be produced.

A squat coloured woman rolls in and is duly sworn in. As the Inspector is about to speak a clamorous cackling rises to the court room, which increases as the constable enters with a beautiful Silver Wyandotte hen under his arm. The Magistrate looks sharply at it.

"Constable, bring that hen here." The tall lean accused casts an apprehensive glance at the Magistrate, then hangs her head. The Magistrate takes the hen and examines it with interest. The hen cackles raucously. The court, wondering what new thing is about to happen, waits breathlessly.

"Stand the witness down," the Magistrate exclaims to the consternation of the whole court. Looking sternly at the two women, he says: "I find each of you guilty on the count of fighting. Five pounds or one month hard labour each."

"You" – he addresses the tall lean woman – "you were my cook last month. This hen is mine. It disappeared from my yard the night you were discharged. Constable, take them both down to the Charge-room and lay the charges already imposed, with an extra one of larceny on . . ." The clerk supplies the name with a wry distortion of his brown face: "Agatha St Louise Walcott."

The court disperses, chuckling.

TORRID ZONE

Malcolm de Castro was walking through Jerningham Avenue on his way to visit his fiancée. He felt supremely happy. Why he felt so happy he couldn't for the world of him say, unless it was the beauty of the night, with a sky adorned by a bright full moon, that entered into his spirit and there wrought the miracle. Not that he was never happy, but since he had become engaged to Felicia Lazarre things had not run so smoothly as to give him cause for perfect contentment. And yet he felt it was unfair of him to expect of all experience, especially love-experience, perfect contentment. He had had quite enough of life – twenty-three years of it – to be able to judge for himself that it was filled with infelicities. But still at times he couldn't help thinking that the path of his love was not running smoothly. There was no doubt about that at all, and try as he might to coax himself into believing otherwise, although at times he succeeded feebly, tonight, despite his happiness, he would not be fooled.

As he reached the other extremity of the Dry River bridge he noticed a couple in the shadow of the wall. Their close embrace thrilled him, and he thought how wonderful it would be when the time arrived for him to hold Felicia like that in the privacy of their bedroom. And what a well-shaped girl she was! He had often in moments of lonely idleness or passionate proximity to her, tried to visualise the contours of her body. How such thoughts would affect his whole being! She was pretty, too; coloured, true enough, but then he himself was coloured, the son of a Portuguese and a mulattress, and in that fact he sensed at times the cause of all the trouble between Felicia and himself, or rather between himself and Van Druten. In spite of the great difference between their ages – for Felicia was only eighteen and Van Druten could not have been much under fifty – sometimes he thought Van Druten in love with Felicia, at other times not. However, whatever the relationship between them, he had soon realized, after his engagement, the immense influence that Van Druten exercised over the whole household; Felicia's mother and sister and even Felicia herself. He vaguely suspected that Van Druten was on intimate terms, very intimate terms, with Felicia's mother. But what made him hate Van Druten more than anything else was the habit he had of flaunting before his face his absolute command over the Lazarre household. That was more than he could bear with composure, and, sooner or later, he knew that all his pent-up anger against the man must find an exhaust. Already, on one or two occasions, he had been on the point of letting himself go, but each time Felicia's imploring eyes had checked him. That couldn't go on for ever . . .

And the man's subtle innuendoes on the score of colour were, to put it mildly, exasperating. Perhaps Van Druten was white, perhaps he wasn't. He said he was a Dutchman, but there was no telling definitely who was white in the island. Still, that was no reason why he should always be condemning girls who married men less fair in blood than they, knowing as he did that he, Malcolm, had so much more negroid blood in his veins than Felicia. His complexion, his hair, his features – though he was quite handsome in a coarse sort of way – were unmistakable, whereas Felicia's skin was olive in colour like a Spaniard's, her features refined, her hair wavy and beautifully black. Oh no, let Van Druten be careful in future! He had had quite enough of the man's domineering way with Felicia. If Felicia's mother didn't mind being bossed about by Van Druten that was her business, but when it came to Felicia, ah, an entirely different matter. Why, the man would want even after they were married . . .

Malcolm found his step accelerating and his anger rising. He looked up and saw the moon. The moon seemed to be smiling at him, to be wanting to tell him by its expression how absurd it was to be losing his temper over a person like Van Druten, but how on earth could he help it? The man's endless flow of braggadocio, monopolising, insistent, was enough to drive you mad. In company he domineered, tyrannised; and the shameful way Felicia's mother and sister kowtowed to whatever he said! . . . The moon could want to tell him whatever it liked, he would put the man in his place sooner or later. He passed his hand involuntarily over his forehead. His hand was cold and trembling.

As he approached the house where Felicia lived he knew that Van Druten was there for he heard his voice, as usual: talking and probably laying down the law. Damn the man! Every night he was there to interrupt his courtship and make it as unpleasant as he possibly could.

He stopped, half-deciding to turn on his heels and return home. He could even go for a walk around the Savannah in the moonlight . . . And then he remembered Felicia.

When he entered he found the family, as usual, listening to Van Druten. As he shook hands with him, Van Druten said: "Your hand is quite cold, Malcolm."

"Yes," he said, "the air is chilly outside."

He sat near to Felicia and the conversation continued; or rather, Van Druten talked and the others listened. The more he talked the more discomposed Malcolm became. He shifted his position in the chair, crossed his legs and uncrossed them, took his pipe from his pocket, filled it and lit it, wore a tired expression, asked for a glass of water and followed Felicia into the pantry for it. When they were there he held her and kissed her passionately, cruelly pressing her to him until she had to ask him not to hurt her. That was one way of relieving his smouldering mixture of love for Felicia and hatred for Van Druten: he must hurt Felicia. If he hadn't done that, he might have done something far worse, far more upsetting.

He saw Felicia handing him the glass of water and he suddenly remembered that he had asked her for water. He regarded her with a crooked smile on his face, not taking the glass.

"Don't you want the water, dear?" she asked.

His expression grew hard. "Water? No," he said; "I want to get away from that man."

"What man?" she asked naively.

The question irritated him, for she knew perfectly well what man he was referring to. He said nothing.

"Come, come Malcolm," he heard her saying; "what's upset you?"

"You ask me that?" he said sharply, looking straight down into her eyes. Her pretty face fading, fading, nearly disarmed him.

"What has he ever done to you that you should ha– . . . dislike him?"

A slight shudder passed through his tall frame. He roused himself.

"Let us not discuss him, dear," he said, deliberately trying to be gentle. "Bring two chairs and let us sit away from them, in here, alone."

She opened her two large eyes wide in astonishment.

"In here?" she said incredulously. "What would Mama say with Van Druten there?"

"Damn Van Druten!" he said, exasperated. "Must he always be here to anger me when I want to be alone with you? What the devil do you people see in the man to charm you so?"

"Charm *me*?" she said in a pained tone, standing away from him. "Can't you be reasonable, Malcolm? What do you want me to do to the man when he has been so kind to Mama?"

"Kind?" he exclaimed.

"Felicia! Felicia!"

"Mama's calling me. Let's go in, Malcolm," and she held him gently by the arm and drew him into the drawing-room.

"As I was saying" – it was Van Druten speaking – "I can stand in front of the Queen's Park Hotel and throw my voice into the Governor's Gardens. I remember, some years ago, making a bet with some friends that –"

Malcolm interrupted: "That's utterly, vocally impossible!"

Van Druten stiffened himself in his chair.

"What did you say, Malcolm?" he asked.

It was as much as Malcolm could do to restrain himself and reply: "I said it is utterly impossible."

"You are telling me that –"

"I am telling you, sir, that you can't do it. It is a vocal impossibility. I happen to know something of ventriloquism,[1] and –"

"Who's talking of ventriloquism?"

"Mr. Van Druten is talking of something else altogether, Malcolm," Felicia's mother said snappishly.

"Something else! I always thought that the art of imitating distant sounds was called ventriloquism."

He puffed violently at his pipe and found that it was cold. That didn't matter; he continued puffing violently.

"My dear boy," – the man's ingratiating manner of address was even more annoying – "you don't seem to know that there is such a thing as actually throwing the voice; of actually placing the vocal organs in such a position –"

"Oh, that's all nonsense!" He was thoroughly angry now. A haze fell over his eyes; a cold sweat suffused his body; the electric light in the room changed its colour, became dismal, with pinpricks of red flashes in it that danced here and there. Everybody in the room receded from him to an impenetrable distance where he could just faintly make out their outlines. And then, suddenly, he saw two eyes, Felicia's eyes imploring him, begging him. His muscles relaxed. His whole quivering frame became limp, as though he had no control over it, as though it belonged to somebody else, and he was levitating in the air.

The grating sound of a gramophone record broke into his brain. He had seen, as in a dream, Felicia's sister rise and go to the gramophone immediately after he had told Van Druten that his theory was all nonsense. She had obviously realized the brittle nature of the moment. Ugh! How he hated the man whom he now saw leaning towards him, glaring; whom he now heard breathing stertorously, like one in a fit. Ugh! How he hated him!

He shifted his position in the chair as a strange man's voice invaded the room. He felt the blood rushing into his dark cheeks, and wondered if anybody was noticing how dark red his face was. The blood pulsated through his veins, the negroid blood with the white blood – by God! He was proud of them both! – rushing through him in a wild fury, chasing the coldness from his feet, his limbs, his trunk, his head, clean out of him, leaving him insufferably hot. The strange voice was like a blur at first, a monotonously drawn-out quaver of guttural sound that gradually settled into periods, into sentences, into words. The strange man was reciting from the gramophone box, reciting from two thousand miles away . . .

He glanced at Felicia. He thought her face was pale, that her eyes held a timorousness in them. He exulted in it. He would make them all afraid of him tonight before he left them!

He listened. The drawling voice continued its sentimental trash of sweetheart this and sweetheart that. Sickening! Chut!

There was no help for it. The voice impinged itself upon the yellow-lit silence of the room. It was better, at any rate, than listening to Van Druten's talk.

The record came to an end without any warning. Van Druten said: "Now I've had many an argument over that record. What would you say Malcolm: that the sweetheart of whom he has been dreaming is his wife or not?"

Malcolm didn't know what to say. He hadn't heard a word of the record, but sweetheart this and sweetheart that. Chut!

"Play it again, Constancia. I'm rather anxious to have Malcolm's opinion."

Constancia put the record on again after a slight hesitation. Malcolm listened. It was the usual shilly-shally of a man thinking over in the quiet of his study an early love affair. The last stanza contained the dénouement:

> But oh, my dream is broken by a step upon the stair,
> And the door is softly opened and my wife is standing there;

Yes: with eagerness and rapture all my visions I resign
To meet the living presence of that old sweetheart of mine.[2]

The record had scarcely reached its raucous end when Van Druten said: "It is obvious that the wife is not the sweetheart; that the wife is only the embodiment of the early, abstract love."

Malcolm gasped, clenched his fist in his lap, bit the stem of his pipe as though he would bite through it, and then: "I don't agree with you," he said with a triumphant acidity.

"How else can you . . ."

"There is only one interpretation to the drivelling verse," Malcolm interrupted.

Van Druten blanched beneath the electric light.

"The wife *is* the sweetheart of whom he has been thinking all the time," Malcolm added.

Van Druten raised his voice a little. "Now you're talking rubbish."

Malcolm half closed his eyes and bit at his pipe. Constancia said looking at him: "I don't know why you should always . . ."

"You shut up!" he commanded her in a loud voice. "This is Mr. Van Druten and I, not you and the whole . . ."

"I will not have this boy always contradicting me in this rude fashion," Van Druten shouted to nobody in particular.

"Malcolm!" Felicia's mother said, severely. "I won't have you being so rude . . ."

But Malcolm's head was now a hissing ball of fire.

"To the devil with you!" he shouted, his eyes bulging, his nostrils dilated, crouching like a lappe at bay. "That's why he's got you all twisted round his little finger! Everything he says, it's as though God Almighty is speaking!" He rose from his chair. Felicia was sobbing hysterically, shaking, calling out, "Malcolm, Malcolm!" but Malcolm could hear nothing.

Van Druten rose, quivering with rage.

"I will not be insulted by this little nigger-upstart!" he screamed, clenching his fists.

Malcolm felt his chest broadening, his arms lengthening, strengthening, his whole body taking on the proportions of a giant.

"To hell with you!" he screamed, putting all the venom that was in him into the scream. There was a red flame waving in front of him, and behind it the gramophone box. A mad desire seized him. Rushing up to it he grabbed it like a feather in his hands, poised it above his head and hurled it at Van Druten.[3]

Van Druten yelled and ducked as the machine flew over his head and crashed against the window, tearing it from its hinges with a smashing noise of breaking panes. Mrs. Lazarre shrieked; Constancia glared at Malcolm as though she would strike him down with her eyes; Felicia called: "Malcolm, Malcolm, Malcolm!" as he rushed out of the house.

NOTES

1. While at school in England, Mendes had become interested in ventriloquism and conjuring tricks, and had performed to considerable acclaim at a school concert.
2. From "An Old Sweetheart of Mine" by an American poet, James Whitcomb Riley (1849–1916).
3. In a videotaped interview with Bruce Paddington c. 1983, Mendes states that this incident actually took place while he was courting Juanita Gouveia, "Nita", who became his second wife.

A DAY OF SORROW

Adelina's mother had died the night before. It was a hard shock for Adelina's father to bear bravely and though he had broken down three or four times, with his ten children clinging to him in a choral wailing that affected all in the house to tears, especially Roberto da Silva, it still could not be denied that he had shown fortitude in this dark hour of his trial. As old Mrs. da Silva kept saying: "No wonder the poor man breaks down when he sees his ten children around him."

And as old Mrs. de Castro remarked: "Theirs was an ideal marriage. They loved each other so!"

All that sad day as the corpse lay in one of the sepulchrally dismal rooms before the funeral, Roberto da Silva was with the family doing what little he could to comfort the children. Adelina, the eldest, a girl of eighteen or nineteen years, was the bravest of them all. Roberto, perhaps ten years older than she was, had always liked her; so much so, that he had often said to his wife that of all the girls he met at dances and down-the- islands picnics, and elsewhere, Adelina was his favourite. There was something in her, something indefinable, which appealed to him. He admitted to himself when he thought about her – and that was seldom – that she was not as pretty as some girls he knew; only her deeply set eyes were large and dark and very beautiful. And strangely enough Roberto realized that she belonged to that type of girl that had never evoked his sympathy, for she was of a religious turn of mind, modest though not prim. Still, subtly, he liked her, enjoyed her company when accident brought them together and danced with her at such functions as often as he could do so reasonably without arousing the jealousy of his wife. And yet his wife was jealous of her. That too, he knew subtly; and it angered him to think that his wife should be jealous when he felt he had given her no cause to be.

When Adelina's mother died, Roberto's wife was in bed, ill. She let him go to the house of sorrow in the morning without attempting to dissuade him; but when, after breakfast, he put his hat on and said he was going there again, his wife said quietly: "I don't see why you should go back again. You'll have to go to the funeral this afternoon. I think that's quite enough."

And he replied: "I must go dear."

"But why?" she asked pettishly.

"Well, in their days of joy I was always with them. You know they always asked us to join them in their parties and picnics. Why should I not be with them now in their hour of pain?"

"But you have been with them all the morning and you have to go to the funeral this afternoon," she repeated a little more pettishly.

One word led to another and there was a row. Still, Roberto went, and as he walked through the drizzle to the house he felt he was justified in what he was doing, first, because he was very fond of Adelina's father, who was ten years his senior, and secondly because he was angry with his wife for trying to prevent him from doing what he thought he ought to do.

When he arrived he found the stricken father in the drawing-room which was cleared of all obstructing furniture. He was dazedly staring on the polished floor. How different everything now was to Roberto! – for there flashed across his mind the memory of an evening some months back when the room was cleared of furniture for dancing. How he had enjoyed himself that night! It was the Carnival season and the disguises had heightened his enthusiasm for the dance. But now . . .

He spoke to the father and then went into the room of death. A priest was there with the children and some sympathisers and relatives praying. The mournful intonation of the priest's voice, the candles burning over the dead body, the somber dusk of the room made Roberto feel so miserable that he walked out of the room and went into an adjoining one. There he saw Adelina on the bed, sobbing softly. He went up to her and put his hand on her head, playing with her hair. He wanted to say so much to her but dared not. He heard the rain outside pattering somnolently on a tree that grew by the window. He bent over the prostrate form and rested his head on hers. She stirred slightly then raised one arm and put it around his neck. That seemed to comfort her for she ceased sobbing and whispered: "You are so kind to me, Roberto."

He could make no reply. So they lay until the solemn sound of the priest's voice subsided.

The rain continued to fall all through the afternoon and despite that the funeral was a splendidly attended one. Adelina's mother had been a favourite with the Portuguese community of the island, always entertaining them to dances at her house; and whenever she went down to her seaside residence on the Teteron coast for a holiday she would have large numbers of her friends down for the week-ends. She was charitable too; but charitable in a searching, inquisitive sort of way that precluded the undeserving sharing with the deserving in the alms she gave. And so there were all sorts of people who followed in the cortège: Negroes and Indians and coloured men and women, all of whom remembered her for the way in which she had helped them out of their difficulties at one time and another.

Just as the people began to arrive at the house for the funeral it was discovered that no press reporters were present, this detail having been overlooked in the stress of grief and confusion. As it was a Sunday and too late to summon them Roberto offered to do what he could by taking down the names of those attending. In this he was helped by Adelina, a form of employment that encouraged her to be brave. Looking at Roberto once with moist large eyes, she said: "You are so kind to me!" and Roberto thought he saw in the look she gave him something more than gratitude, and was thrilled by it – but the next moment realized what a fool he was to be interpreting Adelina's expression in such a way when her soul could be filled with nothing but grief.

As the last clods of muddy earth were being heaped upon the grave Roberto found himself standing beside Adelina. Her whole body was quivering with suppressed sorrow, though all her sisters and brothers were sobbing uncontrollably. Her father, too, was beside himself with grief, his face drawn, pale and twisted into ugly contortions by weeping. Roberto rested his hands on Adelina's shoulders and whispered into her ear that she must be brave for the sake of her father and little brothers and sisters. She controlled herself with a great effort, as he could see, and asked him: would he come this evening to the house? "Oh Roberto," she murmured huskily. "I shan't be able to stand it tonight. Here it is all right, but at home after this . . ." and she looked suddenly away from him, shook her head as though trying to throw something from it and her large eyes filled with tears that trickled down her cheeks. He asked: "Do you really want me to come?" laying a slight stress on the word "me".

"I do, Roberto."

"Very well, dear," – it was the first time he had called her "dear" – "I shall try my best."

When all the wreaths were placed over the mound of earth, in which cere-mony Roberto took his part, and the family was getting ready to go away in the car, Adelina gently drew Roberto in with her and sat him beside her. It was a large car, so it held them all. She took his hand in hers and clasped it tightly, till they arrived at his home. She whispered to him as he was about to alight: "Please come tonight?" and the imploring look in her eyes was enough to make him decide to hazard all risks to be with her that night.

When he told his sick wife that he was going back to the house after dinner she grew furious. Roberto was disturbed, for the doctors had said that his wife's lungs were weak and that she must be kept as quiet as possible. He tried to calm her by argument that sounded to him sympathetic and reasonable. But she would not be calmed and told him many hard things: that she could not trust him after that affair of some months back and that other affair of two years ago. She told him he was cruel to think of leaving her when she was her-self on a sick-bed from which she might never rise. Had she stopped then, Roberto might have been brought to a sense of duty, but when she went on to abuse Adelina saying, among other things, that she was just like those women who intrigued men away from their wives, he became angry, took his hat, and walked out of the house without having had his dinner.

As he walked through the drizzle thoughts rushed into his brain wildly. What unreasonable creatures women were! Why should a man not be allowed to do in peace what he considered was his duty? And yet, even now he did not feel quite comfortable in what he was doing. It would have been so easy for Inez, his wife, to have given her smiling assent: instead of which, for no earthly reason so far as he could see, she had chosen to make it as unpleasant as she possibly could for him. God, why? And she was ill too, which made it even more difficult for him to be at ease with his conscience. How cruel of her to be taking advantage of her illness, a fact which she knew perfectly well should have nothing at all to do with his returning to the house. Had not Jao, Adelina's father, been very kind to him in the days before this appalling tragedy had befallen him? And now, well, Jao was in need of a friend's support . . . Perhaps, after all, he had been a little heartless in his treatment of Inez. Poor Inez! He could see her now, sitting up on the bed, her face pale, her large eyes looking angrily at him this minute, the next with pain in them. How could he have left her like that, alone? Oh yes, he knew he loved her today as much as on that afternoon, seven years ago, when he had married her.

"You are leaving me on a sick-bed, from which I might never rise again!"

she had said to him sobbing. Supposing she should die? The doctor thought her condition serious. Still, he didn't feel there was cause for much anxiety for she was bright and her laugh so rang through the house occasionally that the whole neighbourhood could hear it. Poor little Inez! After all, it would be just as well for him to turn back. Inez was his wife and Adelina's father only his friend – and just as Roberto was about to swing on his heels and retrace his steps he found himself before Adelina's house. Pushing the gate, he walked in.

When he entered the house he found it brightly lighted. Jao was on a sofa in the drawing-room, sobbing. Roberto approached him, sat by him and tried to talk to him, but found him inconsolable, for he kept saying that life could no longer be of any use to him without his loved one, and moaned and moaned and moaned as though he would never stop. There was no one else in the room and Roberto wondered where Adelina could be. His attention was so centred upon trying to catch her voice in any part of the house that he almost forgot the presence of the disconsolate man beside him, until he heard him suddenly give vent to a loud outburst of wailing. He put his arm around him and told him he must try and show a bold front as he had others to consider. But still he sobbed loudly. Roberto was beginning to feel depressed for he could now hear the children softly weeping in another part of the house. Outside, the drizzle had developed into a rain and it seemed to Roberto that all the trees were weeping too. Two or three moths blundered about the electric light. He felt more depressed than ever and the grief of Jao so affected him that tears actually welled up to his eyes. And then Adelina appeared at a door; but she hesitated, as Roberto could see, in order to gain full control of herself. Roberto gazed at her and thought her really beautiful at that moment. His heart beat fast and the blood seemed to be running through his veins in a desperate sort of way that left him cold. Now she was looking at him with the same expression he had once before seen on her face. Rising, he approached her. Just at that moment the front door opened and a priest entered. The priest went up to Jao, sat by him and began talking to him.

"I am so comforted to know you have come," she said sadly.

"I had to come, Adelina. You asked me to come, and so I am here. How do you feel now?"

"Comforted by seeing you," she said simply. "Come and talk to me." She was gripping his hand as though that was the only way of easing the pain in her heart.

She led him into the same room where, earlier in the day, he had inadvertently found her. There was no one else in it, and the reflection from the drawing-room light made it possible for him faintly to see the objects in it: the dressing table, the washstand, a chair here and there, the bed. She sat on the bed and drew him down beside her. Impulsively, she said: "O Roberto, Roberto, this is awful: more than I can bear. What is to become of me now?" And she looked up at him with her bobbed hair all dishevelled and her eyes wild. It was all he could do to resist putting his arms about her and holding her to him desperately, passionately. Instead he said quietly: "You must be brave, dear," and immediately realized how futile the injunction must have sounded to her. It was so commonplace, so stereotyped! – but it was all he could find to say at the moment.

For a long while they were silent. Adelina was staring before her, her eyes distrait, the dimly reflected light gilding her face with a pale tint. Roberto gazed at her. The rain still fell outside. Now and again Roberto could hear the wind howling, and it seemed to him that all the world was weeping over this tragedy that had come upon it this day. He found himself wondering what tragedy – for he had actually forgotten for the moment that Adelina's mother was dead and buried.

"Will you always be kind to me, Roberto?" he heard Adelina asking, in a voice that came from very far away.

"Kind to you, dear? My God!" He was surprised at his own vehemence and checked himself from doing something rash. Then, modulating his voice, he asked: "Why do you ask?"

"Oh Roberto, Roberto, you must know why: my sorrow, and, and, –" she trailed off into silence.

He glanced at her quickly and found her eyes on him.

"Tell me. Tell me," he said, gazing fixedly, challengingly into her large eyes. She lowered her head and mumbled something that he did not hear. He was gripped suddenly by an agonizing ecstasy; and before he could do anything, she rose and walked away from him, towards the wooden partition, murmuring: "God, God, how am I to bear this?"

For a long time they were silent in the room whilst the wind whined like a hungry dog and distant thunder began to growl. She leant against the partition, her head resting on her raised arms. He could not move. Never before had he felt like this. Even if he had tried he could not have moved at that moment. And yet his heart was filled with feeling, bursting with it, until he wondered at his immobility, despised it, derided it, stood, and went rapidly towards her, without any fixed notion as to what he was going to do, but with a full knowledge of what he wanted to do.

For a second or two he stood before her, and during that pause she turned to meet him. He saw only her eyes like two small flames levitating before him. As he extended his hands clumsily, they rested on her breasts, and the next instant she had put her arms around him and he was kissing her on the lips.

IN A RESTAURANT

He walked in briskly and looked down the long narrow room of the Merry Widow in Frederick Street.

"Hello," he said with a disappointed look on his face.

"How d'you do," the man addressed replied. "Come and have a cream."

"Thanks, but I really can't. Am awaiting somebody."

"Oh, sit down, anyway."

He sat down facing the entrance door. Pedestrians of all colours and classes were passing to and fro, to and fro, unceasingly.

"Well, when are you giving us another book of verse?" he was asked.

"Oh, by the way," he replied, not looking at the man sitting opposite him, but into the street with a searching eye, "why the devil don't you review my last book?"[1]

"Thought you wanted Daly[2] to do the job."

"Not necessarily," he said, rising slightly with an expectant look in his eyes, speaking as though mechanically. "When Daly went away I thought the review column would have to await his return to the island, and so I suggested to the editor . . . Excuse me a moment," and he walked to the entrance door rapidly. He stood there for a few minutes, bare-headed, his long black hair neatly combed back, his dark face ugly but for his eyes that were deeply set, looking out as from far away, his short body turning this way and that with an impatient, nervous abruptness. Glancing up he noticed the time on the large clock suspended from Stephens Ltd.[3] Half-past twelve. "I wonder if she will come? I wonder if she will come?" he was thinking, excitedly. Standing on his toes suddenly, he strained forward for a moment, dropped back on his heels, walked inside the restaurant, resumed his seat, his fingers twitching, a cold shiver running through his body, a hardly perceptible ruffle on the somber calm of his eyes.

"You were saying, da Silva . . ."

"Oh yes." His stare was fixed on the entrance door. "She is coming, she is coming," his heart said, and he thought his companion heard his heart speaking. This was his chance with Helen, he realized, his one chance, perhaps, from which might blossom a new experience. He must prepare the soil properly. When he spoke again, he heard his voice coming from a great distance. "Review the book, my dear fellow. Daly will be away too long, and he wrote me telling me when I sent him the volume that his locum tenens . . . Excuse me," he broke off and rose to meet the lovely little woman, like a wisp of cloud on a sunny day, dressed all in white, coming towards him with a smile on her pretty face.

"At last!" he greeted her with.

"Why, am I late?" – ingenuously from her.

"Well, not exactly." She glanced at him with an un-understanding smile, and followed him up the long narrow room, between the two rows of tables at some of which sat people of divers races. They chose the extreme end-table of the room, beyond earshot.

"Well, Helen, and how do you feel after last night and this morning?"

"A bit tired and so sleepy . . ." The coloured waitress stood expectantly by their table.

"Yours Helen?"

"Vanilla. And what are you taking?"

"Really" – rather tiredly, and with a fatigued cast of countenance – "I don't feel well." He watched her face closely and smiled within as he heard her say: "Don't feel well?" He could see that she was concerned and his heart glowed.

"Nothing much. Too much whiskey last night." To the waitress: "Get me a glass of milk."

"We has none sir."

"Beer then – and two glasses of water."

"Tell me the truth Peter," she said, regarding him earnestly, as the waitress retreated from their table. "Did your wife tell you anything – because of me? You know, you danced three times with me."

He heard his wife telling him that morning that she forbade him to dance with Helen more than once on any future occasion.

"Oh no," he said, after a pause, "nothing at all."

"Sure?"

"Quite."

"You know, Peter, I am afraid of her."

"Are you? So am I."

"I don't know why." She laughed nervously. "Perhaps it is because I think she is jealous of me."

"Absurd. Why should you think so when last night was the first time we met at a dance. We have seen very little of each other – you and I."

Quietly she answered: "Yes," as though it pained her to utter the monosyllable.

The waitress returned with their order, set the glasses before them and left them.

After a sip of beer, he said, looking fixedly at her: "Why didn't you treat me roughly when I came to you this morning to ask you to meet me here? I asked that of you last night as a favour."

"You remember that?"

"Oh Helen, I wasn't drunk, only tipsy."

"I don't mean that, but I thought . . ." She paused, glanced at him, at her ice-cream, awkwardly.

"I really don't know what I thought, Peter."

"You thought I wouldn't come, perhaps?"

"Yes."

"You were surprised to see me then?"

"Yes, and glad."

He gazed at her silently for a moment.

"You couldn't tell me to go away then?"

"How could I when I was wanting you to stay?"

"It isn't everything we want that is good for us."

"Yes, but it is difficult to discriminate at times, isn't it?" she asked simply, not looking at him.

"Very," he replied bitterly. Then he braced himself and asked: "You – would meet me again if I asked you to?"

A pause. "I don't know. Where?"

"How about the Look-out?4 We won't be disturbed there."

"When?"

"Oh, any old time that suits you. Tomorrow, about this time."

Another pause. "Are you very anxious for me to say 'yes'?"

"Of course, silly!" and he smiled, passing his hand through his hair.

They lapsed into silence, sipping at their glasses as though that were the only reason for their tryst.

At last he said, straggling the words: "Tell me, Helen, er, are you – a flirt?"

She looked at him quickly, but before she could reply, she heard him saying: "Helen, your eyes are neither grey, nor green, nor blue. Now what lovely new colour are they?"

"Does the colour of my eyes tell you anything about my temperament?"

"Nothing at all, only, well – the intense beauty of their colour I noticed for the first time – at that moment." Then leaning forward, the tips of his fingers touching the tips of her fingers: "Are you a flirt, Helen?" he asked again.

She thought before replying: "Aren't you in a better position to judge than I?"

With a shrug of the shoulders he replied: "I have known you for such a short time, Helen. Our acquaintanceship can be said to have started only last night, and here we are . . ." He didn't finish the sentence.

"But why do you ask me that, Peter?"

Indeed! He asked himself the question: why did he ask her if she was a flirt? . . . All sorts of reasons hopped into his mind until he couldn't recognize one from the other. He gazed at her, his eyes half closed, wondering if she could be more than ten years his junior – perhaps she was twenty, he decided. Twenty, not more.

"It would be rather dangerous if I grew to care for you and realized afterwards that you were – well – one of the more fickle irresponsible sort."

"Don't talk like that Peter. You could never grow to care for me."

"I could, Helen," he answered quickly, almost in a whisper.

He could see her expression change but he could give it no interpretation. He flung his arms to the back of his head carelessly and remarked with a yawn: "Perhaps, everything taken into consideration, I should not be talking to you like this."

By this time there were very few people in the restaurant. He heard a step behind him and asked: "Who is that coming in?" She caught the anxiety in his voice, for she answered quickly: "I don't know the couple. Are you afraid?"

"I am. Aren't you?"

"I don't care!"

"But supposing my wife should . . ." he broke off abruptly and shook his head violently from side to side. "Chut!" he exclaimed.

"Life's funny, isn't it?" Her ingenuousness was disarming and – fascinating.

"You find it so, Helen – and not interesting?"

"Anything that's funny is interesting." He added, chuckling, "And sometimes dangerous."

She took him up immediately. "Why?"

"Oh, this is a small community; and too, I am a rather dangerous person." He spoke seriously, very seriously.

"I have heard nothing of you that leads me to suspect danger lurking in you," she said, glancing at him through the corner of her eye, coyly.

"You have heard nothing . . ." In his mind flowed a repetition of the sentence: "She has heard nothing, she has heard nothing."

"There is nothing to hear, Helen," he pronounced finally.

Followed a silence. The room contained only two other persons now, and they were too interested in each other to take any notice of them.

"I want to ask you a question, Helen."

"You may," she said invitingly.

"But – will you answer it?"

For reply she gazed at him, her face cupped in her hands.

"For God's sake Helen, don't look at me like that."

She straightened herself and pulled the front of her hat down over her eyes. "Does that suit you?"

He smiled as he said: "I really don't know, Helen. You are teasing me."

She dropped her hands and exposed her eyes, with the same expression in them.

"That's better," he said. There was a short silence during which they gazed at each other, became confused, and sipped at their glasses.

His manner suddenly changed. He was watching her intently.

"I wrote a short story last night, Helen. Just before going to the dance. I call it 'Shango,' all about a Negro and his vestigial instincts. "[5]

"I have read some of your stories in a local magazine. I think some of them awfully good, Peter. Have you had any printed in England?"

"Yes," he replied, "in one or two of the better-class magazines. It's a steep climb, Helen, that climb up the literary mountain, but I am determined to get to the apex, sooner or later." His eyes glowed as he added: "I am after immortality, immortality of name."

She looked at him admiringly, but said nothing.

"You know, Helen," he continued, "I think I have the power within me but it takes hard, assiduous labour to bring it to its fullest development, and I feel that I shall succeed one day. Do you wish me luck?"

"With all my heart!"

Again his manner changed abruptly.

"For Christ's sake, Helen, don't let me see you too often. I shall fall desperately in love if I do."

She hung her head as she said: "I am thinking the same for myself."

"Helen!"

"Do you think badly of me for telling you – that?"

He held her hand and raised it to his lips. He could see her blanch, quiver, her pretty lips parted, her grey-blue-green eyes sleepy.

A house bird hovered about the window sill and poised on it chirping. Its "cheep, cheep" fluttered about the room with a delightful insistence. They neither saw it nor heard it, though.

"Helen, kiss me." There was no pleading in his voice; it was a command.

She looked at him for a long time, bending towards him.

"Your breasts – God! Don't let me see them!" She didn't move. Everything became blurred before him, her fair face receding from him, like a fading portrait.

"Kiss me, Helen!"

"Do you really mean that, Peter?" she asked huskily.

"I do, dear."

They both leant forward, the bird still cheeping in the room occupied by them alone, and as he kissed her lips his arm knocked over one of the glasses of water. The water flowed onto a neighbouring chair.

"An accident, Helen," he remarked. "But supposing they think I had wee-weed the chair?" he asked, smiling.

She laughed aloud to conceal her confusion.

NOTES

1.   A long poem, *The Poet's Quest* (London: Heath Cranton, 1927).

2.   Mendes may have been thinking of W.H. Dolly, editor of the *Quarterly Magazine of the Richmond Street Literary and Debating Association*.

3.   A department store on Frederick Street.

4.   May refer to a small concrete platform in the St Ann's Hills, approached through the Botanical Gardens, and with a panoramic view of the city of Port of Spain and the Gulf (Lise Winer, *Dictionary of the English Creole of Trinidad and Tobago* [Mon-

treal: McGill-Queens University Press, 2009]). A viewing point on the Maracas Bay main road, also known as the Look-out, seems less likely in this context.

5.   "Shango" was published posthumously in Alfred H. Mendes, *"The Man Who Ran Away" and Other Stories of Trinidad in the 1920s and 1930s*, ed. Michèle Levy (Kingston: University of the West Indies Press, 2006).

FAUX PAS

In South Quay,[1] three men stood in front of a provision store door chatting. The youngest of the three, a tall black-haired man of twenty-two, was the head clerk in the store. He was jacketless and his sleeves were rolled up to above his elbows. The other two men had been passing by when the clerk had called out to them and they had stopped to have a chat. One was a white man, stodgy, with a pair of small eyes that blinked all the time. He was a commission agent. The other was a coloured man, with bad hair[2] and a muddy-looking skin. He too was a commission agent.

"How's business?" the white man asked.

"Things dull," the clerk said. "No crop, no money. All the Chinese and Indians hard-up."

"Yes, out of crop everybody hard-up," the coloured man said, picking his nose.

"That's so," the white man said. "And, of course, no black-eye peas this year: the rains spoil everything. The coolies round Penal[3] must be seeing hell."

"You right, man, those people must be seeing hell," The clerk said.

"Yes, hell", the coloured man said, examining the finger he had just taken from his nostrils.

"Serve them right," the white man said, blinking and shading his eyes with his hand. The glare was strong. The pitched street was steaming.

"If it serve them right! They work like hell, they make money, they don't spend it. Why they should make more money?"

"Money not made for people like that," the coloured man said, sniffing.

"And the Chinese – they go in the bush, behind God's back, make a lot of money and take it all to China with them."

"That's true, they take all of it with them when they go to China."

"That's a damn shame," the white man said. "Boys, boys, look!" he continued excitedly. The other two looked in the direction his eyes indicated. A flashily dressed woman sauntered along. She walked past them showing all her charms. The clerk gave a deep breath; the white man half-closed his eyes; the coloured man leered at her. Then they looked at each other, grinned salaciously and winked.

"Some stuff," the white man said, adding a lewd remark.

"Some stuff," the clerk said. "Never seen her before."

"No, never seen her before."

They fell into a silence, each thinking his own thoughts. Their thoughts were very much of a piece.

They gazed about them: at a tram-car passing; at an inspector of police on horseback, trying his best to look like a most important personage; at a big black policeman lazily resting his weight on one leg; at a mule micturating.

Some pigeons were excitedly gleaning the multitudinous grains of oats which had leaked from a torn bag on a passing cart, when another cart, rattling up the road on its way to the railway goods' shed, passed over a leg of one of the pigeons. The wounded pigeon flapped its wings in vain between moments of rest. Then it lay panting. A little black boy, ragged and dirty, darted into the street from the railway station, and, picking it up, bolted up the street. Three other ragamuffins started off full pelt after him. They disappeared round the corner of Charlotte Street.

"That's a good joke," the coloured man said wryly. "Pigeon-pélau to-night."

The others agreed, the clerk adding: "Helps to brighten up this God-forsaken job."

"By the way," the white man said, blinking, "see there's a hell of a row over that harbour scheme."4

"Oh, dry up," the clerk said irritably. "Let them talk. They like to hear their own voices. When I go away, d.v."5 – he winked and then chuckled – "I want to have a fine jetty to land on when I return. That's all I care about with that scheme."

"That's all I care about it too."

"And I, of course."

"They're all damn fools to talk so much," the clerk said, gazing at a policeman taking the name of a lawless bus-conductor.

"You right, man," the coloured man said.

"Damn right."

Two women turned the corner and came down the street along the pavement towards them. One was young, the other middle-aged. They were both dressed up to the nines, in bright colours and nicely rouged. The clerk saw them first.

"Christ, boys, look at that, look at that!" he whispered hoarsely, excitedly. "How's that for a –"

"For God's sake," the white commission agent said, glancing at the women and then at the clerk quickly, "shut your damn mouth! That's my wife and daughter."

NOTES

1.   The business quarter of Port of Spain. Mendes's grandfather Francisco's provision store was located on the Almond Walk, now Broadway, which debouches into South Quay.
2.   That is, tightly curled African-type hair.
3.   A town in the south of Trinidad.
4.   A proposal for waterfront development, a deepwater harbour scheme which had been disputed by conflicting interests for some years. It was begun on 6 March 1935 and came into full operation on 12 February 1939. Michael Anthony, *The Making of Port-of-Spain*, vol. 1, *The History of Port-of-Spain, 1757–1939* (Cascade, Trinidad: Paria, 2007), 208.
5.   Latin *Deo volente*, God being willing.

NEWS

In Trinidad everybody is a cricket enthusiast when a West Indies team is touring England.[1] An atmosphere of excitement seems to pervade the town of Port of Spain during that time, for everywhere you turn you observe groups of various sizes gesticulating and talking loudly of the match in progress. Even the cartermen, the porters, the messenger boys, the cabmen discuss the game with evident enthusiasm. Business is conducted as usual, it is true, but you feel as if it is not *the* most important concern of the island's life then. In the delivery of an order a piece of news reaches the clerk – usually false – and he must pass it on. If it is good news, you will hear the carterman, receiving the order, brag in a rasping voice of Constantine's[2] performance two years ago in Barbados, of Small's[3] century in England some years ago, of Challenor's[4] reputation for being one of the six best batsmen in the world. There is for once a bond uniting the cosmopolitan peoples of the island. What considered legislation so often fails to do, cricket does, for the people become, what is so much better than no relationship at all, a cricket family . . .

In the office of de Souza & Co., a group of six men was gathered. There were the two de Souza brothers, an Indian clerk called Sankeralli, two commission agents, one a European, the other a coloured fellow, and Joe Anzora, sportsman and man-about-town. It was a Monday morning, and the clock in the office registered eleven o'clock. Business was dull, as it always is on that day in the provision line.

"Boys," Anzora was saying, his Chinese cast of features puckered up with excitement, "we must win that match. Challenor is going to make a century and Fernandes[5] will score well. The two white men will score, I tell you," he added with emphasis as though someone was contradicting him.

McPherson, the coloured commission agent, said, pulling at his bushy moustache nervously: "We must win that match by an innings, man. News couldn't be better: one for a hundred and seven and all crack bats to come yet."

"Didn't we lick Derbyshire last tour?"[6] Sankeralli asked.

"No," Anzora said, "abandoned through rain." Anzora knew the whole history of West Indies cricket. It was a pleasure to hear him discourse on Learmond, Acton, Sydney Smith, Goodman.[7] He could make the topic interesting to the most apathetic, with his dry voice and picturesque gesticulations.

"When do we expect more news?" the white commission agent asked.

"Well," Anzora said, "Fred Brown of the *Sporting News* was telling me only last night at the *Standard* that he had made arrangements for news twice a day."

"Damn good," one of the de Souza brother said. "It's a shame the way the Cable Board gives us news."

There were murmurs of assent.

"That means," Sankeralli said before going off to attend to a Chinese customer, "news is about due."

"What was the English score again?" McPherson asked.

"One hundred and fifty-nine. We are fifty-two behind with nine wickets intact," Anzora said in a triumphant tone, emphasising each word as though they were all deaf or dull of comprehension.

Just at this minute Halliday entered the office. Each member of the group looked searchingly at his face, for Halliday was known to be so interested in cricket that one year he had actually gone to the expense of having private cables sent out to him. Everybody who was anybody in the town knew Halliday. He was a popular intercolonial umpire, and his authority was regarded with respect. What Halliday had said on such and such an occasion was the means of settling many a dispute on the Savannah. He was a little man, red in the face, with a touch of the negro in his hair and features.

As he walked in all saw that there was something up, for Halliday was biting his underlip and winking rapidly. These were sure signs that he had something to tell.

"Boys," he said, breathing heavily, "four hundred and twenty-one for four wickets. Fernandes a hundred, out, Challenor one hundred and seventeen."

The little group gasped like one man.

"God! Great!" Anzora said.

"Damn fine!" the younger de Souza brother said.

"Record score!" another said.

Sankeralli came rushing up. When he learnt the news a yellow pallor suffused his almost black face and he forgot all about the mean, bartering Chinaman to whom he was attending.

Anzora left the office with quick strides. His keenest desire now was to spread the news. What a pity he hadn't asked Halliday how he had come by it! It couldn't have been the *News* or the Cable Board, he argued mentally, for he noticed no excitement around. There was only one way left: Halliday was getting private cables. Clever dog, that! Great fellow, great sport, Halliday! – to be able to creep into any gathering of gossiping prognosticators and give them authentic news! On more than one occasion Anzora had known Halliday do that, and there were many others in the island who could substantiate this by personal reminiscences.

As Anzora walked, he hardly realized he was walking. He felt as if he was treading on air. The news was simply breath-snatching, and he hoped, yes, prayed God that his son, now going to St. Mary's College, would develop into a good cricketer one day. What more satisfying old age could he spend than by hearing people talk of Nello[8] Anzora; than by reading in the cablegrams of how Nello Anzora had scored a century in a Test Match against Hobbs, Sutcliffe, Hendren[9] and that lot? How he would . . . His dream was rudely interrupted by his bumping into a man. The man said: "Why the devil don't you look where you're going to?" Anzora replied: "Heard the news?" – moving off hurriedly, and almost shouting back: "Four hundred and fifty for three wickets!" The man shouted back: "True?" But Anzora was already too far off to hear him. He was hungrily looking out for some cricket friend with whom to share the news, one who would react to the news as he himself had reacted to it. That would give him one of the supreme moments of his life . . . The first match of the tour and the team to be doing so splendidly? That augured well, for the morale of the boys would be sound, high, and there was no telling what they might not do, in the matches to come, with so good an opening. There was nothing like having your men in high spirits. Initial success spelt ultimate success. It acted like a tonic, inspired confidence . . . Four hundred and . . . wait a minute; he couldn't quite remember what Halliday had said . . . or was it five hundred for . . . Again there was a halt in his mind. How many wickets had Halliday said? Either three or four. How he hoped it might be three wickets! Of *course*, it was three wickets, four hundred and fifty for three wickets. That made an average of, er . . . a century and a half to each man. Great! Splendid! – And then he spied Zorana[10] walking hurriedly through Marine Square. He would hasten to him and let him share the good news. Or perhaps he knew already? His pace was suspicious of excitement, and excitement now could mean nothing but excitement over cricket. He doubled into a run and caught up with his victim. Zorana started to the slap on his back.

"You know already?" he flung at him. Zorana's blank stare of amazement reassured him.

"Four hundred and fifty for three wickets. Challenor a hundred and seventy, not out. Fernandes a century," he gasped out of his frail body as though that was the last sound it would make on earth.

"Out?" queried Zorana.

"Who?" asked Anzora.

"Fernandes," said Zorana.

Anzora paused for the fraction of a second, and decided to say yes.

"What news?" asked Zorana.

"Private cable," said Anzora.

"Whose?"

"Halliday's," triumphantly said Anzora. "Halliday's," he repeated, realizing how important the name was in a matter of this sort.

"Damn fine!" Zorana spluttered, taking out his watch. "I was just hurrying to the Cable office. Thanks old man, thanks. You have saved me a little walk. I'm off to the club. Sure to meet some fellows there. So long!" and he turned to the left, making straight for the Union Club. All the morning he had been working on figures, going over his income tax papers, as submitted by his book-keeper, to see how he could best reduce his income to a reasonable amount for the purpose of the tax. His head was a seething mass of symbols, numerals, ciphers now. Little figures kept jumping, prancing, dancing in his head like marionettes. They played hide and seek round the corners of his brain. He had no control over them . . . Good fellow, Anzora! to give him such splendid news . . . Five thousand, four hundred pounds . . . Nonsense! Five hundred and fifty! . . . That little bet he had with Lorrimer! . . . And how he had nearly missed it! – it was only Lorrimer's bragging cocksureness that had made him take it up. Conceited Englishman, Lorrimer, to be thinking that the West Indies couldn't put up two hundred in their first match! Depending on their not having found their land legs after the long sea voyage, eh? Blithering idiot! He didn't know the boys or he didn't want to know them! Fifty dollars, the bet. Not so bad . . .

He would order a case of champagne as soon as he got to the Club and treat the crowd. *Moet et Chandon*, nothing less . . . Five hundred and fifty! Or was he getting mixed up with that five-thousand-pound-entry on his income tax sheet? "Let me see, let me see," he said to himself. "Five thousand, five hundred. Yes. Anzora distinctly said five hundred and fifty. I can see the movement of his lips now. For two wickets or wasn't it three? Heavens, if it could only be two! Halliday's news, absolutely *bona fide*. Great fellow, Halliday! If only I could find him now to let him share the champagne with us at the club! I wonder where he is, I wonder where he is?" He vaguely heard a voice say: "Good morning, sir," and as vaguely saw a cap tilted to him as he mounted the steps of the club.

"Oh, good morning, James."

"Any news, sir?"

"News?" he shouted. He was already on the top landing. Bless his soul! He would pat the fellow on his back if he were near enough to him. A pity creation had limited the reach of his arm. "Five hundred and fifty for two wickets, James," he shouted down on the old black attendant. Each word fell like a bomb on James's head.

Already somebody was at the door.

"What do you say, Zorana?"

But Zorana would not be baulked of his desire. He wanted the whole crowd of fellows to hear the news from him with one resounding triumphant sentence. He pushed past the intruder, and entered breathless, hot and perspiring. He saw a crowd before him, at least thirty, and they appeared to have been waiting for him for there was intense silence in their midst.

"Boys," he said in a stentorian voice, like a footman announcing guests, "boys," he repeated impressively, "five hundred and fifty for two wickets!"

The whole crowd gave an audible gasp and the room was immediately filled with questions and cross-questions.

"Wait a minute, you fellows," he said, "until I order the champagne." James shambled off with the order as quickly as his rickety legs would allow him.

"Yes, yes, I've seen the cable myself. Anzora – you know Anzora?" Everybody nodded. "Anzora showed me the cable. Halliday had lent it to him . . . Where's Lorrimer?"

"Lorrimer!"

"Lorrimer!"

Zorana felt himself a hero. He had only to ask for Lorrimer and a thousand voices would shout the name until it reached the very skies, and God heard it.

But Lorrimer was nowhere to be found.

"He was here a moment ago," someone said.

"The beggar!" Zorana muttered within his teeth.

Waiters were busy handing round the champagne. When all had been served, a voice shouted: "A toast, Zorana, a toast!"

A thousand voices took up the words. "A toast, Zorana, a toast!" Gone were the troublous figures of his income tax calculations. He cleared his throat raucously, holding his glass up.

"Boys," he said, "boys . . ." but he got no further, for Lorrimer rushed in at that moment wildly waving a piece of paper in his hand.

"Zorana," he almost screamed in his excitement. "Zorana, listen, my boy! News from the Cable Board. Just through. West Indies, one hundred and fifty-five.[11] Slater,[12] the Derbyshire crack-bowler – I'm from Derbyshire . . ."

NOTES

1. The tour of England by the West Indies cricket team in this story took place in 1928.
2. Learie Nicholas Constantine, Baron Constantine of Maraval (1901–71), brilliant cricketer, broadcaster, administrator, lawyer and politician, and a close friend of C.L.R. James.
3. Joseph Small (1892–1958), Trinidad.
4. George Challenor (1888–1947), Barbados.
5. Maurice Fernandes (Maurius Pacheco Fernandes) (1897–1981), British Guiana.
6. 1923. The match was drawn.
7. George Cyril Learmond (1875–1918), British Guiana; Edward Vincent Joseph Acton (1871–1912), Trinidad; Sydney Smith (1881–1963), Trinidad; Percy Arnold Goodman (1874–1935), Barbados.
8. A teasing tip of the hat to C.L.R. James, whose nickname was "Nello". James, a lifelong enthusiast, tried hard to interest Mendes in the game of cricket in the early days of their friendship (see Letters, this volume). Mendes's thoughts on the subject may be read in his autobiography (34, 35).
9. English cricketers: Sir Jack Hobbs (1882–1963); Herbert Sutcliffe (1894–1978); Elias Henry "Patsy" Hendren (1889–1962).
10. An anagram of Anzora.
11. On this tour the West Indies team lost all three tests by an innings and won only five of the thirty first-class matches played.
12. Archibald Gilbert Slater (1890–1949) played for Derbyshire between 1911 and 1931.

OVER THE TOP

Rain falling all day: an incessant soundless drip on the mud-sea of the Salient.[1] In the morning we shall wade (perhaps) waist-deep in slush and beneath the water-levelled pock-marked ground the shell-holes will be hidden to suck us in; and some, no doubt, shall be drowned, whole in body, swollen indecent corpses, instead of being neatly and decently punctured by bullets from lurking men's rifles and loud lurking machine-guns – for in the morning we attack. Now it is three o'clock, but there is no sun to be seen, only a faint, white, mist-white luminosity dampening all the sky above, and it is cold. Autumn. October. Were you ever in the Ypres Salient in Autumn, in October? No? Well then, you were never in a hell whose torture is mud and shells and mud and more shells, where the shell, before exploding, sinks deep, deep: and then the unholy ugly miracle of a shower of mud spouting swiftly from the rocking earth and then falling down. Out of the line (luck, maybe, if you are) your face, your hair, your whole tunic is mailed in mud. Rifle cleaned, pulled-through, shining in the sun: and then yourself, spick and span, with the fleas hunting in your tender parts. Such is the topsy-turveydom of war hygiene.

Squatting tents on the suppurating ground and in them squat men, khaki-clad, making the best of a bad business with desultory bawdy talk. An officer makes his rounds.

"Tomorrow morning, boys. Ready for the show?" He pokes his head into our tent, exhaling plumes of smoke.

"Bloody revue-show," someone mutters when the officer's head, with its plumes of smoke, is gone.

Menacing bursts of black smoke from high-explosives, some so near that you hear the kraoump and then the swift-sailing swish of the shrapnel about you; some distant, like distant sounds thundering the lust of Moloch.[2] Now and then, high up in the mist-white sky, the bee-drone of an aeroplane. We envy the pilot clean in his cockpit, maybe a thousand feet above this mud in which we squat, our bodies damp and the maddening fleas biting at our tender parts. The maddening fleas biting, making a meal of our tender parts.

We are two kilometres behind the line – such as it is: shell holes joined up by nothing, – and through the black night we move, heavily, warily, wearily, wondering what zero hour will bring us. My eyes are wide open, wide as they can be, but they see nothing until, in the distance, a Verey light[3] vomits its flame and reveals the tatterdermalion boles of trees here and there, like petrified bodies of men. And, too, the desolate horizon. Level ground and squelching limbs moving through it. Squelch, squelch. "The bloody 'ell!" Squelch. "Blast war." Squelch. "'Arf a mo, wot the 'ell you're doin'? You think this is the bloody Strand[4] at night?" Squelch. Squelch. Squelch.

And then we are here.

Where, no one knows. Perhaps, though, the officers do, who loom before us like deep black shadows whispering words that have in them the pulse-beat of fear. And we listen, not hearing, hearing only the occasional crack of a rifle or the staccato chatter of a Lewis gun.[5] These tell us that we are "here", that the enemy is just in front, that we are in for it, each man in his own particular way (the gods are laughing): a bullet through the snout or in the buttock (lucky blighty man![6]), or a shell and you find him no more, unless you aren't fastidious and you will call warm red pieces of quivering flesh "him", or through the searing seventy-two hours without a scratch. Indeed, without a scratch!

And the drizzle, drizzle, the deleting drizzle turning the world to water, and the night hanging before you, behind you, closing you in tight until you gasp for breath and you ask the night, in the silence of your spirit, not to stifle you. But – it is your fear that is stifling you. Ask *that* not to stifle you, if you dare. Ask that huge amorphous shape stalking abroad and in the bowels of your belly not to stifle you!

Some men seek security in darkness.

It is three o'clock, someone croaks. It has taken us from six o'clock to three o'clock to traverse two kilometres. That's nine hours. In hell it takes nine hours to do two kilometres and you aren't tired, only frightened in the clammy silence that has queer hooded noises in it, only frightened like the very devil by those urgent intermittent kraoumps.

But the cold which is clammy with rain-water makes you shiver and you say: "I'm not afraid, it is only the cold making me shiver." In the winter, when the fire is low, I shiver.

Round comes the rum. (Jamaica rum they say. Jamaica, and the sun shines for an infinitesimal second.)

Then something like this: "Takin' your rum, Mendes?"

"You bloody well bet I do!"

"'E's a one, 'e is, when he allus give it me afore."

"Ah, 'e's got wind up, lad."

"Well, why d'you want mine? Double ration, double wind up."

"'Ell . . ."

"Tell 'im it's cold, Mendes, an' you from those tropic lands, far-flung British Hempire. Tell 'im give you 'is. All quiet on the western front,[7] 'e takes your'n, 'e do. Over the top,[8] you take 'is. Fair an' square, that's wot I says."

That's that.

Silence as we drink our ration of rum. Four tablespoons and the blood is roused and the mind lightened, but back of it all you know that zero-hour is on top of you because you've just drunk your rum: rum, a signal even in war for running into the jaws of hell.

"Now boys, once again," our officer whispers through the darkness for the last time, his words falling like another sort of drizzle, "the sunken road twelve yards in front and Poelcapelle[9] a couple of hundred yards after. Don't bunch too much, for Christ's sake, don't bunch too much. Bayonets all fixed?"

Nobody answers.

Slowly, slowly the faint mist-white luminosity returns to earth, lighting it up as a wide glabrous desolation, pustulous, erupted.

And the barrage falls.

Stretching my limbs and gripping my rifle I leave the unhealthy shell-hole and run quickly towards the sunken road.

Down the declivity we flounder and in this second-long grave of safety, the sunken road, we hear the shells howling above us in the riotous open, a uniform din, spraying us over with cold clots of mud. But only for a second this respite from the murderous steel flying about for up the incline we scramble, mouths to the mud, sucking it in, spitting it out, the stink of powder everywhere, gripping as best we can, frantically, aching for the top without being aware that the top will expose us to the enemy's fire.

At last.

A sudden cry to the right.

Fierce fusillade.

The riven and violated earth shivers as a woman in the throes of childbearing. Machine guns spit and bullets scratch the air.

Rat-tat-tat-tat-tat-tat!

P-i-i-i-ing!

I see nothing, I feel nothing, I can hear only the detonating crescendo and now and again a human shriek that tells me some man's face is in the mud. The rum runs through my brain and now I am no longer afraid, only elated because there is a monstrous game afoot,[10] a game of explosive babel and scarred earth and crapulent men. I am moving, somehow or the other, through a horizontal hail of bullets, moving with a muddied rifle in my hand; my hair, soaked in brown filthy water, hanging over my forehead, my ears, my eyes, the steel helmet swaying with each laborious step, my heart pounding like fury inside of me.

And the drizzle drops as if it had a mind never to cease. But it makes no difference now. It is neither wet nor dry, warm nor cold. It is only a word: drizzle.

Down I go, splashing in the mud, fighting for a foothold which I find at last. Not two yards in front of me a shell buries itself with a bitter sneaky snort and does not explode. A dud.

Now the smoke has merged with the mist and you know not which is which. You can smell the smoke though, a smell that would turn your stomach sick if you were not in the midst of war's hullabaloo. But what has the stomach to do with this business? – unless it is torn open, with the bowels staring at the sky, drinking in the drizzle through a raw gut-gaping throat.

"Don't bunch, you bloody fools, for Christ's sake don't bunch!" This is a yell that, luckily, we hear, and the five of us (when we ran down to the sunken road we were fifteen) spread out with startled looks in our eyes. Perhaps it is two minutes since we left the sunken road, and perhaps we have done twenty of the two hundred yards to Poelcapelle.

And then suddenly I see him. He is aiming at me, not twenty yards away, but down drops the man next me on my left with a throttled cry, and because he was young and strong the blood spouts from his mouth at least six inches, making a little circle of warm red in the cold brown waste. But there's no time to look at him and he's obviously dead, so we move on and I scream excitedly, pointing at the grey figure crouching in the shell hole, taking another aim. The bullet pings past my head, an inch off, and without knowing why, a mad anger takes hold of me and I scream and scream, floundering towards him with my mud-dull bayonet swaying in front of me. Another bullet pings past my ear and then I'm on top of him with my bayonet boring its way through his left eye. As in some sudden dissolution he rolls over, leaving my bayonet clear and red.

And the rolling detonations continue.

We are three in the shell hole, the still warm body of the dead Boche,[11] on its back across the top of the crater, making a hideous fourth. His right eye, wide open, is turned to the damp misty white sky. He looks as if he died cursing.

Multitudinous burr of machine-gun fire as we crouch in the shell hole looking at our captain, wondering what next. Crepitations of machine-gun fire, crepitations. The captain gingerly peers over the rim of the crater. I do too. Nothing to be seen in front, except smoke and mist and higher up patches of evil-looking black bursts that suddenly appear and float along with a lazy motion, changing shape, changing shape, thinning and then disappearing altogether. And now, silhouetted against the sky like an old mammoth comb, directly in front, the jagged remains of a village: Poelcapelle, no doubt, our objective, tantalizing like a mirage. How get there? And to the left some dozens of men. One crumples, then another, then two and three in a heap. On the right nothing, not a living thing. A necropolis.

"We'd better stay here," the captain says.

Well, that's worth all travail to hear. Blessed sentence, blessed command that hides us from the Avernian[12] wrath! The thick everted brown lips of the crater are no longer forbidding, for do they not invite us to a kiss of peace, short-lived though it be? And the drizzle now is welcome for it cools the hot flaming cheeks and keeps in check the hot blood.

It is difficult to be angry and passionate in the rain.

But the enemy's retaliation had long ago started so that the flights of shells, crossing in the air, fling agonised greetings to each other that keep the tired mind tense, the weary body on tiptoe of awareness. A clot of mud is like a bullet, a spoken word like the challenge of a shell-burst.

The last shrieks of the dying, beyond all ghost of succour now, streak the air.

"Ma-ohhhhhhhhhh!"

"Ma-ohhhhhhhhhh!"

A little silence, and then: "Ma-ohhhhhhhhh!"

"A man with the top of his head blown off: I saw him a moment ago," the captain says, screwing his face up like a man reaching to retch.

"Ma-ohhhhhhhhh!" – weaker and weaker, and then no more.

Sky pregnant with pain. Earth too in pain, vomiting all her entrails, rocking in pain, shells pounding her brown-bleeding bosom, putrid nauseous stench rising from her open wounds, wounds huge as houses, ragged-edged, a thousand wounds in which live men accoutred for war: smoking rifles, red-hot pistols, blood-red bayonets, wounds oozing pus, nauseous putrid stench rising, soaking, air soaked with nauseous putrid stench, saturated. And "It's half past seven," the captain says, eyes blinking over a watch.

"Good God! And zero-hour was a quarter past seven: we've been in the attack for only fifteen minutes."

Time, measured in agonies, ekes itself out interminably.

"And now for the counter-attack," the captain says, again peering over the rim of the crater. When he speaks he shouts to let himself be heard.

For the next five minutes I attend to my rifle. So does the other fellow who now, I see, does not belong to my regiment at all, and the captain peers over, searching for any sign of Boche activity, and we are standing nearly to our knees in water, and the cold is beginning to creep into me, so I rub hard on my rifle, rubbing the mud and the water further in, but I see to it that my barrel is clear, and would you believe it? my magazine is full of bullets for I have not fired a single one since the beginning of the attack. However, I shall need them, I know, in a short time and all the others I have with me, but the cold is not to be stayed. Now that the body is motionless it is a new enemy to deal with and I do believe that I prefer the living enemy to this impersonal everywhere one.

That is what is so agonising: this inactivity, this waiting-for-something-to-happen. And if the enemy does not choose to counter-attack we must freeze here till dusk and even then pray for relief.

The uproar is incessant. My brain lurches like a pendulum. The earth is rocking. The sky is overcast with an opaque grey-green verdigris. Here and there black smudges of smoke appear, cracking the earth from pole to pole, giving the pattern a bizarre weirdness.

Naked congregation of shattered houses on the skyline. Poelcapelle. Shattered houses praying in the mud. Our objective: that fantastical comb that has passed through the hair of all the Negresses in the world.[13]

And the Boche, where are they? Where are our enemies? But *are* they our enemies? I was at school with a Hamburg fellow and I loved him very much. His name was Uhlandt.[14] His father was a rich ship-owner. Is *he* my enemy? But when we parted, a little over two years ago, we shook hands and clapped each other on the back and swore to see each other again. "Come to Hamburg," he said, waving his hand from the railway carriage, "and I will give you a good time."

"The enemy is getting ready. See, see?" excitedly whispers the captain.

I see nothing.

"Good God, man, there, there . . ."

P-i-i-i-ing!

We drop like two jacks-in-the-box.

The captain is all right. So am I.

And now we are done for. We dare not raise our heads above the rim of the crater and look out on the ruin of the world. We must be quiet, just wait, wait until the enemy's barrage falls, when everything will again be higgledy-piggledy, when human beings will be massed flesh to be fired into, and this waiting, this hiatus in time and space is more fearsome then the noisy nacreous bluster of battle.

"Ma-ohhhhhhhhh!"

Christ, and we thought he was dead! Why should the man go on shrieking like that, making more hideous the hideous day? There he goes again!

"Ma-ohhhhhhhhh!"

But he is all of a piece with the tormented screeching earth.

A queer silence. Our ears noisy with explosions. All the echoes of the last fifteen minutes' explosions reverberating in our ears. We crouch in the shell hole, water to our chests, trapped maybe until the enemy comes. We are waiting, waiting, blind men waiting for armed seeing men.

Clench your teeth and wait.

Make the best of a bloody bad, bloody hopeless, bloody . . .

It's a long long way to Tipperary.[15]

Keep the home fires burning.

Mademoiselle from Armentières.

Three cheers for the red white and blue,

Three cheers for the red white and blue.

Three cheers . . .

Listen to that man screaming again. Block your ears and shut his scream out.

He can't die, poor bitch!

A flight of bullets searching their billets. Here are no human billets. Not now. Everything human is in graves: mud, mud, mud. Let bullets lodge themselves there and welcome.

"Five to eight," the captain says, "time they come." His hand, with the wrist-watch turned towards his eyes, shakes. I hold my hand out, away from the captain, and it shakes too.

And the Boche barrage falls.

Kraoump, kraoump, kraoump.

Kraoush, kraoush, kraoush – and almost their thundering crashes drowned in the sibilant swish of their trajectories.

Now's the time to see what's happening. The trap-door is open wide.

You wouldn't have thought there was so much life in this palaeozoic filth.

Our disconnected shell holes burst into life with rapid fire.

Rapid fire, rapid fire! Grey bending running figures dropping one by one, two by two, three by three. Grey figures dropping, coming, coming, dropping, dissolving into their native earth. Earth mother of men. Green earth stripped naked to grieve for men: sackcloth and ashes and wild gnashing of teeth.

Rapid fire!

That's the bloody stuff to give 'em, boys!

Rapid fire!

Rat-tat-tat-tat-tat-tat-tat!

Rat-tat-tat-tat-tat-tat-tat!

That's the bloody stuff to give 'em, boys!

The air shouts itself hoarse with victory.

The counter-attack is repulsed.

NOTES

1. The Ypres Salient in Flanders, site of fierce battles in the Great War of 1914–18. The town of Ypres was defended by troops of the British Empire.
2. A Canaanite deity whose worship involved the sacrifice of children. One of the devils in Milton's *Paradise Lost*.
3. A signal flare fired from a pistol.
4. A street in London famous for its theatres and restaurants.
5. A light machine-gun.

6. "Blighty" was soldiers' slang for England and home. A "blighty man" was a soldier who had been wounded severely enough to be sent back to England to convalesce.

7. A reminder of the famous novel *All Quiet on the Western Front* (1929) by Erich Maria Remarque, which examined the Great War experience from the perspective of ordinary German soldiers. Mendes's own experiences were coloured by his association with working-class English soldiers or "tommies" from the north of England.

8. That is, over the wall of the sheltering trench and away from its protection.

9. A town in the Ypres Salient which endured persistent fierce fighting.

10. Shakespeare, *Henry V*, 3.1: "The game's afoot. / Follow your spirit, and upon this charge / Cry "God for Harry! England and Saint George!" An apt quotation, given Mendes's circumstances, and the battle fury now coursing through his veins.

11. German, especially a German soldier (slang).

12. Lake Avernus, near Naples in Italy, was believed by the ancient Romans to be an entrance to the underworld.

13. A fantastic image, probably the result of the rum that they have all been given to stoke their courage.

14. See Mendes, *Autobiography* 35, 36.

15. This song and the three which follow were popular during the Great War.

FIVE DOLLARS' WORTH OF FLESH

It was morning, but the sun could not be seen, for a drizzle fell from a sky covered with grey matter. The sky looked like a northern one: it looked as if it were preparing to snow, but the temperature was eighty, for the island lay about eleven degrees north of the equator. Some stevedores, returning on a barge from the ship they had been coaling all night long, their black faces made blacker with coal-dust, the rims of their eyes red from sleeplessness, muttered amongst themselves as they glanced up at the sky that it was raining all over the island. "You carn' see San Fernando hill," one said, showing his white teeth as he peered through the mist and drizzle to the south of the Gulf. "San Fernando?" another remarked in a grating voice. "Chris' man, whey's Port o' Spain, whey's Port o' Spain? San Fernando miles away, man; Port o' Spain right in front us an' you ain' name man see it!"

In the town the church bells were striking half past seven. The rich merchants, the well-to-do lawyers were being speeded to their offices in their closed-in cars; the clerks and clerkesses crowded the Belmont, St. Clair and Four Roads tramcars on their way to their occupations. Several pedestrians, some with umbrellas over their heads, others wearing rainproof cloaks, hurried along the paved sidewalks grumbling at the rainy weather. Motor car horns tooted, tramcar gongs sounded. In the business quarter of the town store doors were being opened by yawning porters who regretted that it was not Sunday as the dreary drip of the drizzle made them feel that this was a day for bed and lazy lolling.

In a little two-roomed cottage in St. James, Isadora Guerra lived with her husband and two children. Isadora sat on a box, staring out at the window. She saw the water dripping from a tree a little way off. She saw a little Indian boy, wearing only a shirt, walk along the road in front of her house to the public pipe, fill the bucket he carried with him, place it on his head with an effort and walk away along the road out of sight. She saw Camachie, the young East Indian woman who lived but a stone's throw from her, pass by with a tray of provision on her head on her way to town. And then she heard her year-old baby cry out in the adjoining room.

She rocked the baby in her arms walking up and down the small room, trying to calm it, but the baby whimpered and kicked its legs out as though in pain.

"Oh God," she said to Ignacio, her husband, giving the baby her breast, "dere ain' no food in de house. Dere ain' no food in de house. You come in late las' night. You eat everyt'ing las' night when you come in. Now it ain' got not'ing."

"Wha' you wan' me do?" Ignacio answered, sprawled upon some bags on the floor: his bed.

"Wha' you wan' me do?" He yawned and rolled over on his side, his face away from Isadora.

"Buh, I tell you dere ain' no food in de house! It ain' got not'ing. You come in late las' night an' eat everyt'ing. Why you carn' get work? Everybody else get work. I carn' ask Gheesa for a bread again. I carn' beg like dat. You lazy, Ignacio, Oh God you lazy an' all of us goin' starve because you lazy. You don' wan' to find work . . ."

"Who don' wan to fin' work?" Ignacio turned his head towards his wife. "Who don' wan' to fin' work? I walk me soul-case out all yesterday, all de day before, all dis mont'. Dere ain' no work, I tell you, no work."

"An' where you get dat money from for dat spree night before las'?"

"I ain' tired tell you is friends dat I spree wit? I ain' spen' a damn cent. I ain' have it."

"You lie!"

Ignacio growled and turned again on his side, this time facing his wife. He pretended to close his eyes but kept one slightly open and studied his wife. She was still handsome, in spite of all the hell she had seen with him. My, she had seen hell with him! He was always out of work; he was often drunk; he beat her when he was drunk; he cut her across the cheek once with a horse whip; there was seldom food in the house; the baby was sick, had had fever for the past month, that's why it was so thin now; there was no money to take the baby to a doctor; the other child, a boy of four, was a holy terror. All day long he was in the yard; he threw dirt over his body, he ate mud once and nearly died from suffocation. Now he had a bad looseness of the stomach. He would wake just now, hungry. He would beg his mother for food; there would be none; he would begin by crying, then he would scream, throw himself on the floor and scream for all he was worth: a holy terror. God, but life was hell! And look at her – she was still pretty; her figure was still there. Only recently he had noticed a crude fellow stare at her as she swung down the road, stare at her as if his eyes were dropping from his head. And the rent. The rent was two weeks overdue and Mr. Simpson was not a man to trifle with. But what could he do? What more? You could only look for a job, that was all. If you didn't get one, well, that wasn't *your* fault! Hell of a life! Hell of a life!

"You sleepin', Ignacio, you sleepin'? You ain' goin' out to look fo' work? It getting' late. Get up, man, get up."

"It rainin'," Ignacio said, his eyes closed.

"Rainin'? Wha' dat got to do wit' looking fo' a job? Wha' dat got to do wit' looking fo' a job?"

"It rainin'," Ignacio said, opening his eyes and blinking,

"Yes, you belly full, You get a square meal las' night. Wha' Antonio go eat when he wake up? Is you chil'; you wan' him to die of starvation?"

"Ah-h-h-h!" Ignacio yawned, his large mouth opening wider and wider. Then he sat up, rubbed his eyes and looked at Isadora.

"Why you ain' do wha' I tell you?" he said at last.

She put the baby down on the floor, stood up and watched him for at least a minute in silence. Her left breast was out of the bodice, luscious, firm, brown. Although Ignacio had so often seen it, he looked at it again.

"Oh, you damn, wutless, good-fo'-not'ing!" she said. "Viper, viper!" she hissed at him, then cast her eyes to heaven and made the sign of the cross.

He gave her an indolent sleepy stare, shaped his mouth and spat through the window. The baby yelled suddenly. She picked it up and commenced rocking it in her arms again, but all the time she paced the floor to and fro with it she was speaking. Her voice was mellow. Her face was very pretty, brown, with large black eyes and on one cheek a slight scar. She was twenty-six. Her long straight black hair fell to her waist. She had five bloods in her veins: Spanish, Negro, East Indian, Red Indian[1] and Chinese.

"You know I try me bes'," she was saying. "You carn' expec' to open parlour in St. James and sell. We'se strangers here. Nobody buy from us because we'se strangers here."

"Because you ain' do wha' I tell you," he interrupted, stretching.

"I wash, I iron, I sew, buh wha' sort of work like dat you go get here from these people? They poor, too poor."

"Look Gheesa, look Maharaj at de 'Green Lion,' look de Souza, de Potegee man, dey rich. Is because you ain't do wha' I tell you."

"Oh Chris', Ignacio, oh Chris', Ignacio!" She made the sign of the cross. "If me father could see me now he turn in his grave."

He left the house half an hour later saying he was going to look for work. She watched him from her window as he moved slowly down the road, hoping he would not return drunk, hoping he would get a job and bring home some money for food. Little Antonio was at her side, tugging at her dress asking for bread and coffee. He was a thin, bony child, with a yellow skin and long matted hair. He suffered from worms.

"Mammie go get bread for you jes' now, Tony," she said. "Don' cry. Go in de yard an' play." But Tony cried until he was tired; then he went into the yard, into the drizzle, half naked and began to make mud balls.

At nine o' clock she called out to Olive, her neighbour's eldest child, a girl of fourteen, and asked her to stay with the children while she went to town to look for a job.

She walked from St. James into town, a distance of two miles. One or two men stared at her from shop-doors as she was walking up Tragarete Road.

She tried some residences for a nurse's or maid's job, without success. She entered a parlour in Queen Street where a sallow-faced girl waited behind a counter for customers to come in.

"Whey you want?" the sallow-faced girl asked in a harsh voice.

"I want to see de boss."

"Mr. Texeira, Mr. Texeira," the sallow-faced girl called out. A white man, stodgy and well-dressed, appeared at the door, "Look somebody askin' fo' you." The sallow-faced girl wore a sneering expression.

Texeira came round to the front of the counter.

"You wantsh me?" he asked, leering at her.

"I lookin' for a job," she said.

Texeira glanced slyly at the sallow-faced girl.

"What you can do?" he asked in an undertone, glancing from her head to her foot and then at her bosom.

"Anyt'ing."

"Well" – he glanced again at the sallow-faced girl, "I ain't got anything here. I knowsh somewhere where they wantsh somebody. Go there now." He took her to the door of the parlour and gave her an address.

She had some difficulty in finding the place. It was a two-storey building in

George Street, giving straight on to the pavement. She knocked at the doors, but there was no response. The windows were shut and the place looked empty. Perhaps he had meant upstairs. She went to the gate and pushed. The gate yielded. She entered and found herself in a passage. She advanced cautiously and at the end of the passage she came upon the stairway leading upstairs. She mounted the steps. When she arrived on top a door opened and Texeria appeared. She was puzzled. He beckoned her with a finger. She stood where she was, gazing at him.

"Come inside," he said, in a low hoarse voice.

"Wha' for?"

"You ain' want money?" He dangled a five-dollar bill before her. "This is yoursh if you come here. I like you. I like you as soon as I see you. I go treat you well. Come in. Nobody here." His face was lascivious, his eyes half-closed. He breathed heavily. She could hear him breathing from where she stood.

Her dull mind at last saw what he was after. Anger rose up within her. She wanted to rush at him, hold on to his hair, scratch his eyes, his cheeks, bite him until the blood came, but she was afraid there was somebody else in the house, perhaps waiting there to help him overpower her, so she said furiously: "Because you white you t'ink you can do as you like!", turned on her heel and walked down the steps deliberately. When she got into the street there was a lot of stir and noise and she felt safe again. As she walked away, she began to think of the five-dollar bill Texeira had offered her. A queer idea came into her head: she could easily have snatched it from his hand and run away with it. What could he have done in that case? She must have money. Today she must get money. Snatching a five-dollar bill like that – well, wouldn't that be stealing? She muttered an *ave maria* and made the sign of the cross over her mouth three times. She thought of her baby at home, starving; of Tony, hungry and in the yard. She hoped he wouldn't try to eat mud again. She hoped Olive would take good care of the two children. She had asked Olive to stay with the children often. She could trust her. She thought of her husband and wondered if he had succeeded in getting anything as yet. But if even he did get something, ten to one he would drink it out; so that the responsibility of finding money was hers. But how? She tried two more parlours. She tried a small dry-goods store. The clerkesses gazed at her and giggled amongst themselves. She didn't mind: she wanted work, she wanted money. She saw a sewing shop and went in. The lady in charge looked her up and down before saying, icily, that there was no vacancy now; no, there would be no vacancy in a hurry, didn't she hear? All the machines in the room stopped at once. "Go on with your work, please!" the lady in charge said sternly. When she was once again outside, she regretted that she didn't let the lady in charge know what she thought about her.

She walked along, not feeling in the least tired. All her desires were centred upon getting a job, and thus money. Yesterday she had had only one meal and for the past year seldom had she had more than one meal a day. On some days she had nothing in the house and Olive's people, who were themselves poor, would in some miraculous fashion know of her plight and send her over a loaf of bread, a little butter, a cup of milk (they kept a cow) and sometimes a plate of soup and dumplings. She would never forget how kind Olive's people had been to her, and often, during her moments of prayer, she prayed God to bless them. She didn't mind so much for herself: she thought only of Tony and her baby.

She had given up crying over spilt milk. At first her father and mother had warned her against marrying Ignacio, and then they had got angry with her, had said bitter things to her, and had had nothing to do with the wedding. Soon after, her father (who was a Venezuelan) had taken the family to Venezuela and she had heard nothing from them since. Often she had thought of writing to them, but her pride would not allow her to do so.

She arrived home at two o'clock, exhausted. Tony was covered from head to foot in mud, and crying. Olive was soothing the baby by walking it up and down.

At six o'clock Ignacio came in, drunk. He wasn't as violent as usual, but he cursed her at the top of his voice and threatened to beat her if she didn't do what he wanted her to do in order to get money. She was very much afraid of him when he was drunk, and at such times she dared not open her mouth.

In half an hour he was sprawled along the floor, in his usual spot, fast asleep, and was snoring stertorously. Little Tony clung to her dress, gazing at his father with wide open, scared eyes. She patted his head with one hand while, with the other, she rocked the baby.

Tony began to wail, saying he was hungry. Olive brought in a bowl of milk and a loaf of bread. Tony snatched the loaf of bread from Olive's hand and ran off into the yard to eat it.

It was growing dark and the drizzle began to drop again. She lit the stump of last night's candle. It lit up the bare room and gave her a feeling of intense misery. The baby in her arm was hot with fever. She drank a little of the milk, afraid to take too much, she didn't know why for she could have swallowed it down with quick, greedy gulps, and put what was left down on the table beside the candle. Olive was gazing up at her, not understanding.

She gave the baby her breast then, but as there was little milk in her breast, the baby began to whimper again. She listened to its weak, whimpering cry and remembered Texeira. She saw the five-dollar bill being dangled before her eyes. She shook her head and shuddered at the thought that came to her. She mumbled an *ave maria* and made the sign of the cross. Olive watched her, not understanding. She looked through the window and saw it there too; at Olive, and Olive's face was a five-dollar bill. It would give her food for days, help her with the rent. It would do this, that and the other. She planned wildly.

A moment later she asked Olive to go over and tell her mother that she wanted to say something to her. Olive went willingly.

"So he drunk again?" Olive's mother was saying, looking down at the prostrate form of Ignacio with an expression of disgust. She was a stout black woman, very ugly.

"Yes."

"I always says, gie me a man who run after women to a man who run after rum."

"You right, Mrs. Thomas."

"Never min', darlin'." She laid a hand on Isadora's head. "God good. You know de ol' saying: 'In God we trus', in man we bus'. All us women got dat burden to bear. But God good. Put you trus' in Him and all go come right."

"Yes, Mrs. Thomas, I know dat. But you min' keepin' Tony and baby fo' me while I go out? I got a job, you see, a job in town, an' I have to go jes' now. I go come back early, Mrs. Thomas."

"Yes, me chil'. Le' Olive bring dem over when you ready, an' I glad you get a little somet'ing to do."

"T'anks. Good night, Mrs. Thomas."

"Good night, darling." Mrs. Thomas shambled off.

Isadora got on her knees then and prayed. She prayed for a long time.

When she rose, she dried her eyes, fixed herself up, sent over Tony and the baby to Mrs. Thomas, and walked out of the house, up the road, until she arrived at Texeira's parlour. It was brightly lighted and she stepped in.

NOTE

1.   Amerindian, probably Carib.

SCAPULAR

As a boy, I lived in Sangre Grande, a village about thirty miles to the east of Port of Spain. My father managed a small dry goods store in the village, but our house was a little outside the village, on the Manzanilla road. The river Cunapo flowed past at a distance of not more than a hundred yards from our house; and when the Cunapo was in flood, in the rainy season, we boys had great fun. About twelve miles up the river Mr. Francois, a creole of French extraction, owned a tidy acreage of forest land: balata and crapeau and purple-heart and cedar and so forth. As soon as the rains came Mr. Francois, in order to save time and expense, employed a few men to launch his innumerable logs into the swirling waters of the Cunapo. At the Manzanilla road bridge their further downward passage was impeded by a huge wire net stretched from bank to bank; then the logs were dragged up to the road, loaded into lorries and taken down to Port of Spain for local sale and shipment abroad. We boys, unknown to our mothers, used to tramp the twelve miles to Mr. Francois' plantation, watch the launching operations and, no sooner was Mr. Francois' back turned, board the logs and sail down the river on their precarious surfaces. Usually, with a good current, the twelve miles were covered in four hours, and fours hours of such excitement as I have, in no other activity since, known. It was a dangerous game, as you may well imagine, but only once did we ever have an accident that looked for a moment like being fatal: and it is that story I shall now relate.

Anthony was a school friend of mine. At the time, we were both about fourteen years old. Although so many years have slipped by, I can still picture Anthony as he was then: tall and gawky, his face yellow almost, the cheekbones sticking up from under the tightly drawn skin. There was, really, nothing remarkable in his appearance: but his behaviour, his character was so religious (unusual for a growing boy) that he came to be known in the village as Saint Anthony. Every morning you could see him, if you were so minded, walking to early mass, his chaplet dangling from his hand, his prayer book bulging out his pocket. Once a week he went to confession and as often took communion; and this was everybody's wonder: what did Anthony find sinful in himself to confess? I need hardly tell you that we chaffed him at every favourable opportunity, but he took it all kindly, smiling his saintly smile and sometimes saying, quite seriously, that he would pray for us. In spite of his complete difference to me – to be frank, I was a little pagan – I liked Anthony. We were not often together. Once or twice he came to our house, and my mother, good Catholic that she was, was never tired of holding Anthony up to me as an example after which I should be striving. But I could not be often with Anthony because he took no interest in the things of which I was fond. I loved cricket, I loved football, I loved mischief of all kinds; whereas Anthony was seldom seen on a cricket field, never on a football field (it was a savage's game, he said), and any play that smacked of adventure and risk he refused with a pious smile. And yet I liked him and felt, also, that he liked me. So that when, that morning so many many years ago, Peter came up to our little group and suggested that someone should ask Anthony to accompany us to Mr. Francois' plantation, everybody looked to me as being the only one who stood any chance of success with the proposal.

"You can't do it, Auguste," Peter said to me. "You'll never get him."

"It would be fun having him," Joe said. "Can you picture him on one of those logs?"

Everybody laughed.

"Auguste'll never get him."

"I bet you I do." I said, in the manner of a boy accepting a challenge. And I walked off.

Arrived at Anthony's house, I called him out into the yard and persuaded him into joining us. Of course, at first he refused. Then he said he would have to ask his mother, at which my eyes opened wide with fear; but, a brilliant idea jumping into my mind, I said: "And supposing your mother was dead, who would you ask then?"

"All right, all right," he said, shuddering. "But let me put on my scapular first."

Anthony went into the house and returned in a moment with the scapular in his hand. I was curious and asked him to show it me. Attached to a braid was a small woollen disc, the size of a penny, and into this disc the pattern of a head was knitted.

"Is this you?" I asked, pointing to the head.

His eyes turned up in horror. "No, No." he said. "That's Saint Anthony." He took it away from me and adjusted it around his neck, inside his clothes. "My patron saint," he added, smiling his saintly smile.

"But why do you wear it?" I asked, moving into the street beside him.

"It keeps me from harm. It was given me by Father O'Brien when I took my first communion."

I remember wondering why my mother did not get one for me so that I, too, might be kept from harm.

When we arrived at Mr. Francois' clearing on the river bank, all was hustle and bustle. Dressed in a khaki suit, an old white helmet on his head, Mr. Francois himself was there superintending the work. A dozen or so burly black men, their naked torsos perspiring and shining in the sun, moved to and fro. Now and again Mr. Francois raised his voice angrily, giving orders. For a while he took no notice of us, but suddenly he strode up to where we were standing and addressed Anthony in a stern tone: "Now look here, you little vagabonds, it has come to my hearing that you are in the habit of riding down the river on my logs. I cannot prevent you from doing that, but I can tell you this: if any of you get drowned, that's not my business." Saying which, he turned right about turn, stamped down to his men and gave his attention to the labour once again.

Anthony stood open-mouthed, blushing up to his eyebrows. We all looked at him, poked each other in the ribs and laughed. Mr. Francois' mule, tethered to a nearby tree, knocked the turf with his forefeet and neighed, whereat we laughed all the more.

"Don't laugh," Anthony said. "When a mule neighs like that, it means bad luck."

"Saints can't get drowned," Peter said.

"Especially saints who wear scapulars," I put in. As young as I was, I regretted the remark immediately I had made it: Anthony's face clouded over with a most painful expression; I thought he was going to cry. I said nothing, however, but the others took the cue and continued taunting him. Anthony didn't seem to mind them for his expression changed into a saintly smile, and he remained smiling like that until they were done taunting him.

At last the logs were all launched. Mr. Francois wiped the perspiration off his sunburnt face with a huge coloured handkerchief, gave us a last menacing look, threw himself astride his impatient mule, flicked his whip and disappeared down the bridle path at a quick canter.

In a moment we all woke up. Running down the bank to the water's boisterous edge, I cried, trying to make amends for my ugly behaviour of a minute before: "Anthony, there's a fine log for you. Jump."

"It's too far out," he said, gazing helplessly at the retreating log. With a spring, I landed on it and nearly lost my balance. I shouted out to Anthony, drawing his attention to another sailing past within his reach. Awkwardly he clambered aboard it and in a short while we were side by side, slowly gliding down. All the other boys had already found berths and there was a hullabaloo echoing and re-echoing about the thickly wooded banks. Keskidees, darting from high green sanctuaries, sang shrilly, and wood doves cooed in lofty excitement. On each side of the river, not more than fifty feet across, the trees rose tall and stately, their overhanging branches intertwining to make a majestic arch through which sunlight fitfully slanted. The current of the river was strong here and noisily bubbled about the jostling logs. Great clumps of bamboos, creaking like hundreds of cicadas when the wind shook them, here and there bordered the river. And a solitary deer, no doubt recognizing us for what we were, with one leap disappeared into the forest.

Meanwhile, we shouted across to each other, a regular fusillade of tease and counter-tease. The buoyant waters played ducks and drakes with our logs, but all of us, by dint of long practice, had become adept at the game. Not so Anthony. By this time he was kneeling on his log, grimly holding on to its sides. His face betrayed his inward panic. His scapular had somehow or the other escaped from under his clothes and was now swinging from his neck. Our logs had earlier sheared apart, and I was screaming out frantic instructions to him, but he did not seem to hear me for he took no notice of me. He simply held on, his log swerving this way and that, every now and again rising on the crest of a dashing current.

"Can you swim?" Peter called out to him. He did not answer.

"Can you swim?" I screamed.

Without looking at me, he nodded – and with that nod lost his balance. His log rolled over and the next moment he was in the water. I saw one hand lifted high, like the hand that gripped Excalibur,[1] then it splashed the water and he sank. By a miracle of luck I sprang from log to log without mishap, until I landed on his. The others looked on, their voices for once silenced. My heart beating very fast, I ran to the stern-end of the log. Gasping for breath, Anthony rose, one hand beating the water. I threw myself flat along the log, leaned over and grasped him by the collar. After a long and difficult time, the other boys and I managed to navigate the log to the bank and we helped Anthony on to dry land.

As soon as he recovered, he pulled the scapular from around his neck and threw it into the river. Dumbfounded, we stood gaping at him. All that he sputtered, however, was: "That damn thing nearly made me drown. My hand caught in it. The damn . . ."

NOTE

1.   King Arthur's sword, which was given into the keeping of the Lady of the Lake upon King Arthur's death.

He was a small fair man, with sharp features, the nose perhaps a little too long for the face, was always dandily dressed, and walked with so sprightly a step that people were in the habit of turning their heads in the streets to watch his retreating figure. In short, he wasn't a man you could look at once only. The way he would suddenly turn his head, quite naturally, giving no impression that he was suffering from St. Vitus's dance,[1] the dainty movements he would now and again make with his hands while speaking, the queer cock of his head in listening to an interesting story, that delicate walk of his, and above all his panache – all this made you look at him twice. And once you got to know something about him: for instance, that although he died at the age of forty-five he had never been known to fall in love; that all sorts of women, the cream of the island's society really, had made unmistakable overtures to him (there's no wondering about that when you remember that his income was four hundred dollars a month) – when you knew this you became more interested than ever. So that when he died, and the scandal swept over the town like a stifling heat-wave giving everybody, so to speak, a moral prickly heat, some people said that they knew all along that there was something strange, a few that there was something mysterious, and most that there was something evil in his nature. His name was Rose, quite congruous considering that he was never seen in public without a bud in his buttonhole.

After the very first interview, Mr. Levitt decided that Rose was just the man for the job. Seated before his desk that morning so many years ago, Mr. Levitt was wondering what would become of a particular department of his huge, complicated commission business, for since Letchworth's[2] retirement the sales of the department had lamentably fallen off, when Rose's written application, posted from Barbados, reached him.

Dear Sir, I think that I am the very man you are looking for. Wire if you think so too.

    Respectfully, Marshall Rose –

That, and nothing more, and Mr. Levitt had immediately wired: "Come."

Three days later Rose stood before him and he was immensely impressed by the smart, dapper figure of the man. It seemed to radiate energy.

"You are a Barbadian, Mr. Rose?"

"I am, sir," Rose said.

"But you don't speak like one."

"I was in England, at school, sir, for eight years."

That pleased Mr. Levitt. "Had any experience in this line before, Mr. Rose?" he asked.

"Three years, sir, with Hankey & Son Ltd. of Bridgetown."

"And why did you leave?" Mr. Levitt could not think of Rose as having been dismissed from any job.

"Oh, they didn't want to pay me, that's all," Rose said, adjusting the bud in his buttonhole.

"A lady's man," Mr. Levitt said to himself, noticing at that moment the bud adorning the lapel of Rose's coat. "I see," he continued aloud, "they didn't want to pay you. That is a characteristic of most firms in these islands, Mr. Rose. Most firms recognise only one sort of morality. With us, that is, the firm I represent, business morality is as sacred as any other sort of morality." Mr. Levitt felt quite at ease speaking like this to Rose. After a pause he asked: "Married?"

Rose's thin lips twisted into a smile as he said: "Oh no, sir."

"What, now that smile for instance: the inference I draw is that you're—"

"Oh no, sir," Rose interrupted. "It's only that I'm not married, that's all. Maybe I haven't found Miss Right as yet."

"Hah, I see, yes, of course, I see." Mr. Levitt was a bit uncomfortable. He felt that he had been saved from committing a faux pas by Rose's tact. He didn't like to hurt people's feelings.

"Well," he said at last, "d'you think you would like to come on with us?"

"I should very much like to, sir," Rose said, looking straight into Mr. Levitt's eyes.

"A fine fellow, a fine fellow," Mr. Levitt said to himself. Then, remembering Rose's application and smiling wryly, he said aloud: "Well then, Mr. Rose, I too think you're just the man we're looking for."

"I thought you'd think so too," Rose said; and gracefully sweeping his arm, he passed his hand three times, with the affected touch of a dandy, over his well-combed hair.

"There's one other thing," Mr. Levitt said, tentatively. "I hope you don't mind my asking you this question?"

Rose waited while Mr. Levitt shifted his pen from the writing pad on to the inkstand.

"Are you by any chance a religious man, Mr. Rose?"

"What exactly do you mean, sir?" Rose asked quickly.

"Well, d'you go to church and that sort of thing?" Mr. Levitt asked, replacing the pen on to the writing pad.

"Oh yes, sir," Rose said. "I am an Anglican."

"Good, very good. You see, it's like this. We always try and make it a point to employ men of sound moral disposition and as it is only religion that can give them that, we naturally prefer to employ religious men. This firm, I might tell you, Mr. Rose, was built up by my father who was a man with a strong religious sense, an Anglican, in fact. And in these days, what with the spread of loose and wild thinking even in this island, it is difficult to find the sort of man we would like."

"I don't think you'll find me wanting," Rose said.

For one month Mr. Levitt watched Rose very closely and was satisfied. One night he said to Mrs. Levitt at the dinner table: "You know, Elizabeth, I must be a very clever man."

Elizabeth looked at her husband with a meek evangelical look. "Fancy," Mr. Levitt continued, "my being able to judge of a man's capacity for work when he was in Barbados and I in Port of Spain!"

"Oh, you mean that new man?" Elizabeth said, still regarding her husband in a soft, admiring way.

"Yes, the new man, Mr. Rose. He has odd little ways. In fact, I always have to pull myself together in his presence and consciously accept his little mannerisms for what they are worth. But what a worker! What a conscientious and prodigious worker! And I was so sure of him that I cabled him in Barbados to come for the job. That's what more businessmen need in this town, Elizabeth: perspicacity for judging character by the shortest letter, the least word."

"I saw him in church yesterday morning," Elizabeth said, passing the napkin across her mouth.

"Every Sunday since he has been here I've seen him in church," Mr. Levitt said. "And, what is more important, his department, in that short time, is doing fifty per cent more business."

"I don't like him," Richard said. Mr. Levitt regarded his eight- year-old son very sternly.

"You mustn't say that, Dick," Elizabeth said. "And he gave you such a nice cricket set only last week."

"I'm always telling you," Mr. Levitt said to his wife, "not to let the boy have dinner with us. He is far too young. When I was a boy of his age, I was still going to bed at seven o'clock, and it's now nearly eight. These new-fangled ideas will be the ruin of young people." Mr. Levitt appeared to be quite angry. Elizabeth was meekly flustered.

"And he asked me the last time I saw him to go for a walk with him," Richard said, apparently not noticing what was passing between his father and mother.

"I hope you were not rude, Dick," Elizabeth said.

"I told him no, I wasn't going."

"But why, Dick?"

"I don't like him, Mother."

"But why?"

"I don't know. I don't like him."

About a fortnight later Mr. Levitt was strolling down Frederick Street on his way to the office from the barber's, when he stepped into Marsden's Dry Goods Store to have a chat with Mr. Marsden. Him he found in the haberdashery department, going through some invoices; but as soon as Mr. Marsden saw Mr. Levitt, he left what he was doing and came over to him.

"Hello Levitt," he said, his paunch giving him the appearance of a contented man, his face bursting with the blood in it, "how do you find business?"

"Dull," Mr. Levitt said.

"Dull like hell," Mr. Marsden replied.

That was what Mr. Levitt always found so objectionable in Mr. Marsden: his habit of swearing. He himself was never heard to use a single swear word; and when once in a moment of anger, he had said: "Confound you!" he was troubled for days.

"By the way," Mr. Marsden said, resting one hand on Mr. Levitt's shoulder," I see you've got a new man down from Barbados?" Mr. Levitt said yes, that he had got a new man down from Barbados, and what did he, Mr. Marsden, think of him?

"By God," Mr. Marsden said, failing to notice Mr. Levitt's wince," I envy you that fellow. A real live wire. A real live wire. The finest salesman walking on two legs in this town today, Levitt, the finest salesman. How did you manage him?"

"Oh," Mr. Levitt said, quite nonchalantly, " I used my head, got into touch with him, knew that he was a good, an extremely good man by my short correspondence with him and wired for him. He has given every satisfaction, I might tell you, Marsden. In fact, I seldom make a mistake in matters of that kind. I know a good man when I see him. I was telling my wife that only a few days ago. A businessman should be able to read character. It's his chief asset, more of an asset than thousands of dollars."

"Straight, he is a damn good man, Levitt, and no flattery," Marsden said. "He's worth a lot to you. I congratulate you on wangling him." And Mr. Marsden gripped Mr. Levitt's shoulder quite painfully to show how much he meant what he was saying.

But that was only the beginning. Into every store Mr. Levitt went afterwards, the heads would approach him and congratulate him on his wonderful shrewdness in procuring the services of a man like Rose; so much so, that Mr. Levitt, at the age of forty-nine, was beginning to think that he had always been too humble in the estimate he had made of his own astuteness, and too magnanimous in the estimate he had made of other men. In fact, he was actually beginning to believe that it was himself who was clever and then Rose, a long way behind; that it was himself who was the bright and brilliant salesman who had caused such a flutter in the town. And one cannot really blame him, for there is that sort of man who will keep flattering himself with such consistency that he ends up by believing that the adulation has all come from his friends.

When Mrs. Levitt, one Saturday afternoon, gave a cocktail party in her beautiful home in Cascade, Rose was asked. Mr. Levitt, some nights before, had insisted on Elizabeth asking him, "For," he said, "it is immoral not to show a man a little social attention when he is giving you such dedicated, such profitable labour."

"But surely you're paying him for that?" Elizabeth said meekly.

"Paying him, paying him?" Mr. Levitt snorted and blew his nose loudly. "What does a woman know of matters of that kind that she should make such a remark?"

"And what does a man know of a cocktail party that he should interfere?" Elizabeth showed not the slightest discomposure. Mr. Levitt continued to snort, regarding his wife indignantly. However, he made no reply, so Elizabeth remarked, gazing down on her lap: "And he is a complete stranger to the place. What does anyone know of his family? What are his family connections?"

"I was talking to Bascomb in town only yesterday and he told me that Rose comes from one of the best families in Barbados," Mr. Levitt said with a little note of triumph in his voice. That wasn't the truth, but still, it served the purpose, for Elizabeth raised no further objections.

Mr. Levitt's house was perched on a little shoulder of land in the Cascade valley, about a hundred yards from the road. Hills, some hundreds of feet high, rose at the back of it. It was really a very beautiful house. When it was hot in town, it was cool up there. Little gay-plumaged birds sang all day long in the trees around, starting from early in the morning; but as Mr. Levitt was a businessman he could never listen to the birds singing without becoming irritable and fidgety. Elizabeth liked to listen to them. Richard was in the habit of throwing stones at them.

As the Levitts moved in the island's best society, they had only nice people at their party.

Rose, with a yellow bud in his buttonhole, immaculately dressed, arrived with Boret, a young, handsome student from the Imperial College at St. Augustine. They came in a huge car, which made so monstrous a noise as it laboured up the incline that everybody looked at it. Eileen Brinig, a pretty Jewess, turned to Mrs. Levitt and asked her who was that funny little man just driving up with Boret; but not more than an hour later Eileen was herself ogling Rose. She said afterwards, when she saw that he was really not interested in her, that he was a fop and a conceited ass.

Rose created quite an agreeable impression on the females present at the party. The girls said he was such a jolly sort, and when Mrs. Levitt inadvertently mentioned to Eileen's mother that Mr. Rose, "D'you know my dear," was getting as a start three hundred dollars a month, "But please" she added, "this is strictly *entre nous,*" he rose in the estimation of every girl's mother. It intrigued them all to notice how evenly he shared his attentions around, and they were amused by his dainty ways and mannerisms of speech. Even his voice, they said, was like a flute's. The men thought him a coxcomb, but the elderly ladies, mothers all, were charmed by the dapper little man and expressed surprise that he was yet single.

"However," Mrs. Brinig whispered to Mrs. Levitt, fanning her pretty face, "I'm sure, with all *these* lovely girls here he'll soon be caught!" And Elizabeth gave one of her meek smiles to show how true she thought the remark.

After that, Rose was asked everywhere, and it soon became apparent that he was one of the most popular men amongst the ladies in town. The men regarded him with suspicion, no doubt resenting his coming into their midst and gaining such admiration with so little to show for it.

The buyers in all the stores on Frederick Street found it impossible to refuse buying from him, so that Mr. Levitt was able to boast in less than two years after his employment that Rose's department was doing one hundred and fifty per cent more business than ever. Mr. Levitt was immensely proud, of himself first and then Rose, "For," he said to Elizabeth one night in bed, "to judge and test a clever man, it takes a cleverer man."

Every Sunday morning Rose was seen at church by Mr. and Mrs. Levitt, and when old Barlow died, the miser who had a seat in the Levitts' pew, Rose took it over, much to the satisfaction and pride of Mr. and Mrs. Levitt. Indeed, Mr. Levitt felt it quite an honour having Rose sitting in the same pew with his family. Still, he always regarded himself as Rose's patron, and was never tired of telling Elizabeth that were it not for him, with his intuition and influence, Rose would probably still be in Barbados, unknown, unhonoured and unsung.

As time moved on, Mrs. Levitt grew to be fond of Rose and was vexed with herself for ever having harboured reservations about him. Often she had him up to dinner, and even little Richard at last was able to say that he liked Mr. Rose. He went walks [*sic*] with him very often, long rambles up the Cascade road and across the hills, arriving home red in the face, his clothes all covered with sweethearts,3 and wet through with perspiration. Both parents agreed that Rose was having a healthy influence over the boy, and encouraged the relationship as much as possible.

Elizabeth would say: "Well Dick, and how did you enjoy your walk?" and Dick would relate, in his characteristically shy manner (he had inherited much of his mother's shyness), what a fine time he had had, and how Mr. Rose had helped him over the steeper portions of their climb by taking him on his back, and how Mr. Rose had given him sweets to eat along the way, and what wonderful stories Mr. Rose had related to him, and how Mr. Rose, seeing that he was tired, would turn back for home. And the parents would laugh, feeling happy in their knowledge that a man like Rose was so fond of and kind to their little boy.

"You mark my words," Mr. Levitt often said, "that boy must have something in him, Elizabeth, for a man like Rose to be so attentive to him."

One Christmas Eve night, some years after Rose's arrival, Mr. Levitt gave a large dinner party at the Queen's Park Hotel for his friends. Some of the best people in the island were there, even government big-wigs with their wives. Rose, with a flaming-red bud in his buttonhole, was the life and soul of the party. Anything he said caused roars of laughter, even amongst the men, for they had all by this time admitted defeat and accepted him as their leader.

The dining-hall was beautifully decorated with multicoloured streamers, and all the flags of the American and European nations fluttered to the clean, pure breezes passing in on their way from the hills to the sea. Every table was taken. Expensively dressed women laughed and sang until they were hoarse. Now and again girls rushed across from other tables to adorn Rose's person with some clown's cap or gaudy paper-necklace or huge artificial bouquet until only the small fair face, with the nose too long for it, could be seen.

Well in his cups, Colonel Bartington, the pompous Chief of Police, shouted across the table to Rose: "Ah, Marshall, my boy, the ladies are adorning you for the altar. Now who will be the bride?"

The cry was taken up and flung from table to table: "Who will be the bride, who will be the bride?" and in a moment dozens of girls came surging and clamouring over Rose like a prismatic wave. And poor Rose, buried beneath this beautiful wave, the champagne shaking his head to dizziness, could do nothing but fight his way through it until he stood on the table, toppling his glass over in the action, and scream drunkenly: "No, no, not the altar, not that! I warn you . . . I warn you . . . By God!"

It was quite a dramatic scene, the girls billowing around Rose's feet, Rose standing on the table with his hands tragically thrown out and all the guests gazing at him through crapulent eyes.

Mr. Levitt said afterwards that the only thing he didn't thoroughly enjoy in the little scene was Rose's blasphemous "By God!"

But long before anybody could decide what Rose meant, Colonel Bartington laughed his sonorous laugh and called on Rose for a speech; whereupon Rose put his hands to his head, obviously to collect his thoughts, and delivered one of the wittiest after-dinner speeches ever heard at the hotel. It was the first time he had spoken in public since his coming to Trinidad. Subsequently, it was always taken for granted that the chief attraction of any dinner was Rose's speech. Colonel Bartington told Mr. Levitt that night that he would, "Yes, by George!" he would walk miles to hear Marshall, and Mr. Levitt mumbled, "Yes, of course, yes", putting his thumbs into the armpits of his waistcoat and feeling just as if the Colonel had paid him a personal compliment. The ladies clustered around Rose immediately he had uttered the last word of his speech, and the young men, taking him on their shoulders, walked around the hilarious hall with him. And he, like an important personage, kept making mock salutations to those standing and sitting beneath him.

Mrs. Levitt, who had been persuaded by Mrs. Brinig seated to her left at table, to take a little champagne, now forgot to be meek in demeanour and evangelical in look. She clapped her hands and shouted as any modern girl. Mrs. Marsden, who was considered "fast" by everybody, and of whom it was said that once she had set out to make a capture, the capture was as good as made, seeing Mrs. Levitt's strange behaviour, leaned over to her neighbour and murmured: "Isn't it perfectly marvellous what a drop of champagne will do for some Anglo-Anglicans, darling?"

And then the dancing started. It was midnight when Mr. Levitt found himself leading Mrs. Brinig from the dance hall. He was fanning himself with his handkerchief, feeling hot and tired and uncomfortable, but persuading himself as old men will who hate to think of themselves as old, that he was happy and strong enough to do all that the young men were doing. Watching them alone injected him with a vicarious vitality. Mrs. Marsden, slim and smartly dressed, looking no more than twenty-five when she had already passed thirty, came sailing up to Mr. Levitt and, without so much as an "Excuse me" to Mrs. Brinig, took hold of Mr. Levitt's arm, tugged him, and sailed away with him on to the dance floor.

Rose, passing by just then, distinctly heard Mrs. Brinig mutter between her teeth, venomously: "The Bitch!"

As Mrs. Marsden escorted the panting Mr. Levitt from the dance floor she whispered: "*Entre nous*, what does that semitic lady have that draws you so frequently to talk to her?" And she playfully tapped him on the stomach with her fan. At which Mr. Levitt reminded her that Brinig's firm bought goods in large quantities through his firm.

"Ah tut!" Mrs. Marsden said, playfully striking Mr. Levitt across the stomach with her fan again, "and you call yourself a Christian?"

Mr. Levitt's first impulse was to be rude, but the lady giving him that irresistible look of hers, that look which had long since cowed Mr. Marsden into child-like submissiveness in her presence, controlled himself and said: "To be a Christian is not always to be human," at which Mrs. Marsden's bird-like voice rippled into laughter.

"You're a witty man!" she said, and this time kissed her fan and gently touched his lips with it.

Mr. Levitt's heart warmed to the lady and he pressed her hand tenderly.

"Now tell me," Mrs. Marsden said, when she had at last controlled her laughter, "tell me, do you think Mr. Rose left a sweetheart in Barbados?"

Mr. Levitt was puzzled.

"Well then, is he a misogynist?"

"Ah, you ladies, you ladies!" Mr. Levitt said, shaking his finger at Mrs. Marsden, "because you cannot, with all your Delilah-wiles, immediately trap a poor fellow you call him a misogynist!"

Mrs. Marsden was silent for a moment, gazing at Mr. Levitt with open curiosity. Then leaning back in her chair and blowing threads of smoke into the air, she murmured: "Of course, you know what a wicked reputation I enjoy?"

A mild panic simmered in Mr. Levitt's heart. He began to wonder where Mrs. Marsden was leading him with her strange questions and oblique talk. Sensing danger, he softly said: "I think I see what you are driving at."

"Of course you do," she replied. "But I'm ashamed to say that I failed."

Mr. Levitt looked down at his shoes to hide his bewilderment and mortification. The confession, if he understood her correctly, also shocked him. Being what he was, he could discover no escape from the snare into which Mrs. Marsden was guiding him. He must bring this exchange of alarming pleasantries to a close at once.

"Well," he murmured, "all I can say is, bravo for Rose."

Mrs. Marsden sat in silence, glancing at him with alternating expressions of pity and contempt.

At the Christmas table next morning Mr. Levitt told Elizabeth how pleasing it was to have people notice that Rose was fond of their Dick. "Even Mrs. Marsden," he added, "was telling me recently that she had heard so."

Two weeks later, reading his early morning paper before driving down to the office, Mr. Levitt's attention was drawn to these headlines:

> Prominent City Salesman in Brawl
>
> Men in Women's Clothing
>
> Smart Work by Police

Mr. Levitt read on and was surprised to come upon the name of Marshall

Rose. He gathered from the report that the police had for some time been receiving complaints from certain residents in Carenage about the noisy and peace-disturbing behaviour of a number of young men who were in the habit of renting a house in that district and there celebrating nightly orgies. The police, awaiting their opportunity, had the night before last raided the house and had discovered, in varying stages of inebriation, at least thirty young men, some dressed in women's clothing, others in male attire, dancing together and shouting and singing at the top of their voices. Among the names mentioned, the only one Mr. Levitt recognised was Rose's. At first he was extremely puzzled that any man should find pleasure in wearing a woman's dress. But when later in the day, he had casually asked Rose what it all meant (by this time he had grown to respect Rose so much that he dared not assume the employer's attitude towards him) and Rose had smilingly dismissed the matter with the remark: "A lark, Mr. Levitt, a lark!" he was able to say to Elizabeth that evening when he got home: "Boys will be boys, my dear, boys will be boys!"

"But surely Marshall is old enough to know that that sort of thing isn't done here?" Elizabeth said in a quiet tone, not glancing up from the piece of crochet she was engaged on at the moment.

"What sort of thing?" Mr. Levitt asked, surprised, for it was seldom that Elizabeth failed to agree with him.

"Why, going about drinking with ordinary coloured men," Elizabeth replied quietly.

"Who said they were ordinary coloured men?"

"Read the list of names in the newspaper, do you recognise any other name but Marshall's? And surely we know every young man who's worth knowing here!"

But Mr. Levitt's mind was already set. "Boys will be boys," he repeated. "I used to do the same thing myself, when I was his age."

"What, with that sort of person, and wearing ladies' clothing?"

"At Carnival time, my dear, yes."

"Is this Carnival time?"

Finding himself at bay, Mr. Levitt displayed annoyance and again said, tersely: "Boys will be boys!" and Elizabeth, observing that she was upsetting her husband, said nothing more.

There was much gossip at the clubs, hotels and élite homes of Port of Spain over this incident. And when, two weeks later, there was a big dance at Government House in honour of the officers belonging to the flotilla of American warships then in the harbour, Colonel Bartington was the first to start teasing Rose.

"Ah Marshall, my boy, dissatisfied with your sex when you've been so successful with it?"

"Why is it, Colonel, that you always envy us bachelors so?" Rose said, sweeping his hand over his hair and winking mischievously at Mrs. Bartington.

"He knows why," Mrs. Bartington said piquantly, glancing at the Colonel through the corner of her eye.

Even the young girls teased Rose and asked him: were they not pretty enough for him that he must needs go dressing up mysterious young men in women's clothing? But Rose completely disarmed them all by his naïve replies and charming manner. He danced all night; and when, late in the evening, the Governor was seen tête-à-tête with him, everybody said what a fine and interesting fellow Marshall was. In the privacy of their rooms, however, they criticised him. Anybody else, they said, behaving in that fashion would immediately be ostracised by society; but because Rose was popular and possessed a personality, he escaped open condemnation.

And then it was that the cat was let out of the bag, as the saying goes.

At two o'clock one afternoon, soon after the Carenage incident, in the heart of the business section of Frederick Street, just in front of Marsden's Dry Goods Store, Marshall Rose dropped bonelessly to the pavement, and was dead within three minutes. Anybody can imagine what a shock his sudden death caused, and some of the ladies' eyes grew quite moist the following morning when they read in the papers how this "popular social figure and pre-eminently successful salesman" had died with a red bud in his buttonhole.

Mr. Levitt was distracted for days. Richard wept and could not be consoled. Elizabeth bore the bereavement with Christian fortitude.

A week later the will was read, and much to the surprise of everybody, Rose left but a paltry two thousand one hundred and thirty-five dollars lodged in the Royal Bank of Canada. This he bequeathed to an aunt in Barbados. The will also mentioned a trunk, the contents of which were to be destroyed in the presence of his executors. So, on the appointed day, Mr. Levitt and Mr. Marsden, joint-executors under the will, met and opened the trunk with two or three witnesses standing around. The trunk was discovered, much to their bewilderment, to be crammed with odd pieces of female attire, and right at the bottom a small packet, neatly wrapped and tied with a length of red ribbon, was found. It was Mr. Levitt who opened it, with Mr. Marsden and the others full of curiosity looking over his shoulder, for here at last they thought were the love letters that would explain the secret of the dead man's escape from marriage. Dozen of snapshots slid from Mr. Levitt's trembling fingers onto the floor, all taken by sunlight as well as flashlight, of naked young men and boys in varying stages of erotic excitement.

"And do you know," Mr. Marsden said to his wife that night, "at least a dozen of them were of young Richard, Levitt's son!"

NOTES

1. An old name for Sydenham's chorea, a disorder characterized by involuntary jerky movements.
2. Letchworth, a "new town", was located about two miles from Hitchin Grammar School in Hitchin, Hertfordshire, England, where Mendes went to school from 1912 to 1915.
3. The sticky seeds of a weed, the sweetheart bush, which cling to one's clothing on contact.

AT THE BALL

Everybody of importance in the island was present at the ball. All the best
French, English, Spanish and Portuguese families were there. Jean de la Roche,
entering with his wife, felt very important. He liked to know that he was privileged to associate with Trinidad's best company, and there was nothing else
that gave him more satisfaction than exercising that privilege. He knew that
somewhere in the early days of his ancestors' settling in the island, a negress
had somehow or the other got mixed up with the family; and, although he could
pass for white in any part of the world with his dark complexion and refined
features, the fact of his having a touch of the tar-brush worried him immensely.
He had been educated in England and there nobody had guessed that he was
coloured, but in the island of his birth it was, of course, different. Everybody
knew everybody else.

When he entered the ballroom the first dance was already in progress, so
he took his wife and danced with her. While dancing he kept looking around
to see who was who so that he could book up his programme as soon as possible. Because of the huge crowd, he threaded his way through the revolving
maze of dancers with difficulty. He was nodding, waving and saying: "Hello,
hello, how are you?" all the time he was dancing with his wife. Once or twice,
bumping against other couples, she swore at him under her breath. After the
dance he left his wife with some friends, booked a few dances, and decided to
go to the bar for a drink. On his way he met Goodliffe.[1]

"Hello, Goodliffe, have a drink?"

"I don't mind, de la Roche."

Goodliffe was a young Englishman who had recently come out to Barclay's
Bank. De la Roche was working at the Royal Bank of Canada and they had come
to know each other because of business connections. They were not too

friendly, but on a night like this when everybody would notice with whom you danced and with whom you drank, de la Roche considered it his luck to be seen drinking with Goodliffe.

"Damn fine crowd, Goodcliffe, eh what?"

He always conveniently remembered to add "eh what" to whatever he said, or to use expressions that told his listener that he had been educated in England, especially when the person to whom he was speaking was English. At his own home he was creole in speech and intonation of voice, but there it didn't matter. At a function like this it mattered, for it gave him prestige.

"Fine set here to-night," Goodliffe agreed.

"Perhaps, my dear fellow, you've not been out here long enough to realize our difficulty. Socially, I mean. The colour question: so damned difficult, don't you know, to keep the coloured people out of any dance. They push themselves where they're not wanted. Very trying."

"There aren't many here to-night."

"No, thank God. Well, cheer-ho!"

They drank and stood chatting. A moment later Horton, an American oil-driller from down South, passed by. It was a long time since de la Roche had seen Horton. He hailed him loudly and pompously. Horton approached and was introduced to Goodliffe.

"Have a drink, Horton," de la Roche said.

"No, no, this is mine," Goodliffe said.

De la Roche waved the suggestion aside with his arm. "That's all right, my dear fellow, that's all right!" he said. "This is my pleasure". And he beamed on them both. As they drank St. Hill, a clever coloured barrister, advanced. In the early days de la Roche had been to school with St. Hill and at that time they had been friends. Now, however, he pretended not to see him. He dreaded that St. Hill would fail to notice the "cut". A minute passed and he once more breathed easily.

Soon he rejoined his wife. The music striking up, he waltzed off with his partner, an English girl who had married a big-wig government official. He enjoyed the dance immensely.

After the third dance he was sitting in the gallery with his wife. She was sipping a crème-de-menthe. Again he had occasion to "cut" St. Hill. That was the only discomforting feature of dances and other social functions that were open to the public: you had to be constantly on the look out in order to avoid contact with certain people.

And then it was that he saw MacDonald walking across the dance- hall with a young woman on his arm. Mac, as he was popularly known, in spite of his iconoclastic ideas, or because of them, perhaps, was a great favourite with everybody. Ever since he had come out to the island to a sugar estate several years before, he had been doing strange and unconventional things. For instance, once at a Government House ball he had turned up in an ordinary white suit. When asked by some friends if he had lost his senses, Mac had said:

"Oh, go to hell! I'm comfortable." And because of his popularity, he had got away with his dress and his rudeness.

De la Roche called out loudly to MacDonald. Mac approached with his young woman-friend. De la Roche thought that she might be a Portuguese or a Spaniard for she was dark and very beautiful.

Slapping him familiarly on the back, de la Roche asked Mac how he was. Through the corner of his eye he could see everybody looking in his direction. For Mac to have noticed him before anyone else in this large and important assembly! This was indeed a great victory he had scored, and pride swelled within him. Mac introduced the strange young woman and stood chatting. In the excitement he had failed to catch the young woman's name. He glanced at his programme and saw that the fourth dance was booked, but this was too fine an opportunity to be lost, so he scratched the name out and asked Mac's friend to dance it with him. She smiled consent, and for the first time he saw her large black eyes, her rosebud mouth, and her black, wavy hair.

They stepped off to the tune of a fox-trot.

While dancing he observed couples gazing at him and whispering to each other. Others were smiling sarcastically. They are envious, he thought – and danced with more verve than he had ever danced before.

When the music ceased he felt sure that he had made a hit, for he noticed everybody looking at him and whispering. He wondered why they scowled whenever he caught their eyes. The band began to play and Mac took his woman-friend off. De la Roche glanced at his programme and went in search of his next partner. He observed her sitting a little way off. He went up to her and offered her his arm. The lady rose, gave him a scornful look, murmured something which he did not catch, and walked off with her head high in the air. De la Roche stood gazing before him, nonplussed. Then, feeling sick, he went to the gallery and leant against the rail. Never before had he been snubbed so flagrantly, and search his mind as he might, he could find no cause for it. He was interrupted in his gloomy reverie by someone saying to him in a low voice: "Heartiest congratulations, my dear de la Roche! I didn't dream you had it in you!"

He turned round, recognizing the voice. St. Hill was standing beside him, smiling. It was impossible to escape now, so he said sharply: "What the devil do you mean?"

"Oh, nothing, nothing, except this!" St. Hill said airily. "Don't you know that every young man, *every young man in town,* knows intimately the young woman with whom you just danced?"

NOTE

1.   A name borrowed from Mendes's school-days in England. Robert Goodliffe was a close friend of Mendes, and the latter spent several school holidays with the Goodliffe family.

A LIFE

When Camachee was ten years old she arrived in Trinidad on board the S.S. *Ganges* from India. Her parents came out indentured to "Bacolet",[1] a large sugar estate in Caroni. Camachee landed with wide-open scared eyes, shrinking within her mother's broad skirts as if to hide herself.

On the estate, life was not so bad. Her parents, between them, worked for forty cents a day and somehow or the other managed to save half their earnings. Camachee grew quickly, and when she was thirteen years old her figure had already taken on the rounded outlines of womanhood. As there was no school near enough, she never went to school. Instead, she romped about the yard of the barracks all day long with other East Indian children. In the mornings, as her mother had taught her, she swept out the room in which the little family lived; and in the evenings, again as her mother had taught her, she cooked the rice, so that when the parents returned home tired and sweating from the day's hot toil in the fields, they found the evening meal ready.

Camachee, in her dark fashion, was pretty. Her face was an oval with large almond-shaped eyes, small mouth and slightly turned-up nose. The hair, worn in a plait, reached down to her waist; black and glossy it was from the use of coconut oil.

Just as she turned fourteen, Camachee had a baby for a Scotsman named McGuire, one of the overseers on the estate. The baby had a light brown skin, grey eyes and regular features.

Camachee's parents were proud that the father of their daughter's baby girl was a white man: *buckra* man, as they put it. They went about their daily task with heads higher and hearts lighter. In the evenings they played for long minutes with the baby, and were never tired showing it to everybody, saying: "Dis we gran'chile. Fader *buckra* man."

They even walked one Sunday to the nearest village, five miles away, to show the baby to some people they knew there.

In the fullness of time, Camachee's parents died. That happened when little Rampatia, the Eurasian, was five years old. Camachee, hankering after Port of Spain about which she had heard so much, decided to go to the big town with Rampatia. McGuire's contract with the sugar company had long since terminated and he had returned to Scotland, broken down by drink.

Camachee found a room in St. James, the Indian suburb of Port of Spain; and with the little money she had inherited from her father and mother, she was able to live comfortably. Because she was vivacious and still physically attractive, she made friends quickly. One of these friends was Monir, a young East Indian carterman, handsome and debonair. Within a year of their first meeting, they were married in the St. James's Catholic Church. Camachee that afternoon was more pretty than ever in her multicoloured *oranee* or veil, her voluminous skirts and bare shapely feet.

But the St. James's people knew what they were saying when, wagging their heads, they foretold disaster for the marriage. One month after the wedding, Monir resumed his heavy drinking and begun to beat his pretty wife. Camachee would not have minded so much if he had been kind to Rampatia. When he began to beat the child too, she left him, very much impoverished, for Monir had succeeded in drinking out nearly all of her little fortune.

Some time after the separation, she managed to get a job in a large provision store in town. As the store opened at seven o'clock, she used to rise at five, feed Rampatia, take a little herself and walk the two miles into town. Her pay was thirty cents a day for cleaning rotting potatoes and onions. At first, after walking back to her room in St. James she was in the habit of scrubbing her hands for long minutes in a vain endeavour to wash off the horrid clinging smell. However, she soon got accustomed to it. Only Rampatia complained, but she too got accustomed to it.

Camachee was happy enough until the clerks in the store where she was employed began to molest her with undue attentions. One of them she grew to like: her blood took to his, as she phrased it. He was a white man, tall and dark-haired. In course of time she gave in to his importunities and had another baby.

She was at her job up to a week before the confinement; and the clerk was so kind to her that he took her back in the store when she was well enough to work again.

The years went by and with them Camachee's drudgery. She lived only for her two children. Her earnings were so small that she could not, even occasionally, take the tramcar to or from her work. More exhausted every day, she still continued her morning and evening tramps.

During her week's cleaning, she carefully put aside the onions and potatoes too bad for sale in the store. Every Saturday, after inspecting them, the clerk allowed her to make a parcel and take them home. These served her for the week; and sometimes, when the supply was more than usual, she was able to sell a few cents' worth, which gave her cigarette-change.

Rampatia, at eighteen, was the handsomest girl in the suburb, and all St. James's dandies flocked around her. This was the most unhappy period of Camachee's life: she watched her daughter with apprehension and warned her repeatedly. But such adulation as the young woman received could do nothing but turn her head. She went off to live with a young Indian grass-cutter, who soon got tired of her and threw her out of his room to take in another, more desirable.

Rampatia, knowing where her value lay, straightaway donned European dress and went on the streets. Camachee remonstrated with her time and again, but the young woman was obdurate and continued in her way of living.

That was the beginning of Camachee's decline. Her grief gnawed at her strength. In one year she looked old; but, always remembering her other child, she toiled on at her job and struggled to make two ends meet. Her neighbours commiserated with her, but whispered ill words about her amongst themselves. Of course, they were jealous of her two fair-skinned children and in their heart of hearts always wished her misfortune.

Rampatia, the ghost of her former self, knocked at her mother's door one night and begged her to take her back. Camachee threw her arms around her daughter's neck and there was a brief period of happiness for the old woman.

Soon, however, Rampatia, tainted already by street-life, took to drink. Every penny she could steal from her mother went into the till of the rum-shop nearby. Camachee could hold out no longer and herself began to drink. The alcohol quickly took toll of her emaciated body and she died.

The villagers, because they had watched her struggles for so long a time with secret satisfaction, now relented and passed round a subscription list. With this money they gave the old woman as fine a funeral as had been seen in St. James for many a year.

NOTE

1.   "Bacolet" was the name of a property owned by Alfred Mendes senior in Tobago. It was managed by Alfred H. Mendes's brother Walter.

A LITTLE CARGO

On a mean street in downtown Port of Spain, stood a dance-hall. Its five piece orchestra, in the throes of a hot calypso number, blared away. The musicians sweated, their black faces shining under the glare of the electric lights. Ranging in colour from deep black to near white, the dancers swung wildly to the syncopated rhythm of the music. They swung around the large room in wild abandon, their animated faces betraying the ecstasy that gripped them. It was Friday night, nearing eleven o'clock. Every Friday night these dances were held, and to them came the ne'er-do-wells from all over: from John John Hill, from Belmont, from Corbeautown.[1]

Tonight the dance-hall and bar-room were packed. Multicoloured streamers straddled the ceiling. Chinese lanterns were suspended from the light-fixtures, three large but torn Union Jacks adorned the walls. Above the din of the music rose the chatter of human voices, the rich singsong cadences of Negro talk.

"How you, Jojo?"

"Fine an' dandy, Estelline."

"Make you' feet fly, sweet boy!"

Sensuous laughter.

Fats Small was leaning over the bar, drinking the best brandy in the house. Everybody called him Fats; nobody knew his real first name. And he *was* fat. Confirmed gamblers had been known to make bets on his weight, but no one had ever won or lost because Fats could never be persuaded to step onto a scale. Perhaps he weighed two hundred and twenty pounds: he looked it. And he was certainly the most repulsive-looking Negro in the city. His face was blue-black, his nose broad and flat, his mouth, the lips blue and bulbous, protruded well beyond his nose, his chin receded to his neck, his eyes could scarcely be seen beneath their layers of flesh. His belly was as large and round as a barrel. His kinky hair was plastered down with scented pomade.

But Fats Small, despite his physical handicaps, or more likely because of them, dressed in the loudest taste. Indeed, among his own people he was considered the dandiest dresser. Tonight he wore a silk suit, double-breasted, the cut of it in the latest fashion. And always he could produce from his pockets thick rolls of notes. No one knew where he got the money, but all suspected that there was something shady in his activities.

As he lounged against the bar now, alternately mopping his perspiring brow with a perfumed handkerchief and sipping his brandy, his little eyes roamed among the dancers gyrating in the adjoining room. He was interested in the women. He appraised them with the flair of a connoisseur as they revolved past him. Every now and again he walked to the large arched opening leading to the dance-hall and glanced around as if he were looking for someone.

A slip of a brown-skinned girl, dressed in green and embraced by a huge Negro, lightly skipped by. He fixed his attention on her, up on his toes to follow her with his eyes to the far end of the room, and smiled at her as she came abreast of him. The girl returned the smile. Fats smacked his lips, made up his mind, and returned to his brandy.

The noise, the movement, the colour, the foetid atmosphere – all excited him. But above all, the women. The odour of their bodies seeped through the imprisoned air. He inhaled deep draughts of it, then sipped his brandy. A few of the guests exchanged pleasantries with him; he laughed raucously, his belly rolling.

Mari entered the dance-hall. The musicians were approaching the frenzied end of the piece, so she waited until the music ceased and the dancers had dispersed. Then she moved across the deserted floor towards the bar-room. Her imposing figure was clad in a tight-fitting red dress which heightened the colour of her bronzed face. Her features displayed a mixture of bloods: the aquiline nose Spanish, the high cheekbones Indian, the full mouth Negroid. Her hair, parted in the middle and drawn to a knot at the nape of her neck, was black and straight. Her beauty was striking.

As she walked across the room, there flashed into her memory the night of her meeting Toni in this very place over a year ago. How she wished he was with her now!

She took a seat at a table near the bar. Fats blinked as his eyes fell on her. He stared at her for a while, looking her over. The girl in the green dress slipped from his mind. His interest in Mari was immediate, and while his scrutiny of her lasted he stood oblivious to his surroundings. He came to with a jerk. Loudly he ordered drinks for the house, ostentatiously extracting a roll of notes from his breast pocket. Mari raised her head and gave him a languorous look as a waiter hurried to her table.

"How is Mister Toni?" the waiter asked her after his greeting.

"He still in New York," she said, her voice low and mellow.

"You must be missing him a plenty. Miss Mari."

Mari smiled with her lips; her eyes held a faraway, nostalgic expression. She ordered a soft drink, them gave herself up to memories of Toni.

What an intense thrill she got out of coming here and thinking about Toni! Here she had met him, here he had made his first advances to her, here she had accepted him as her lover. She could see him now: his black handsome face, his powerful frame; she could hear him singing his calypso songs, singing them with verve in a deep sonorous voice. His fame as a calypso singer had spread throughout the island, and even the white people came to hear him during the carnival season. A bottle of rum beside him, the tent crowded to suffocation, the acetylene lamps blindingly bright, he would stand on the improvised stage and lift his head and sing with gusto, competing against the other singers and emerging triumphant always.

And then the crazy notion had seized him to go to New York and there commercialize his songs. Mari sighed. She remembered the day he sailed – and the emptiness within her ever since. The emptiness and the growing realization of her great passion for him, the deepening desire to be with him once again. She had written telling him of her resolve to join him in New York. She was saving money, he wouldn't have to worry about his failure, she would have enough to set them both up in a little business in Harlem. They would marry at once and settle down to raising a family.

She didn't care how she came by the money. By fair means or foul, she would get it, enough and to spare. Her charms would see to that.

The waiter plonked down a bottle of champagne before her. She looked up in surprise.

"Mister Fats . . . dat's de big gentl'man over there, Miss Mari . . . he send it to you wit' his compliments." He lowered his voice like a conspirator to add: "He have a lot of money, Miss Mari, a lot of money."

Mari said nothing. Turning her head, she gave Fats the suspicion of a smile. His little eyes twinkled, he smacked his lips. Brandy in hand, he strutted to her table. Her languorous expression excited him.

"Excuse the liberty," he said. "My name is Fats Small." He rested the glass on the table.

"Good evening, Mister Small."

Fine, he thought, fine. "No, no," he said aloud. "Call me 'Fats.' That's how everybody does call me."

"You . . . you don't mind de name?"

"Ho! Ho! Ho!" Fats boomed. "Fat, thin, big, small . . . a man hasn't to worry about things like dat. But a woman . . ."

Mari uttered a little snort of laughter. "You here now, you may as well sit," she said. "Have a glass of champagne wit' me?"

"Sure thing, sure thing." Pompously he hailed the waiter.

"Take dis brandy away an' bring a glass, Gustus. An' let me pay for de champagne now." Ostentatiously he pulled out a roll of notes. "An' now you'se here, Gustus, bring another bottle of champagne, the best." Puffing at a fat cigar, he handed the waiter a twenty dollar bill. "Have a cigarette," he said, passing a gold case to her. He watched her closely as the flame flickered before her lovely face.

"That's a pretty case," she remarked.

""You wants it?"

"I . . . I never take things from strange men."

"Ho! Ho! Ho! How you can call me strange? I'se a stranger to nobody, especially a fine woman like you. Here, take de case."

"Thanks," she returned, "but I can't. It's against my principles."

"Okay," he said as Gustus appeared with the glass and another bottle of champagne. Clinking glasses with her, he murmured: "Here's to no stranger business between us."

They drank.

"Where you been hidin' all dis time?" he asked at length.

"What you mean hiding?"

"I saw you last month here but I didn' get no chance to talk to you. I been coming here ever since then, lookin' for you, every Friday night. Ask Gustus, ask de people who does run dis place."

"Looking for me!" She exclaimed in mock surprise. "What you want wit' me?"

"What any man want wit' a beauty like you? You have it in you to charm a judge, much less me."

"You making fun, Mister Fats."

He frowned. "I don' like de 'Mister.' Call me plain Fats. I tell you I like to be friendly."

"But I don' know you. We only just meet."

"I'se willin' to call you by you' first name – if you tell me what it is."

"You're a fast traveller, Mister Fats."

"Ho! Ho! Ho! Dat's a good one! You ever know a man to get anything in life unless he travel fast? Now then what's your name?"

"Mari. M-A-R-I."

"A pretty name, a pretty name. An' it spell even prettier." He refilled the glasses. They drank. "Tell me, Mari, what you doin' here alone, a beautiful young woman like you?"

"How you know I'se alone?"

He looked around. "I don' see nobody here good enough for you," he announced.

"Present company included?" she teased.

"Ho! Ho! Ho! Dat's a different matter, Mari. I hasn' got de looks, but I has what every woman does love."

"You mean money?"

"Perhaps I does, perhaps I doesn't. You know which perhaps."

"Perhaps you right," she said, averting her slumberous eyes. Already the champagne was rising to her head. She began to feel gay.

"Last time you was all alone," he remarked. "It have me puzzled, a beauty like you."

"I living wit' a Chineeman. He don' like dis kind of life."

Fats sat up. "Livin' wit' a Chineeman, eh?" he mused, now more intrigued than ever. This was what he gloried in, this was his speciality: to pursue and possess other men's women. "I does business wit' Chineemen, you know, an' I lookin' for a couple right now."

"What kind of business?"

"Private business."

"You mean funny business."

"Ho! Ho! Ho! Funny Business! I like dat!"

She leaned towards him, put her hand to her mouth and whispered: "There's only one kind of business nigger can do wit' Chinee – opium."

The music struck up again and the dancers were whirling around the hall.

"You'se a smart girl, Mari," he remarked, his little eyes searching her face. "So it's true, eh? I guess right?"

"I do an' I doesn' deny it," he said. "We all got to live, an' every man have his own way of makin' money."

"My man have a shop, down by Carenage."

"A shop, eh? A big shop?"

"Big enough. He gone out tonight to . . . to get a little cargo. I don' have to tell you what. Dat's how I come to be here."

"While the cat's away, the pretty little mouse will play." He laughed, and refilled the glasses.

"I has to leave soon," she said, "before he get home."

"Who is dis Chineeman? Perhaps I know him."

"Sing Hop."

His little eyes glittered and he whistled through his teeth. "A gorgeous woman like you livin' wit' pint-size Chineeman!" His tone was derisive.

"You knows him?"

"Sure. Ten cents worth of God help us."

She drained her glass before she asked, coyly: "You can do better for me than Sing Hop?"

Fate looked at her, excitedly. His little eyes danced and his thick lips parted. She could hear his heavy breathing.

"When I put over de deal I have in hand now," he said, bending over to her, "I can set you up in fine style: a little house, a maid – anything you want."

Mari, the sparkling wine coursing through her veins, narrowed her almond eyes. "You don' know Sing Hop," she remarked, casually. "You don' know how jealous he is. He would kill me if I try to leave him."

"So you 'fraid him?"

"You not afraid of knife?" she asked with a shudder.

"Me?" said Fats. "Me 'fraid of knife? Hunh, I carries a gun, here," and he placed his hand over his hip.

"I don' like men who does carry guns," she murmured.

"Oh, dis is only for business, Mari, *my* business. Some men has pen an' ink; I has gun." He paused. "A woman like you shouldn' 'fraid Sing Hop," he added. "He isn't even pint; he's half-pint, an' you strong, you look brave."

They fell silent. Fats refilled the glasses and hailed the waiter for another bottle of champagne. Again he pulled out a roll of notes, flourishing them before Mari. She was sufficiently tipsy now to stare at them, deliberately. He noticed this – and prided himself on his way with women.

She broke the silence. "If . . . if you think you can rid him for me . . ." and she glanced at him warily.

"Look at me, Mari, look at me. You makin' a suggestion there . . . I don' know if I get you right. Supposin' I get rid him, what . . ."

"We can't talk about that now. We'll talk afterwards an . . ."

She trailed off into silence.

"You mean you like me, Mari?" Fats asked huskily.

"Sure," she replied. "I like you."

Fats was breathing heavily, regarding her through eyes inflamed with drink and desire. He puffed violently at his cigar. The girl in the green dress, leaning on the arm of the huge Negro, sauntered to the bar, passing close to the table at which Fats and Mari sat. She glanced at Fats, but he did not see her. All his attention was now concentrated on Mari, his whole being focussed on her. The people moving about, the chatter, the stifling air, the clatter of glasses, even the music – he saw, he heard nothing of them. Perspiration shone on his forehead. Never before had he had such a beautiful woman sitting tête-à-tête with him. And bargaining with him! He could scarcely believe his eyes, his ears. Nothing, nothing could stop him now. And a kept woman at that, of all types the most desirable. He looked at her skin: a golden brown, a lighter brown than had ever fallen to his lot.

Mari's head was going round and round, but her mind was steady, anchored to her purpose with an unbreakable determination. Toni – nobody else mattered. She wanted him, she needed him as she had never needed anything else in life. She loved him as she had never loved anything in life, including herself. What if Fats were repulsive, sickening to her? Obviously he had money, obviously he made a lot of it, and money was what she had to have, as much of it as she could lay hands on. Fats was a free spender, she could see that. It would be easy to get as much as she fancied from him – and into her bank account it would go. The account was rising, and Sing Hop had certainly helped her there. But Sing Hop was stingy and she was becoming more and more tired of trying to squeeze money out of him. The typical oriental, he never discussed his business affairs with her and she wasn't even sure that he had much cash left. She had tried to find the hiding place of his bank book: in vain. With the passing of the weeks her heartache for Toni became more intense and the necessity for money was aggravated. She had arrived at the stage where she wanted it at once, in a large sum. She knew her charms, her only asset, she was prepared to use them – for Toni.

"You ever do business wit' Sing Hop?" she asked, her almond eyes as slumberous as ever.

"I never do business wit' him direct," he replied.

She turned her head away to murmur, "You . . . you know how de police feel about opium smuggling."

"Hunh, I know too good. But they never catch Fats, they'll never catch this Fats, you can bet you' bottom dollar on dat!"

"Good." She spoke slowly, with a changed inflection in her voice. Her dark eyes were fixed on him now. "Why you don't make a deal wit' Sing Hop, eh?"

"You mean . . ."

"I mean . . ." she laughed lightly. "I mean what you have in mind." Then she leaned over to him. "You . . . you like me now, you only like me now, but later on, if you find a way to shake him off for me . . ."

Fats' brain began to work. The wheels of it started to spin furiously. Placing the glass to her lips, she drank, pretending indifference now. But she sensed his preoccupation, sensed it as if she were looking into his mind. She said nothing. She drew on her cigarette, deeply, inhaling the smoke down to her lungs.

The cigar had gone dead in his hand when he said: "Let's dance, Mari."

"With you?" she asked, tauntingly.

"Not because I fat I can't dance. I 'se de lightest man on feet in dis hall. Try me."

"All right. But only one. Then I must go."

They rose. Fats extended an arm, she took it, and proudly he led her onto the dance floor.

⌐

Early the following morning Mari and Sing Hop were up and about. The shop was already open for business. The building itself was low and deep, and in the front room Sing Hop ran his general store. Strings of Madeira onions and Mexican garlic festooned the ceiling. One shelf was stacked with firecrackers, the others sagged under the weight of cans and packages containing salt, sugar, flour, peas, and so on. There was a pungent odour of saltfish. An open barrel of salted pork squatted behind the counter. Against the back partition was nailed a small clock decorated with cobweb. The shop faced the main road running through the village of Cocorite.

In the rear were three rooms, their living quarters, the last one their bedroom. Some hundred feet in back of the building stretched the sea. A few coconut trees, their pendulous leaves waving gracefully in the morning breeze, raised their heads high above the yard. Hens clucked, cocks crowed. Every fifteen minutes a trolley car rattled by, creating a deafening din.

The bedroom was in disorder. The bed lay rumpled and Mari's clothes were in little piles here and there. The furniture had not been dusted in days. Looking at it all, you saw that Mari was not a good housekeeper.

But Mari herself was already dressed and tidied up. Sing Hop, wearing a pair of baggy pants and an undershirt, slippers on his feet, looked little more than five feet tall. The jaundiced skin was pulled tightly over his cheekbones, his close-cropped hair stuck up like thin wires, and his eyes seemed to hold little darting beads in them. He moved with nervous energy, quick, precise.

"But I tell you I must have de money!" Mari was saying, her mellow voice subdued.

"Mali, Mali,[2] one hunderd tollars! Where I goin' to get it?" Sing Hop wailed.

"Get it! You have it, man. If you haven't got it, you must get it, somewhere. If what I askin' you for now was for me, I'd understand. But I tell you it's for my mother in Couva.[3] She sick. She owe rent. She must pay doctor. She have to buy medicine. She must have it."

"You allays spendin' money, Mali. Allays spendin', allays."

"If you didn' think I was worth it, why you make me come an' live wit' you?"

"What more you want me to do for you, Mali? Before you come, I was satisfy wit' de little s'op, de little place here. But no. You mek me puy new bed, new buleau, new chair, new lug. You mek me puy a car an' build galage fol it. I learn to dlive it for you. Look de clothes in your closet, Mali. I puy all, I puy all for you."

Mari laughed, contemptuously.

"Don' laff, Mali. Before you come, I was satisfy wit' de s'op, de money I make wit' it. Evely month I put a few tollars in de bank. Since you come you spend all, all. An' lemember what I doin' for you more. You know how I flaid de sea, de police. But no. Now I go out in boat to smuggle op'um to mek more money for you. An' still you complainin', still you . . ."

"I tired hearin' all that," she broke in impatiently. "You goin' to give me de money or you not goin' to give me de money? Say which, an' say it quick."

Sing Hop wrung his diminutive hands and gazed pleadingly at the angry woman. Never had he had anyone like her. From the first moment of seeing her he had fallen for her, completely, abjectly. Her voluptuous figure, her cold

manner and sleepy eyes, her reserve, the struggle he had had to win her . . .
But with each passing week the fear of losing her had been growing within
him, and hand in hand with this went an ever deepening intensity in his passion for her. He disliked her, disliked her untidiness, her unthriftiness, her
lack of affection, but he hungered for her maddeningly. His jealousy at the
prospect of losing her was so overwhelming that he mistook it for love. Above
all, the conviction was dawning on him that in order to hold on to her he must
give her money, more money and yet more money. His reserve fund was something sacred, put away against the day when he would return to China. About
this sum in the bank she must know nothing, and so far he had succeeded in
keeping her in ignorance of it. He was prepared to let her have what he made;
but he now realized that he would have to make more to keep her content. He
dreaded losing her; he dreaded it because he would prefer to see her dead first.
His Mari in the arms of another man? The thought made him frantic, turned
his stomach sick; and it gave him a feeling that was dangerous, very dangerous
– and frightening.

"An' suppose I tell you I can't giff it to you because I haven' got it?" he asked
despairingly.

"Maybe I'd leave you," she said, quietly.

Sing Hop's slit-eyes narrowed, his thin lips quivered, he went taut. He made
one agile step towards her, then stopped, glaring at her with a look she had
never seen before. She stood her ground, her sleepy eyes roused to full wake-
fulness.

His anger went as suddenly as it had possessed him, and he fell to his knees
before her, clutching at her skirt, cringing before her like a terrified child. Her
eyes grew cold, her lips curled. His squeaky voice rose.

"No, no! you can't do me that! . . . All light, all light, I find it for you . . .
anyt'ing you want I giff you. Anyt'ing . . ."

The sound of a step reached them from the shop. Sing Hop leapt to his feet.
Mari had turned from him in disgust and gone over to the window facing on
the sea. He fixed her with a harassed, perplexed stare; then he lowered his head,
brushed the dust from his pants, and shuffled out.

Clad in a white linen suit, a panama hat sitting on his head at a rakish angle,
Fats lounged at the far end of the counter, whistling a popular tune. He greeted
Sing Hop familiarly and noisily.

"Hello, Mister Fats," said Sing Hop. "You velly early."

"What time you does open up, Sing Hop?"

"Half pas' sick."

"You don' call dat early? In business you must be early." He laughed. "I come to see you on business."

"So?"

"Sure. Real business. How is sales?"

"Not velly goot, not velly bat."

"Dat's de perfect Chinee answer," said Fats, his features distorted in a smile. Then he grew serious. "I'se come to see you private an' confidential."

"Plivate? About what?"

"Look, man, when I say private I mean private. I have a proposition, a first class proposition."

Sing Hop glanced nervously over his shoulder before saying: "You tell me here?"

Fats, his little eyes fixed on the door leading into the rear of the shop, snapped petulantly: "If you don' want to hear it, an' it's big business, you hear, big money, I can take it to Lee Sang up de road," and he made as if to go.

"All light, all light, Mister Fats," Sing Hop squeaked. "Don' get vex. I leady to listen."

Fats smiled. Sing Hop raised the trap in the counter and Fats squeezed his large girth through the opening. They moved into the bedroom.

Mari faced them as they came in. There was nothing in her manner to show that she had ever met Fats. The Negro breathed stertorously, his small eyes dancing with excitement.

"Dis gentl'man want to see me private, Mali. Mind de s'op till we finish."

Mari walked out of the room. Sing Hop shuffled to the door and closed it.

"So?" he said.

"Give me a chair first, man. Your bank manager don' offer you a seat when you go to see him? I can't talk to you standin' up. I not your size, you know."

"Ekcuse me," Sing Hop murmured, and drew up a chair.

Fats sat, mopping his brow with a red silk handkerchief. Sing Hop sat on the edge of the bed, his legs dangling an inch from the floor.

"Now then, Sing Hop, I come to you because I wants to put something good your way, big profit . . ."

"An' big lisk?"

"No risk at all, man, none. It's opium."

"Eh?"

"Don' stare at me as if you never hear dat word before. You interested?"

"Tell me more firs'."

"Good. The thing so big, I'se forming a syndicate. I has t'ree Chineemen in de deal already. I needs t'ree more – unless I find one man brave enough to take de whole thing."

"So?"

"It's a Venezuelan sloop. I been doin' business wit' de captain a long time. De sloop been beatin' about de gulf now two days, ten, twelve mile off shore, waitin' for me to close de deal."

"So?"

"All right, man, give me a chance to finish. Don' get excited. I has made all arrangements for goin' out to de sloop. De captain say he can't wait no longer. We have to get busy – tonight."

"How much?"

"Ha, my boy, now you coming down to brass tacks, now you showin' dat you is a business man. Opium? What's wrong wit' opium? De white man himself does drink rum till his insides rot away. De Chineeman like opium. What's de difference? An' rum does make you sick: opium does give you dreams, sweet dreams, nice women, not so?"

Sing Hop nodded, his faced screwed up in anticipation.

"Good. Now don' jump out of you' skin when I tell you how much it is. It's big money, but big money does make big money, just like if I have a child it bound to be a big child." He chuckled, heavily. "Take de deal, Sing Hop, an' you make a fortune. You know better than me how you can double you' money in dis kind a business, quick like dat," and he snapped his fingers. "Take it an' sell it to your Chinee friends."

"How much?" He glanced at the door and added: "Speak easy."

"Six t'ousand dollars!"

The Chinaman opened his eyes wide, but the Negro was quick.

"You not telling me you have courage like you' size? Look how you' countrymen fightin' de Japs,4 man. I did think all Chineemen was brave, brave like lions. You know de speedboat I does hire? American make. Fastest in de harbour. Forty-eight miles a hour. De police launch?" He made a deprecatory gesture with his right arm. "Only twenty miles a hour at de most. Big money, no risk. Safe as de man in de moon. What you say?"

Sing Hop dropped to the floor and shuffled noiselessly to the door. Placing his ear to it, he listened for a while and returned to the bed.

Fats held his sides and laughed without a sound, his belly rolling. "You right, man," he remarked. "I know women. They all de same. Some things they mustn' know if you wants to keep right wit' you'self."

"Sick t'ousand tollar! Plenty money, plenty money."

"Sure is plenty money. But six t'ousand dollars can make six t'ousand dollars in dis sort a business. You know dat better dan me. If I had de cash I take it myself, right off. An' look de nice woman you have. I sure she does want money; all de nice women want money, they does dribble for it. *I know*. Look how happy you can make her. A handsome present, a diamond ring, a gold bracelet, a new car – she will love you forever an' ever, man. An' look how much trouble it will save you, how much risk. Every week you goin' out in boat to . . ."

"How you know dat?" Sing Hop shot at him.

Fats chuckled. "How I know dat! Show me de Chineeman in dis town who don' do dat' an' I give you . . . I give you some of my fat, man. Every week you goin' for five hundred dollars. To make six t'ousand dollars you run twelve risks of jail, maybe even of bullets. Think of dat! One stroke, one risk – an' is no risk wit' de speedboat I have – an' you make six t'ousand dollars! What you say? Speak up, man, before I go to see Lee Sang up de road. He'd jump on it like cat on a mouse."

The Negro was breathless with talk, but his eyes were glued to the Chinaman.

"All light, I take it," Sing Hop said at length.

"De whole deal?"

"Sure."

"Dat's de way to talk, boy. Dat's real business sense. But wait, you have de money in ready cash?"

The amount represented his sacred fund for his trip to China, but he did not hesitate to say: "Sure," in a low voice, glancing at the door.

Fats rose, ponderously. Sing Hop shuffled ahead and opened the door. When they entered the shop, Mari was standing at the far end of the counter, looking out into the street.

"Mali," Sing Hop squeaked in a happy tone, "dis is Mister Fats."

Fats raised his panama hat grandly. Mari bowed slightly, cast him a languorous look, and retired inside.

"Huh, my boy," Fats remarked expansively, "you Chineemen know how to choose good. Dat's a handsome woman."

Sing Hop smiled. "So?" he said.

"Till tonight. We drive down to Carenage5 in your car from here?"

"All light. What time?"

"Ten o' clock sharp. Watch out for me. I'll be seein' you."

They shook hands. Fats broke into an ungainly run to catch the downtown trolley car.

~

A half moon looked down from the sky on an outlying district of Port of Spain. Sing Hop sat at the wheel, driving carefully.

"Just de right kind a moon," Fats remarked.

A cool breeze blew in from the sea. It was nearing eleven o' clock. Coconut trees lined the shore to their left; to their right was hilly land, yellow-green with moonlight. They rolled by an occasional dark house. The street was deserted. At times they could see the sea through the coconut trees. The two men were silent for most of the way.

"Here, to the left," Fats said. "Go slow. This is de shack where de Greaser does live. Let me out here. Drive straight on down de road a little way, where a tall coconut tree does bend over de road. On de right is a narrow track. Drive de car in there an' hide it in de bushes. Then walk back to de beach, stand behind de trees an' wait there for us. We'll be there in five minutes."

Fats alighted and Sing Hop drove off.

The Negro, wearing a dark suit and a heavy felt hat pulled over his eyes, walked down the path to the Greaser's shack. He knocked.

"Who is that?" came a voice from within.

"Open, man, open."

The door swung open and Fats stepped in. The Greaser, a heavy-set Venezuelan with a big head and a mop of tousled hair, was clad in a pair of black trousers and a dark sweater. A hammock was slung across the room. An oil lamp, standing on a table, cast a feeble light.

"I been expecting you since yesterday," said the Greaser.

"I know, but I couldn' manage before. De syndicate is off. Lucky for us I get one Chineeman to take de whole deal." He paused to light a cigarette. "Look, Greaser, you going to make a extra hundred dollars tonight – in addition to de regular fifty dollars for de boat. What you say?"

The Greaser's tired eyes woke up. "What you mean?" he asked.

"Just what I say. You know me long enough to know dat I always mean what I say. Here," he said , "I have de fifty dollars ready for you. The other hundred you get in about a month. All you have to do for it is to stop de boat as soon as de police fire a shot across your bow. Easy money."

"Police!"

"Yes, police, my friends dis time. Don' get frighten. Safe as de man in de moon. I already notify them of the time an' place."

The Greaser lit a cigarette. "You is turn stool-pigeon now, huh?"

"Call it fancy name if you like: I does call it *business*. An' look, don't ask too many question now . . ."

"But you takin' me by surprise, Fats. I got to ask questions. Who want to get mix up wit' de po– . . ."

"Listen, Greaser! Don' be a damn fool! You an' me is there to set trap for de Chineeman. After de police arrest him wit' de evidence . . . listen good, *wit' de evidence* . . . we got to see dat he have de opium on him when de police catch him in de boat . . . after de police put him in handcuffs de judge goin' to fine him heavy, heavy an' hard – besides jail. I sharin' de reward wit' you. You don' see how safe it is? An' a hundred dollars is a lot of money, man."

The Greaser spat through the window. "Not enough," he announced.

"Ho, ho, you playin' big now! How much you want ?" The Greaser did not reply immediately. "Hurry up, man. De Chineeman waitin' for us."

"Five hundred," the Greaser said.

Fats laughed. "You crazy, man."

"Crazy? Suppose de Chineeman put knife in me afterwards?"

"I tell you not to worry you' head about him. De police goin' lose him in jail, perhaps five, perhaps ten years. When he pay de fine, you get your share of de reward."

"What about Captain Gonzales an' de sloop? Suppose de police find us on de sloop?"

Fats sucked his tongue hissingly between his teeth. "You t'ink I'se a fool? You t'ink I don't know I have to do more business with Captain Gonzalez? De police not goin' to find us on de sloop because I tell them five miles different. T'ink good before you ask me foolish questions. Dis is easy money, man. Fifty dollars for you' boat, de other hundred for jam."

"Five hundred," said the Greaser.

"Look, man, I losin' patience wit' you."

"All right. Get another boat."

Fats knitted his brows and thought for a moment. "You'se smart, Greaser, you'se smart all right. Listen, I play ball wit' you. Let's say two hundred an' call it quits."

They settled finally for two hundred and fifty dollars and Fats handed over the boat rental. The Greaser checked the notes, rolled them, and waited until Fats was outside before putting the money away in his mattress.

"Now look," Fats said as the Greaser joined him outside, "you understand well that you stop de boat as soon as de police fire a shot across your bow, eh? If you don't . . ."

"I know, I know."

"Good. Let's go an' meet de Chineeman. His name is Sing Hop. You know him?"

"All Chinee is de same to me."

Sing Hop was standing under a coconut tree when they came up to him.

"I see jetty," he said, "but I don' see boat."

"She there all right, at the end of de jetty," Fats explained. "De Greaser paint it all black, wit' no name on it. De police never see us. Come, let's go. It's gettin' late."

They walked out on the rickety jetty, Fats carefully picking his steps. The boat, tied up at the end, sat low in the water. The sea was calm. Little waves danced in with soft splashing sounds, their crests silvered by the moon. Away to the left twinkled the lights of the steamships at anchor off Port of Spain.

"How de tide?" Fats asked.

"Low," the Greaser replied.

"Good. Look, Sing Hop, I goin' give de Greaser's boat a extra recommendation, free an' gratis. When you wants to go out again, take his boat. You know how de sea shallow knee-deep two miles out from here. De Greaser boat have only a shallow draft. Look how she sittin' nice on dis shallow water, like a duck. But de police launch . . . how much draft she have again, Greaser?"

"About four feet."

"Get it, Sing Hop? De police launch can't get nearer shore than two miles! Now in de Greaser's boat you can speed in, right into here. Get it, Sing Hop?"

Sing Hop nodded.

The Greaser had already opened up the hatch and started the motor. While Fats was clumsily descending into the boat from the jetty, Sing Hop leapt lightly onto the stern deck and prepared to take a seat.

"Keep away from there," Fats called out to him. "Dat's my place. You can't expect to sit in de same seat wit' a fat man like me. I need a lot a room. Sit in front wit' de Greaser."

Sing Hop jumped onto the hatch, crossed it in three steps, and dropped down into the cockpit, beside the Greaser. With one hand on the wheel, the Greaser slipped into gear and opened up the throttle. Sing Hop idly watched him. "Just like drivin' a car," he remarked.

The boat shot forward, the musical hum of its motor filling the ears of the three men. The bow rose, the stern settled as she gathered speed. Her props[6] churned the water into a seething white mound, the phosphorous glowing in the wake.

Soon they were well out to sea, the wind racing past them. Fats turned his head shorewards and saw the opaque mass of mountain looming up in the moonlit night. Then he felt his hip pocket, glanced at his wrist watch, made himself comfortable, and settled down to think.

Mari possessed his thoughts. The mental picture of her exhilarated him. How cunningly she had given him the idea for this daring scheme! How smoothly it was working out! With the thousand dollars he would receive as his commission on the deal, way beyond any sum he had yet made at one swoop, he would be able to give her all she needed for weeks to come. And his share of the reward . . . the police had assured him of a ten thousand dollar fine . . . ten per cent of that was one thousand . . . two hundred and fifty to the Greaser left him seven hundred and fifty . . . seventeen hundred and fifty for himself! He would get her a cottage in Laventille, furnish it, set her up like a grand lady, buy her jewellery – lordy, lordy, this was the life! Another hour and he would be with her. Yes, as soon as the Chinaman was locked safely in jail he would go straight to her, give her the good news, display the banknotes before her startled eyes, and . . . A thrill passed through his gargantuan bulk.

Sing Hop huddled his knees to his chin, watching the Greaser manoeuvre the speeding boat. Six thousand dollars rolled in his pocket, his whole cash fortune! Fats had come to him in the nick of time. He could see Mari now, the face with the slumberous eyes, the body that maddened him. In six weeks he could dispose of the cargo – that was the way to do business. Then he could give her all she asked for – and she would be his, his for as long as he wanted her. For once he was not afraid of the sea. And how could he fear the police in this boat skimming along as if there were wings to her sides?

The Greaser's powerful hands gripped the pulsing wheel, his eyes fixed on the moonlit distance. No craft was in sight. Ahead the moonlight dappled the scintillating surface. His boat was doing fine. A good investment when he bought her six months ago, the best investment he had ever made. And how well he knew her! Still, he was timid, a bit timid. He didn't like the idea of any shell falling too near his boat. His life's saving's were in it, but who could resist the offer of an extra two hundred and fifty dollars for an hour's work? He would do a lot with it: fix up his little shack, overhaul his boat – and hide the balance away in his mattress against a rainy day. Fats? He had known Fats for a long time and had never once been let down by him. Besides, he knew too much about the nigger and his affairs for him to try any monkey business with *him*.

"Slow down, Greaser, an' flash de light," Fats called out above the hum of the motor. "I calculate we'se about there now. Keep your eyes skinned for de sloop an' make de sign when we see her."

The boat slowed down, her nose dropping in the water. The Greaser stood up with a flashlight in his hand. They cut ahead slowly, the sea gurgling along the sides of the craft. Sing Hop's hand involuntarily stole to his jacket-pocket and felt the notes bulging there. The sudden cessation of speed, of the full music of the motor, the sudden subsidence of the boiling water at their stern, brought home to the men the realization that their expedition was fraught with danger. Even Fats was uneasy. He blinked his eyes and peered into the somber moonlight for the sloop, the cut and jib of which he knew so well that he would recognize her under any conditions. He strained his eyes, but his ears were cocked for sound, the sound of the police motor launch, for how could he be sure that it would not blunder into them at the moment of their boarding the sloop? That he didn't want, and he had done all that he reasonably could to avoid it. Still, you had to take chances in life if . . .

"I see her," the Greaser announced.

"Give de signal – t'ree flashes in quick succession." Fats' voice was tense. A green light flashed some distance ahead. "Yes, there she is."

In a few minutes they were alongside and the gangway was let down.

"Keep your eyes open wide, Greaser," Fats warned as, preceded by the agile Chinaman, he laboured up the gangway.

Captain Gonzalez received them without a word. The deck was a silent array of immobile shadows: boxes, bales, bags, the galley, the wheel-house. Two men sprawled on the galley, another stood at the wheel. The sails flapped lazily in the light breeze drifting from the direction of Port of Spain.

They followed the captain down the companionway into his cramped cabin. The pungent odour of copra assailed their nostrils. Fats coughed, took a per-fumed handkerchief from his pocket and held it to his spatulate nose, inhaling deeply. Sing Hop's face was impassive, but his heart beat violently.

"I been waiting two whole days for you," Captain Gonzalez began in a strong accent.

"I know, I know," Fats cut in. "We can't talk about that now, Captain. We have to get away, an' quick." He glanced at his wrist-watch. "You has de stuff?"

The captain turned to a little safe, fumbled with it for a space, and lifted two large paint cans from it. Both carried make-shift rope handles and each can was labelled: VELSPAR ENAMEL, Inside White. He handed them to Fats. The Negro rested them on the table, drew the covers out, and sniffed the contents. Sing Hop followed. After the cans had been weighed to Sing Hop's satisfaction, Fats snapped: "Pay up, man! Quick! We got to go. No time to lose."

Captain Gonzalez took the roll of notes and checked them. Then he slipped a thousand-dollar bill into Fats' hand, Sing Hop catching this exchange through the corner of his eye. It was all right with him. He wasn't such a fool as to imagine that Fats was working for nothing.

"See you tomorrow in de usual place in town," Fats said. "No time for ceremonies an' celebrations now."

Sing Hop sealed the cans with some adhesive tape and said, quietly: "I leady."

The speed boat's motor was purring as Fats resumed his seat at the stern. He pressed himself against the gunwale and called out:

"Look, I make room for you, Sing Hop." He was taking no chances now of having the evidence thrown overboard by the Chinaman in panic. No evidence, no arrest, no reward, . . . and the loss of Mari. "Here, we has de opium now, better stay together. You can' be sure of what might happen." The motor burst into song and their bow lifted. Sing Hop fell back into the seat beside Fats with an oath. "Move up a little, man," the Negro said. "I have to put de gun between us in case we need it." A clever touch this, he thought, so disarming. He could retrieve it and put it out of harm's way as soon as . . .

"No, no," squeaked Sing Hop. "Take it 'way. I don' want no gun near me. Gun mek trouple."

"An' suppose de police come, you fool?"

"I don' want s'oot. If police come, I tell them we joy-liding in moonlight."

"You t'ink de police foolish as all dat? They bound to search you an' find de opium."

"Hah," squeaked Sing Hop, "if it come to dat I throw it in de sea."

Fats smiled at his own cleverness and placed the automatic on the seat between them.

Their wake was a long line of white foam in the moonlight. The stars shone brightly, no cloud was in the sky. Now they were streaking towards the shore. The sloop was already swallowed up in the darkness. The Greaser sat tensed at the wheel, his nerves on tiptoe waiting for the police shell.

Fats pretended to be taking it easy, his fat legs stretched out, his back against the stern rail. Now and again he glanced over his shoulder. The night air was warm, but the tips of his fingers were cold.

Sing Hop's eyes were closed. At his feet rested the two cans.

They were flying past a group of small islands in the gulf when the shriek of a police siren pierced the hum of their motor. Immediately a searchlight started to rake the water about them.

"Oh God, de police!" Fats cried and ducked his head.

Sing Hop sprang to his feet.

Suddenly the full glare of the searchlight struck the boat and the next instant a shell detonated at their bow, breaking the water into a phosphorescent shower that doused them. The boat shook, Sing Hop fell.

With a trembling hand, the Greaser slipped the clutch. The bow dropped. The white maelstrom of water at their stern quieted and was gone. The searchlight's cone shifted from them, lost them and went agitatedly searching for the white target of their wake.

Fats, his heart pumping, forgot the gun, forgot the opium in his panic, and stiffened up to watch the swaying cone of light.

With a start, Sing Hop leapt to his feet, leaned over the hatch, and hissed at the Greaser: "Put gear in! Quick! Quick!"

"I don't want no hole blown in de side of my boat," the Greaser said, facing the Chinaman. "I don't want my head blown off."

"So? So?" Sing Hop wheezed, his mind spinning like clockwork. His future fortune at his feet, his liberty right here, his Mari . . .

Before Fats knew what was happening, Sing Hop snatched the automatic, flung himself on his belly across the hatch, and levelled the gun a foot from the Greaser's head. The Greaser turned to face him and got the full explosion in his mouth and eyes. He slumped and rolled over.

Fats spun around just in time to see the Chinaman hop into the Greaser's seat. There was a rasp of shifting gears, the bow rose from the water as the boat gathered speed and was off like a 'plane about to leave the surface of the sea.

The searchlight found them again and a shell burst a few yards away. Fats dived into the bottom of the boat and lay there, petrified.

The siren shrieked, more distant now. Fats scrambled to his feet, keeping his head low.

"Stop de boat!" he screamed at the Chinaman.

The boat raced on. A hail of bullets whined over them. Fats crouched, every limb shaking.

As he lay like that, it broke in upon him that if he did not bring the boat to a halt he was lost. He raised his head above the hatch. He couldn't see the Chinaman, so he stretched over the hatch to grab him by the throat. Another hail of bullets ping'd past. One got him in the neck, another in the chest. His bulk shivered and was still.

Sing Hop zig-zagged his course and eluded the one remaining hope of the police – their searchlight. He listened to the song of the motor, to the angry wash of the water as he flew towards the shore.

Once he glanced back and saw the helpless searchlight far out to sea. The pursuit had stopped. The blurred shoreline began to take shape, coconut trees detached themselves, the white crests of the waves breaking gently on the beach shone. The boat grazed the sand and he shifted into neutral.

Lightly Sing Hop sprang out into a few inches of water and scanned the beach. No one was about; not even the coconut trees stirred. The automatic gleamed on the hatch, beside Fats. He leaned over and explored the cockpit with his hands. He could see the horribly mutilated face of the Greaser, one open eye staring glassily up at him. At last he found what he wanted – a rag. Gingerly he wrapped one end of the rag around the muzzle of the gun and with the other end rubbed the butt vigorously. Then with great care he entwined the limp fingers of Fats' right hand around the butt. With a dexterous movement he extracted the thousand-dollar bill from the dead Negro's inside pocket and shoved it into his underwear.

Grabbing the cans by their rope handles, he lifted them out. One in each hand, he made for the beach. At the water's edge he stopped and looked hard at the sand that could so easily take imprints. Then he turned right and, parallel to the shore and ankle-deep in water, he hurried on, the cans swaying rhythmically to his steps.

NOTES

1. Working-class areas of Port of Spain.
2. All of Mendes's working-class Chinese characters have difficulty in pronouncing the letter "r".
3. A town midway between Port of Spain and San Fernando.
4. Fats is most probably referring to the series of Sino-Japanese conflicts between 1928 and 1932.
5. A coastal town on the road from Port of Spain to Chaguaramas.
6. Propellers

GOLD BEANS

The title of this story, like so much else, belongs to an age that seems to have dropped below the horizon of the past. Gold beans . . .
Even now I can see Teelucksingh,[1] tall and wiry and copper-complexioned, his cheeks sunken in from tough and timeless labour in the fields, his hair veined with grey strands. Years before, his parents, indentured to a cocoa plantation, had arrived in Trinidad from India. Teelucksingh was born in the island and had all his life lived on cocoa plantations with men of his own race, and so could speak English only in the fashion of his people.

"Hunh, Sahib," he said to me that sunfilled morning as I stood with him by the shanty in which he lived with his wife and eight children. "Me got-am ten carry land." He made a sweeping gesture with his arms to indicate the twenty-odd acres of land surrounding his home. "Time come, time pass an' Gahd sabby how much plenty work me put-am estate-side. Price so-so. Fambly live. Sumintra . . . good wife, Sumintra, Sahib . . . Sumintra work like hell, make *talcari*, make rice, make *roti*, all fambly eat-am good. Get-am enough copper to buy capra, to buy dress store-side, to keep rain from coming through roof. Dat time cacao same like silver. Today, Sahib, cacao same like gold. Hunh, Sahib, cacao gold bean."

That was in 1929.

I can remember, too, Chin Lee, the undersized Chinaman who ran a provision shop just outside Sangre Grande on the way to Manzanilla. Perhaps he is still there. His shop crouched on a curve of the road that wound through one of the richest cocoa districts of the island, and Chin Lee plied a lucrative trade with the estate labourers around. Also, he bought cocoa in small lots from the small holders – one, two and three bags at a time – and spread them out on the tray he had built at the back of the shop to "doctor" the beans for the Port of Spain market. Once a month he trucked his purchases to town, sometimes ten, sometimes fifteen bags; and because Chin Lee was cautious and shrewd, always his profits were good.

He was standing idly at one of his shop doors the morning I dropped in on him. I knew him well, as well as it is possible for the west to know the east. Often I had dropped in on him to make some last small purchases of a can of this, a pound of that, and ten cents' worth of the other, on my way to my father's cocoa plantation, which I visited once a fortnight to pay the labourers. At such times Chin Lee and I would talk: of the weather, of trade, of crops, of prices.

"How's things?" I said to him.

Rubbing the palms of his pale, diminutive hands together, his yellow face wrinkling into a smile, he said: "Cocoa plice flyin' up to t'e sky, Mr. Mentes. Evelyboty makin' money. Cocoa bean gold bean."

That, too, was in 1929.

Do I have to tell you that I remember my father during those boom years? He had made his money slowly but surely. He had made his money step by step, adjusting his personal expenditure carefully and conservatively to the yearly fluctuations of his income in the vain hope that no force outside of his control would come along and dash him against the rocks of bankruptcy. He, too, in 1929 had said: "Cocoa beans are gold beans."

And they were. Make no mistake about that. The rise from the normal eight dollars per fanega (110 pounds) to sixteen and seventeen dollars had miraculously brought to the proprietors visions of living in mansions around the Savannah, of running two cars with liveried chauffeurs, of sending their children to school in England, of vacationing abroad for three months every year, of pushing ahead in the social scale to hobnob with the small official set popularly referred to as "the Government House clique." For let me say at once that cocoa is to the island what wheat is to larger tracts of the earth's dry surface. When the price of the bean is up, the purchasing power of the people is high; when down, the island is like a sick man coughing up the life from his lungs.

Which is all by way of telling you that I am a native of the island and that I have lived long enough on it to know whereof I speak, particularly of the running of a cocoa estate.

Leaving Chin Lee smiling and still rubbing the palms of his hands together, as well he might, I jumped into my new Ford and resumed my way. The bright

October morning sun was pouring down streams of light onto the dusty road and the thick press of cocoa foliage spread out far and wide on either side. The crop was coming in and the purpose of my visit was not only to pay wages, but to inspect the progress of the gathering of the geese that would lay the golden eggs.

If you've never had a panoramic view of a cocoa plantation, you've missed a sight worth travelling to the Antilles to see. Santa Carlotta estate's great-house, a large, unpainted building of the tropical bungalow type, stands atop a hill. From its front porch I looked down on the 130 acres of the plantation. Tall immortelle trees, scintillating to the touch of the sun, reared themselves up like guardians of the humbler trees huddling beneath to present a greensward to the sky. Or, to change the simile, green sea, capped with yellow waves of immortelle bloom, faced blue sky freckled with white wisps of cloud. And washing it all, sunlight. And silence, save for the sibilant whistle of the wind that blew from the sea four miles away.

"How's the crop coming along?" I said to Renwick, the coloured overseer, as he stood waiting for me to change into appropriate clothes for the foot-tour of inspection.

"Fine, Borss," he said, his brown face beaded with perspiration. "You going see for yourself."

Within ten minutes we were stumbling down the hill into the green and odoriferous shade of the plantation. After the heat of the sun's rays, it was cool. Walking along one of the innumerable paths that criss-cross the estate, I looked at the squat and round-bellied trees burdened with green and brown and red pods. The crop will be fine, I reflected; and with prices as they are, the estate should yield a profit of over fifteen thousand dollars for the year. I felt good as I sprang across drain after drain.

The leaf-carpetted ground was soft and silent to the step.

"We in John-John field, Borss," said Renwick. "Remember that tree?"

Sure I remembered it. Who wouldn't? Year after year it had proven to be one of the heaviest-bearing trees, and here again it had performed the miracle of producing a drooping weight of fruit. We both stood and gazed up at it for a long time, our spirits uplifted by its strength and amazing fertility.

Soon we came upon the first signs of human activity in this green expanse of silence: a group of "pickers." With long poles, to the ends of which were attached crescent-shaped knives, they sent the ripe pods tumbling to earth with deft, stabbing cuts. They wore merinos and old soiled pants; and as they went from tree to tree, they teased and taunted each other like black birds over a dung heap. In spite of their sixty cents a day, they seemed to be happy enough. Now and again their raucous laughter echoed through the tree-lanes and "plop, plop, plop" came the sound of the dropping pods.

"Boodhoo!"[2] shouted Renwick.

A short, sturdy East Indian, with leggings and enormous hat on head, sauntered up. Exposing the white gleam of perfect teeth, he saluted.

"This man had a bad shot of malaria last week," Renwick said to me. And to Boodhoo: "How you feeling today?"

"I feeling good," said Boodhoo.

"How the picking going?"

"I never seen so much cacao in all me life," said Boodhoo – and strode off to his interrupted task.

"Plop, plop, plop," was the last I heard of that sweating gang of Negroes and East Indians.

We were still descending and as we got nearer the bed of the valley, into which the slanting rays of the sun could not dip, the green shade grew greener, the musky odour of earth and decaying leaves muskier. In spite of my having explored the plantation frequently, by this time I had lost all sense of direction. Remember the green aisles shutting us away from the sight of the sun; remember the rectangular ravel of intersecting lanes and drains; remember the sameness of squat tree after squat tree, overlorded at intervals of fifty feet or so by the sameness of lofty immortelles whose tops were lost to us above the roof of our immediate world; remember all this and you will understand my bewilderment. Not so Renwick. *He* knew every hidden recess of the hundred and thirty overgrown acres and could find his way about them through the impenetrable darkness of night with the sure instinct of an animal. That I know because I had been out with him on rare occasions to hunt agouti and lappe long after the sun had gone down. I asked him once: "How on earth do you manage it?"

"By smell," said he – and laughed to celebrate his victory over me in these unfamiliar surroundings.

We passed a babbling stream and saw, at the base of an old immortelle, a dozen or so East Indian women squatting on their hams around a preposterous pile of cocoa pods.

"Salaam, Sahib. Salaam, Sahib."

"Salaam," said I.

They were the "breakers." With their veils wrapped around their heads and their voluminous skirts mantling their legs, they went about their business of slashing open the pods with the precision that comes only after long practice. To watch them was fascinating, almost as fascinating as it is to watch the fingers of a Schnabel[3] pirouetting over the keys of a piano. And as they worked, they gossiped in their native tongue. A pod open, with dexterous scoops of their hands they scraped out the slimy beans and threw them into a nearby basket.

"Remember Rampatia, Borss?" said Renwick. "Look her sitting there, next to Mulemeah."

I knew Rampatia well. She was born on the estate and had grown up on it. At fifteen she was the loveliest girl for miles around. The older women, wagging their heads solemnly, said she was wild and free with her favours and would come to no good end. Boodhoo, with a dozen other young blades of the district, fluttered around her for months. As we say in our genteel society, Boodhoo's "intentions were honourable." He loved Rampatia. He was a serious and sober fellow. At last she succumbed to his flattering refusal to take no for an answer and married him.

Now as I stared at her I could scarcely recognize her. Across both cheeks were nasty gashes that had but recently healed.

"Good God," I said to Renwick , "who the devil did *that*?"

"Sh," he warned. "I hushed it up. I didn't want no scandal on Santa Carlotta with the police."

"But who . . ."

"Boodhoo, of course. It was bound to come to that with her playing with fire every chance she got. One night he caught her redhanded with a nigger boy from the village, and ups with his cutlass and gave it to her good and ugly."

"But aren't you afraid . . ."

"No Borss. You know what these Indians are. He told me he satisfied now. He got his revenge."

"Are they together again?"

"Sure Borss. And she tame like a mouse now. Some women are like that, you know. You have to beat and cut them to make them behave." He paused for a moment and then added: "It isn't what *I* would do, but different men, different ways. *You* know, Borss."

I was thinking over what had just been told me when Renwick, with artless lack of respect for the moment, switched to Mulemeah.

"Now look at Mulemeah there, Borss. You know what I hear last week? I hear she has over six hundred dollars in the bank! And she been working all these years for thirty cents a day!"

That, because I had heard it of others like Mulemeah time and again, did not surprise me in the least.

The pungently sweet odour of green cocoa assailed the nostrils. That and the green shade and the chatter of an alien tongue constituted a *mise-en-scène* that was strange and exotic and tremendously exciting. I had smelt and seen and heard it all before, of course, but always its effect was the same.

Standing by and champing their bits were two mules with their Negro "drivers." As soon as a couple of baskets were full, down swooped the drivers on them and, lifting them, slung them across the back of a mule. The two animals loaded, with loud gee-ups and louder cracks of whips the drivers urged on their burdened beasts to the start of the long climb up to the "sweating houses." They would take a shorter way back than we had taken in, so we decided to follow them.

Laboriously the mules moved onwards and upwards, foam already at their mouths, their nostrils dilated with the pressure of their snorting respiration. Renwick trudged on ahead of me. A tall, thin man he was, perhaps forty, perhaps fifty. His hair was kinky, his nose Roman; his mouth, heavy and well shaped, was a fine acknowledgment of the black and white bloods coursing through his veins. He had come from Grenada, a small island a hundred or so miles to the north of Trinidad, in which there are but three or four families of pure European descent. This is another way of saying that the élite of the island's society is coloured for the most part – and from this set came Renwick. He had been well raised, pretty well educated and his future was bright; but when, like his English grandfather before him, he fell in love with and married a black girl of "ordinary" stock, he found himself ostracized and unable to find work that would afford him the standards of living to which he had been accustomed. So he came to Trinidad, got the job at Santa Carlotta, and raised a brood of seventeen children. The Lord alone knows how he did it on thirty dollars a fortnight! True enough, there was no rent to pay. True enough, the younger ones ran around almost naked for most of the time. And then Celestine, his wife, now grown as fat as a Barbadian cook, did all the washing, cooking and ironing and herself tended the garden of sweet potatoes, yams, tannias and tomatoes at the back of the four-room estate-cottage in which the family lived. Even with all this – and the breadfruit, bananas and oranges that grew profusely in odd corners of the plantation – to have reared a family of seventeen, without a single death, on such niggardly earnings remained a brilliant economic feat – not to mention its significance as a commentary on the appalling lot of the workers throughout the West Indian islands. Appalling, I say, but judged only by the metropolitan standards of the toilet, the telephone and the taxi, for is it not a moot question as to which is the *wiser* way of life?

At last we emerged from the cool of shade-land into the heat of a noonday sun. Still following the mules and their drivers, we panted up the incline, our clothes now saturated with perspiration, the blood bursting in our faces. We plodded past the "barracks" in which the labourers lived, a long row of rooms under a common galvanized roof, apportioned according to the size of the respective families. Naked Indian and Negro children, with big bellies adorned with stumps of umbilical cord, stood and gaped at us, white teeth and whites of eyes gleaming. Their parents in the fields, they were left at crop-time to their own make of mischief and merrymaking. When it rained, they rolled in the mud. When the weather was fine, they romped around the dusty yard – and yet they lived and grew into strapping men and women, strong enough to perform tasks from the mere prospect of which most Englishmen would recoil. Their rice and their *roti* built brawn and, in some cases, brain.

And so we came to the "sweating houses", long, low sheds divided up into large, box-like compartments. To the accompaniment of strident whoas and hooplas, the drivers unloaded the animals of their baskets and tilted the contents into one of the sweating boxes. The heat under the shed was terrific, the odour of fermenting cocoa so powerful and opaque that you felt you could cut it with a knife. Here the beans are allowed to sweat for anywhere between ten and fourteen days; and during that period, the men every day roll up their trouser legs to above the knees and, lustily singing bawdy songs to the lilt of rolling tunes, plunge naked feet round and round into the thick soup of beans to aid the fermenting process. How they survive the baking heat at such times passes my comprehension. Why, to think of it alone brings beads of sweat to my forehead and the blood pulsating in hot waves to my temples.

Hard by are the "drying trays". On sunny mornings you will see wheeled roofs being rolled out to expose the trays to the warmth of the day; then the labourers, shouldering bags and boxes of the steaming beans, move heavily across the open space to the shed and mount the steps leading up into the trays, onto which they dump their burdens. The women are there, ready to spread out thinly the slimy, acrid stuff and begin the long period of "dancing the cocoa" to give it an even polish and colour. For days you will hear them chanting songs of the Far East as, barefooted, they scrape along to the rhythmic jingle of their silver anklets and bracelets from end to end of the tray, turning the beans over and over. They glide with grace, the veils that should protect them from the glare of the sun snatched away by gusts of wind, their sliding feet making a swishing sound. On and on they dance – and you watch them, wondering what the bright London thing would say could she but have seen the soiled feet of these brown pagan women caressing the beans that have gone into the making of the chocolate sweet she is munching.

At last the beans are dry, brown pebbles of rich food, and are ready for bagging. Shovelled into bags, they are taken to the room below the tray and scaled to the tune of a fanega and a half per bag. The trucks roll up, are loaded and in less than three hours their freights are discharged before the doors of the proprietor's warehouse.

Rarely are proprietors shippers. In our capitalistic dispensation the *entrepreneur*, that parasite of parasites, is a necessary evil. And let it not be forgotten that in the function of his activities he is duplicated and even triplicated. The merchandising of the proprietor's cocoa does not escape this system of legalized extortion. No sooner are the bags deposited on the sidewalk than along comes running a commission agent, usually a man of no fixed office-address, a free lancer. This coloured gent you will see of a morning hanging around the railroad station waiting for the East Indian, Chinese and Negro shopkeepers who, like Chin Lee, buy cocoa on speculation from the small land-holders in the country. With grand greetings he accosts Jugmansingh or Lee Hong or Wellington and, to make his relationship with each as intimate as possible, his "How are you?" is cried out in their respective native tongues: "*Ki sahn harl?*" "*Ho la mah?*" "Kyi, Borss?" Extracting a sample of beans from his victim, off he hops to the big middle-men who are the shippers. Always he is wide awake. He knows the contracts of all the shippers, he knows their immediate needs and consequently where he can get the highest bids. His commission is ten cents per fanega and in crop-time his earnings mount to seventy and eighty dollars a week. The cocoa season out, he shifts to the black-eye pea crop, to the corn crop, and so on. During the lean months he is kept by his woman – or women. His way of life would shock a Victorian lady out of her stays. His leisure hours are spent in rum-drinking, gambling, and in the shady hotel dance-halls along Charlotte Street. On Sundays he continues his overnight spree with his women and boon companions on one of the less frequented beaches.

The big cocoa buyer is a horse of a different colour. He comes, as a rule, from the island's "best families." Instead of rum, he drinks Scotch. His gambling stakes are higher. His office, as far as offices go in Port of Spain, is sumptuous. He swings around with his dancing partner to the best music the island can afford, in the best clubs, in the best hotels. The weekend finds him "down the islands," those paradisal islets in the Gulf of Paria used as resorts by the well-to-do. In boom times his profits are enormous; in a bad depression he goes to the wall and forever afterwards will tell you of the days when he was rich.

Gold beans . . . What now in this year of our Lord nineteen hundred and thirty-eight?4 Ask any proprietor, ask any buyer in or from the island – at your risk. Ask me, if you dare.

NOTES

1.   A borrowed name. Sarran Teelucksingh was member for the county of Caroni in the legislative council and president of the Trinidad East Indian National Congress in 1931. He was in favour of the divorce bill which became law in Trinidad on 1 January 1933, as was Mendes.

2.   Mendes tends to use certain names rather frequently in his stories. "Boodhoo" is also the name of Henry Lawrence's illegitimate son in the story by that name (*Man Who Ran Away*). "Rampatia" reappears in "A Life", and "Marie and Rampatia" (*Pablo's Fandango*), and "Mulemeah" and "Sumintra" are the names of the two young brides in "And Then the Hurricane Came" (*Pablo's Fandango*).

3.   The Austrian pianist Artur Schnabel 1882–1951.

4.   Cocoa prices on the world market collapsed 1920–21, and the market crashed in the 1920s and 1930s. This, in addition to the Great Depression (1929–33) caused serious financial problems for Mendes's father in the decade of the 1920s. John Small the cocoa broker in "One Day for John Small" (*Man Who Ran Away*) registers falling prices and knows that he has to be careful. However, 1929 seems to have been a boom year for Trinidad's cocoa.

Section 3

JOURNALISM

For *Trinidad Presbyterian* Mendes wrote *Pen Portraits of the Poets* on a monthly basis from January 1926 until December 1926, with one more in March 1927. The poets he wrote about were Dante, Milton, William Cowper, W.H. Davies, Countee Cullen, J.C. Squire, Walter de la Mare, W.B. Yeats, John Masefield and W.H. Hamilton, Robert Bridges, and William Morris. He also wrote "A Foreword" to the *Portraits*, and a general piece, "Contemporary Poetry and Poets", which is reproduced here along with "Countee Cullen".

"Contemporary Poetry and Poets" is a survey of the schools of English poetry at the time. It is whimsical and impressionistic, and sometimes resembles a catalogue of names, which it drops freely alongside "iambus", "anapaest", and chunks of quotation. Mendes is clearly having fun here. However, the piece is particularly interesting in its treatment of the "Free Verse School" and especially of T.S. Eliot. While Mendes's apparent disparagement of the ending of Eliot's "The Hollow Men" begs the question of what he and his friends considered suitable subjects for poetry, there is a strong grain of truth in his pronouncement on Eliot: "He seems to me to be a man so disgusted with his kind that he must throw mud at it." And Mendes does debunk himself at the end of the article: "Let it not be supposed that because I have written flippantly of the ultra-moderns that there is no good in them." As we have seen in his poems of the *Beacon* period, he was later to find that free verse was the most effective vehicle for his poems of social protest.

Mendes is clearly comfortable with the traditional verse forms used by Countee Cullen, and strongly appreciative of Cullen's revolutionary ideas. His critical method in this "Portrait" is to provide background with some commentary, and to quote liberally and at length from Cullen's work. This was probably necessary as his readers could have experienced difficulty in obtaining copies of the poems for themselves. His criticism of the poet's "passion that is at times so barbarically fierce that he loses intellectual control" is fair comment. Interestingly, though, Mendes is guilty of the same excess in the anti-war poems of the *Beacon*, especially in "Poppy Day", with its queasy insistence on "blood-orgasms".[1]

Mendes wrote to Countee Cullen, enclosing a copy of this review, and received a graceful note in reply. They were to become fast friends later, when Mendes found himself sitting at a desk beside Cullen in the office of the Works Project Administration in New York City.[2]

The opening paragraph of this article will resonate wryly with anyone who tries to make a living out of writing: "There is a fashion in England today among literary circles to exchange praise . . . if Mr. A. will review Mr. Z.'s latest book of verse enthusiastically because he has enjoyed a similar treatment at the hands of Mr. Z., what is criticism coming to?" Ironically, though, Mendes may himself have been guilty of choosing his reviewers, as a short exchange in "In a Restaurant" between the protagonist Peter and a fellow writer seems to show.

"A Commentary", which appeared four years after "Contemporary Poetry and Poets", was written as a reply to critics of *Trinidad* 1, no. 1, and especially in defence of James's barrack-yard story "Triumph". It is a densely argued piece, important for understanding Mendes's own praxis, which he is clearly in the process of working out while defending stories about the barrack- yard and the lives of ordinary working-class Trinidadians. He has moved some distance from the assumptions of "Contemporary Poetry and Poets" when he writes: "we have only to be acquainted with contemporary literature to find ourselves face to face with the fact that the *Zeitgeist* is one of revolt against established customs and organic loyalties". He ponders the meaning of obscenity and launches a broadside against "Victorianism". His interpretation of "Victorianism" is narrow and somewhat exaggerated, and is by no means applicable to the great writers of that period. But the hypocrisy and attempts to cover up human sexuality for purposes of respectability associated with the mores of that time are what he holds up to scrutiny in his anti-colonial poems and stories. When he writes that "Life and Art are very much less pretty than the Victorian novelists would have us believe", he has moved a significant distance from his criticisms of T.S. Eliot and the "Free Verse School".3

"From St. Lucia by Air", written for the *Trinidad Guardian*, is included for its historical interest. It describes a period that is now lost. Travel by air between the islands of the then British West Indies was relatively new, and Mendes's article conveys his sense of wonder and excitement at floating over land and sea in the NYRBA (New York, Rio and Buenos Aires Line) seaplane, with the archipelago of islands unfolding below him "like jewels", at a maximum speed of one hundred miles per hour. Despite Mendes's enjoyment of fast travel (dashing around the Savannah as a small child in his father's buggy) and expectation of even greater speeds than the NYRBA plane can achieve, he is still able to appreciate the beauties of the natural world in the leisurely, drifting flight which he describes. A way of life that has passed for ever is fixed and recorded here.

The contentious letter "What is all the din about" was selected because of its relation to the controversial article "Revolt", which followed ten days later.

Mendes's anti-Catholic prejudices are revealed clearly here, and the reasonableness of his argument is somewhat obscured by his impatience. The intolerance of which he accuses Captain Longridge is evident in his own letter, and the tone of aggression carried through to "Revolt".

This article caused serious offence to Trinidad's Catholics, and generated a slew of indignant letters and articles, at the same time that articles and letters in support of Mendes's position poured in. Behind it are the prejudices formed by Mendes's personal history: the persecution of Presbyterians by Catholics on the Portuguese island of Madeira in the nineteenth century, which led to the exodus of the former to Trinidad;[4] the conflict in his own family between his Catholic mother and Presbyterian father;[5] and the ironic repetition of marital dysfunction in his relationship with his second wife Nita.[6] By the time the divorce legislation had been introduced their marriage was effectively over and Mendes had moved on to other relationships. He would naturally have been deeply interested at a personal level in the outcome of the council's deliberations.

As in the preceding letter, valid argument is weakened by invective. The editor of the *Guardian* himself pointed out that Mendes would have been on stronger ground had he discussed the contributions of the scholars whose names he produced as authorities, rather than assuming arbitrarily that his readers would have been familiar with their work. Name-dropping seems to have been a characteristic flaw in Mendes's critical writing, although in later *Guardian* articles he did take the time to clarify many of his references.

Despite its obvious shortcomings, "Revolt" is an important piece. It shows Mendes in fighting mood, and it also points to the polarization of Trinidadian society during the period leading up to the passing of the Divorce Act on 1 January 1933.

It is little wonder, given the personality that is emerging in Mendes's writing, that the letter which follows, "Flying Inkpots", written three months after Mendes's return from New York, should express approval of an unseemly but very funny fracas in the city council. Mendes's friend Albert Gomes had locked horns with the mayor of Port of Spain, Captain Arthur Cipriani, over the mayor's refusal to allow a political meeting to be held in Woodford Square. Upon being dismissed from the chamber, Gomes had lain down on its floor, thereby forcing the policemen summoned by the mayor to carry him out bodily. At that time he weighed 240 pounds. Importantly for Mendes, this was a sign that "democracy is still alive and kicking" in Trinidad.

Another important democratizing institution for Mendes was Trinidad's annual carnival. As Mendes relates in "Carnival Piece" he had participated in road marches and masquerades from early childhood. And after the restoration of the celebrations at the end of the Second World War he acted as a carnival judge for the *Trinidad Guardian* along with his wife Ellen, who herself had a background in show business, over a period of twenty years. In the letter which follows, written as a response to a letter by Ralph de Boissière praising the calypso, and the successive articles "If Calypso Is Folksong", "Carnival Piece" and the later "Masquerade", he explores the phenomenon of calypso, now known as kaiso, and the nature of carnival itself. He deplores the loss of various folk-figures, and determines the meaning of the experience for himself, and by extension, the meaning which it has for Trinidad's society, rich and poor alike. His ruminations on the liberating properties of masking, on the origins of the music, and that unifying quality of carnival which encourages people to put down roots, though, as he honestly admits, devoid of scholarly authority, are especially interesting when viewed against the serious studies of carnival and kaiso which were published in the latter part of the twentieth century.

Mendes consistently maintained that Trinidad's culture must be of the island's life and scene. His conviction that art and culture precede and encourage political maturity is carried through the three articles on Trinidad's artists which follow, and the later "Art Is Abstraction". In "Five Painters" he floats the idea that art like carnival is a leveller because it promotes better understanding of races and all national communities: "pride and prejudice when brought under the disinfecting force of an art object can be like cloud-clusters before a powerful wind".

The Trinidad and Tobago Art Society was founded on 8 September 1943. Mendes reviewed its shows faithfully. His references to artists active during that period and discussion of their works, which he mentions by name, should prove extremely helpful to scholars working in that early period. He takes special pains with Leo Basso, whom he evidently revered, along with M.P. Alladin and Joseph Cromwell. In "Holder's Creole Extravaganza" he brings Boscoe Holder, painter, dancer and choreographer, vividly to life. His appreciation of what Holder was trying to do is evident even through his disappointment at the patchy quality of the production. A typical touch of flamboyance appears in "Costumes are costly. Casting must be correct, décor daring, music mesmeric, lighting luscious." Such tongue-in-cheek pronouncements make Mendes fun to read.

The typescript of "Holder's Creole Extravaganza" was shown to Boscoe Holder by a member of Mendes's family some fifty years after it had appeared in the *Trinidad Guardian*. Holder was delighted with it, and remarked: "This man [Mendes] should be published!" Holder died in 2007. I am sorry that he is no longer here to see the article in print for the second time.

The four articles on Beryl McBurnie and her dancers, and the "Little Carib", reiterate Mendes's views about the indigenizing of culture. Beryl McBurnie was a close personal friend of Mendes's, and according to the Trinidadian activist George Padmore, she gave Mendes generous credit for being instrumental in the founding of "Little Carib".7 Mendes writes of McBurnie that "She is first of all an artist – and then a commentator on the politics of our age", which is how he saw himself during the period of his creative writing. His excitement on the opening night of the "Little Carib" (25 November 1948), with the performance of the celebratory ballet "Talking Drums", comes through very clearly, as does his awareness of the response of the audience to the dancers. That this was a watershed performance in Trinidad's cultural life may be deduced from the later article "McBurnie's Art Honoured with Stamp of Public Approval", in which Mendes describes the wide cross-section of society that now fills the "Little Carib". His assessment of McBurnie as "a creative creature of the rarest quality" has been borne out by, to use his own phrase, "the verdict of posterity".[8]

The ability to involve his readers in the experience of his response is to be seen also in the splendid vignette of Paul Robeson and the concert which he gave at the "Little Carib". The assertion that "any man who can perform the miracle of generating in a vast audience of people mixed in race and beliefs a mood of oneness, of togetherness, can help lead the West Indian family into a better world" restates the position which he takes in "Five Painters": that great art transcends artificial social barriers and promotes better understanding and unity among people separated by class, colour and creed.

I have selected the article on the Whitehall Players because, out of all of the pieces which Mendes wrote about the theatre, this one deals with the Trinidadian actor and playwright Errol John and his play *The Tout*. John was to go on to write the better-known *Moon on a Rainbow Shawl*, but the performance of this half-hour long play was enough for Mendes to predict a brilliant future for him. Mendes, with his background in writing stories of working-class and barrack-yard life, would have been delighted with an accomplished version of the same presented on stage: "a slum play about uncomplicated, 'uncivilised' folk".   .

Oddly, the only genre with which Mendes did not to my knowledge experiment was drama, although his acute sense of timing and extensive use of dialogue in his fiction indicate a more than ordinary understanding of the possibilities of theatre. Many of his short stories would lend themselves particularly well to adaptation for the stage or small screen.

In addition to writing for the *Trinidad Guardian* Mendes gave talks on Trinidad's radio, and at venues like the Public Library and the "Little Carib". He did pieces for Henry Swanzy's *Caribbean Voices*, and actually took part in a symposium at the BBC in London in 1950. Unfortunately the only scripts that have survived, apart from those written for *Caribbean Voices*,9 are the three included here. And with the exception of "The Man, His Land and His Culture" which Mendes clearly states is taking place on the stage of the "Little Carib", it has proved impossible to discover where the other two, "On the Pre-Atomic Gentleman" and "All My Sons", were delivered. Internal references suggest that they were all three written between 1948 and 1950. They are a great deal more substantial than the majority of articles written for the *Guardian*, with the different medium allowing more time and space for Mendes to develop his arguments. And they are all linked by common concerns: the nature of man, and the elevation of the common man.

"On the Pre-Atomic Gentleman" returns to Mendes's favourite hobby-horses: capitalism, colonialism, institutionalized religion and the guilt of the relevant authorities in propagating war. His scorn of convention and enthusiasm for tackling sacred cows may be observed in his unfavourable comments on Sir Winston Churchill, Great Britain's revered wartime prime minister, and in his approval of Joseph Stalin. Mendes as stated earlier was heavily influenced by the October 1917 revolution, and according to his sons, tended to venerate "the Russians" for most of his life. While in America he worked alongside and socialized with like-minded writers. Many of his friends were members of the American Communist Party. His brother Frank, with whom he lived for much of his seven years in New York, was very left-wing, and enjoyed the dubious distinction of being investigated by the Federal Bureau of Investigation. Against such a background it is possible to understand his apology for a man now known to have been a butcher of his own people on a scale that defeats the imagination. What is especially interesting about this talk is that it must have been given while Mendes was working for the colonial government, although he would not yet have risen to the prominent position which he later occupied at the port.

Similar concern for the common man may be seen in the final two articles in the Journalism section. In "The Man, His Land and His Culture" Mendes is swift to point out the anomaly of an educated middle-class panel, "radical in comfortably cushioned seats", pontificating on the meaning of the West Indian man; and to insist on the inclusion of Trinidadians of Chinese and East Indian descent in such a discussion. It is significant that he refers to himself as a "retired writer", doubtless because the revolutionary conclusion to his contribution would sit most uneasily on the shoulders of a civil servant in the colonial government.

In "All My Sons", a title borrowed as he admits from the left-wing American playwright Arthur Miller, Mendes returns to the themes of the egalitarian society and the brotherhood of man which preoccupy him throughout the different phases of his writing, while setting out a thoughtful analysis of what he wishes for his own sons. His favourite anathemas of capitalism and race prejudice are touched upon, as well as the need for openness to sexuality first mooted in "A Commentary". His analysis of parental responsibility and conversely, the need for the parent to be able to learn from the child, helps to make this a careful, open, and sensitive piece, with an underlying note of pride and affection for his three sons.

NOTES

1. *Beacon* 2, no. 11 (May 1933).

2. Mendes, *Autobiography*, 91–92.

3. James's letter which discusses Hulbert Footner's letter to Mendes, reveals that Mendes had been reading intensively in contemporary modern writing. See Letters, this volume.

4. Mendes, *Autobiography*, chapter 1: "Madeira Prologue, 1846–1897".

5. Ibid., 12–16.

6. Ibid., 69–70.

7. In a letter to Mendes dated 1951.

8. See page 267, this volume.

9. Mendes wrote scripts on "The Origins of Calypso" (16 January 1949), "Carnival" (19 February 1950), and a critical review of "Christopher" by Basil McFarlane (18 June 1950). He also took part in person in "A West Indian Symposium", mediated by Arthur Calder-Marshall, in London (9 July 1950).

Contemporary Poetry and Poets[1]

And now it is time we discoursed of modern poetry, though it is but a trivial incident that has enjoined that necessity upon me. The Editors beg me to apologise for the exhaustion of their supply of photographs. They tell me they have tried their level best to obtain more, but have failed; and they proceed further to reassure me by explaining that the blame must lie wholly with their agents on the other side who have obviously not gone to their full length of enquiry; for it must seem odd to us that such a simple commission fails of effect in these days of business acceptance on the part of agents: and on the part of living poets their anxiety to see their portraits in the papers – be they ever so humble – of the world. For it cannot be denied that Literature has become part and parcel of business; and it follows as a corollary that those poets who are loath to have their faces broadcasted are either timid of Fame, or, what is more to the purpose, fools; which is absurd; for advertisement now-a-days plays such an important role in the filling or emptying of one's purse that it should be allowed a room in the Household of Art; for – may I make bold to say? – such has Art descended to.

It was said of Elizabethan times that England was a nest of singing birds. Today nests of singing birds make England what it is. There are birds singing from the hedges-like W.H. Davies, that super-tramp who turned super-poet. There are birds singing in the air – Shelley-like spirits that have been incarnated palpably with a purpose. From the ocean we can listen to the migratory song of John Masefield as he chants his splendid stanzas of the Dauber.[2] From the streams a newly-born bird sings – Edmund Blunden. Then there is W.J. Turner who flits from shade to light, a very embodiment of chiaroscuro. From the moonlight the owl hoots – Walter de la Mare. From the dung-heap a croaking blackbird tunes its throat – T.S. Eliot.3 From the market-places rises the voice of an individual bird – J.C. Squire. The night too has its song – A.E. Housman. From somewhere on the Olympian heights we hear a sadly satirical strain – Thomas Hardy. From the trenches the soul-splitting melody of Siegfried Sassoon once pierced us. And from innumerable other places songs arise. The world is gone singing-mad. There is an antiphon of sounds that disturbs the ear. It all seems discordant. We must imagine ourselves in a hall (for the world is not so large after all) where a thousand and one persons are singing different words set to differing airs, and all at the same time. Something like the proverbial chattering of tongues at the building of the Tower of Babel. There is the school of the Imagists. There is the Free-verse clique. Other voices are tuned to the traditional key – the Georgians mainly.

Immediately following upon the Beardsley4 Period – that last decade of the nineteenth century – fell a time of comparative silence. The Poet Laureate, William Watson (now Sir William Watson), John Drinkwater, Alfred Noyes and others were marking time. A.E. Housman, who had come like a bolt from the blue on the closing days of the last century, had apparently burnt himself out. And no wonder, for the hammered finish of his work, men said, could not but have exhausted his power and patience. His career has been, so far, comet-like; he has made two appearances; it remains to be seen if his parabola will permit his return this way. Ernest Dowson, Oscar Wilde, John Davidson, Francis Thompson – these were all dead when the march of the poetic legions was resumed. The rest by the wayside had obviously been given a new lease on life; for the march, commenced by a few choice and select favourites, was soon joined by a multitude of curious pagans who had caught the spirit of the central figures and were themselves metamorphosed into tentative singers. Before long the volume of sound was appalling, until today one knows not what it signifies – whether God is being praised for His goodness or the Devil for his cleverness. It is all a jumble of noise and the listener is in that quandary wherein one of our best contemporary poets5 places God:

> God heard the embattled nations sing and shout:
> "Gott straffe England" and "God save the King,"
> God this, God that, and God the other thing.
> "Good God" said God, "I've got my work cut out."

Isn't that dreadful? Indeed has the reader of modern poetry got his work cut out! Let him turn to the right and a voice calls from the left. Let him go straight forward and a summons comes to him from the rear. Let him try to look upwards and subterranean rumblings reach his ear. The world of poetry has constituted itself a macrocosm. There is a conscience to it that has relative positions. Let it be remembered that what is a sin in the West is considered a virtue in the East. The Court in Pepys'[6] day permitted the restored Charles[7] to love my Lady Castlemaine a little too well; and though the Diarist's conscience was against it, the conscience of fashionable England looked upon it with favour and even applause. And the regard of Poetry today is but a relative matter. Einstein[8] – thank God! – has arrived in time. Daily we read of Critics quarrelling with each other over their minions. The poet himself is levelling attacks at his brother. William Watson epigrammatically observes in his publication of this Spring:

> Sing, Nightingale. There will be those who take
> > Thy music to be sweet.
> Chant thine old chant – till the new fashions make
> All melody obsolete.
> I cannot doubt that soon the corn-crake's note
> Shall be to thine preferred.
> What then? – Sing on with thy still golden throat
> Still tolerated bird.

Very true, I say. But then my friend disagrees, and I argue with him that Lascelles Abercrombie and John Drinkwater are perfectly right in upholding in their essays the traditional forms of poetic expression. "Traditional forms?" he replies, incredulously. "All well and good if you are recounting the mythological tales of Greece, those tales that have become atrophied with too much use, as evidenced in Lord Gorell's[9] 'The Spirit of Happiness,' despite what Mr. Squire says of the poem. The modern perspective of life, my dear fellow, is entirely changed. We live in an age of machine-movement. Staccato-movement. Why the iambus? Why the anapaest?" I maintain, by way of argument, that the glories of poetry are as fixed as the fixed stars; that they are incontrovertible; that this age is but a travelling phase, and as such will have passed away from the vision of men in the days that are to come. He denies that and talks of form giving way to matter. I point out that matter and form, being both plastic . . . and so on and so forth, for the discussion soon reduces itself to philosophic presumptions that have nothing to do with Poetry. And for that reason I will spare my reader them.

I had thought in this article to write concerning the living poets, but I find the number of their names so greatly in excess of a cursory estimate that I must content myself with brief, light references. It would be so easy for me to scribble name after name until my allowed magazine space were filled and say to the Editors: "Here is my article for this month." And even then I daresay I could present similar contributions until the end of the year. If that were done some controversial reader would be sure to take objection, murmuring: "Here's a blockhead. What information do we gather from his contributions?" And I would say: "As much as I can give you, my dear friend. For as a bulk of human beings pursuing one course that is as much as I know of them – their names." And that reply, though not the absolute truth (I wonder if Truth has degrees of accuracy? Can a cup be more full of water than another?) would be as near the truth as it is possible for a mediocre mind to get.

There is, of course, the Georgian School. I say "of course" advisedly, for it is but fit that a prosaic King should have a cluster of poets named after him. A man's children all carry his surname, though they be as unlike him as it is likely for them to be. We read of the Augustan Poets, the Elizabethan Poets, the Revolutionary Poets (the kings of Europe were a bit timid then) and the Victorian Poets; and someone has written of the Edwardian Poets, but our sense of aesthetic values has somehow or the other subjected the synonym to oblivion. (There will, I venture to imagine, be soon the "Prince of Wales" poets. Are there not "Prince of Wales" matches and "Prince of Wales" soap and "Prince of Wales" this and that? Then why not "Prince of Wales" Poets? These Georgian Poets (the King[10] is personally acquainted with one or two; W.H. Davies, for example) are fathered by men like Messrs. J.C. Squire, Harold Monro, and Edward Marsh. It is unfortunate that the last named gentleman should have seen it fit to disown all future authority over the brood he has for so many years warmed under his expansive wing. He probably thinks they are sufficiently grown-up to take care of themselves. I would like him to know that Robert Graves is straying from the fold; but still, most of them seem to be taking care of themselves, for they are being well hearthed in the commodious rooms of the *London Mercury*. The *Chapbook*, Harold Monro's yearly, is turning apostate. It is allowing the Sitwell[11] family to enter its threshold.

There is the Free Verse school. To whom they owe filial allegiance I know not. I suspect them to be illegitimate though some of them proudly speak of Whitman and would imply that they take their inspiration from him. Perhaps he is a sort of foster- father to them: though the enquiry is not worth pursuing.

To me they are little children grown wild, if not mad, from want of proper care. They don't wash their faces. Their finger-nails are never clean. Their teeth-ugh! Perhaps they have never heard of tooth-paste! Their latest perpetration is "The Waste Land. "[12] Listen to this from the same book:

> This is the way the world ends
> This is the way the world ends
> This is the way the world ends
> Not with a bang but a whimper.

Will any reader dare find poetry in that? Let him or her (for women are often times more mystical than men) point it out. Why they write at all is beyond me. Silence is more noble than expression through a medium that is Double Dutch. The whole of this last book of Eliot's is nearly the same. He seems to me to be a man so disgusted with his kind that he must throw mud at it.

There are a hundred and one others who are attempting to break off into tangents. Poetry is like Christianity today. Or rather, the fault lies with the pseudo-poets and the quasi-Christians. Each must be a law unto himself until Law has become disorder.

Let it not be supposed that because I have written flippantly of the ultra-moderns that there is no good in them. We shall see otherwise as we proceed month by month to the study of one at a time.

NOTES

1. With the notable exceptions of Thomas Hardy (1840–1928) and T.S. Eliot (1888–1965) the poets mentioned in this article are minor English poets of the early twentieth century.

2. *Dauber* (1912) is a long narrative poem about an artist who goes to sea as a painter on a ship.

3. Cf. the final paragraphs in this article on the Free Verse school. Within a very few years Mendes was to modify his early unfavourable impressions of T.S. Eliot's poetry, and to employ free verse with some degree of success in his own poems.

4. The artist Aubrey Beardsley (1872–98), a contemporary of the Irish writer Oscar Wilde, and contributor to the *Yellow Book*, an illustrated quarterly which appeared from 1884 to 1897.

5. J.C. Squire (1884–1958) was a poet, writer, and editor of, among other things, the *London Mercury*. The quotation is from *Epigrams* (1916)

6. Samuel Pepys (1633–1703), the diarist.

7. Charles Stuart, who was restored to the English throne in 1660 as King Charles II. Lady Barbara Castlemaine was one of his several mistresses.

8. The great physicist and Nobel Prize winner Albert Einstein (1879–1955). The elliptical reference here is to his theory of relativity.

9. Ronald Gorell Barnes, third Baron Gorell (1884–1963) was a politician and author. He edited the *Cornhill Magazine* from 1933 to 1939, and published several volumes of poetry.

10. George V, King of England 1910–36. The Prince of Wales at this time was Edward, later briefly Edward VIII.

11. Edith (1887–1965), Osbert (1892–1969) and Sacheverell Sitwell (1897–1988) were siblings, members of an aristocratic English family. All three were poets and writers. Edith was particularly distinguished.

12. By T.S. Eliot, published in 1922. The following quotation is the conclusion of Eliot's poem "The Hollow Men".

PEN PORTRAITS OF THE POETS

Countee Cullen[1]

I was some three or four months ago reading in a mood of utter lassitude the *Times Literary Supplement*, one of my usual periodicals. I say "in a mood of utter lassitude" for now-a-days it is so seldom that one reads an enthusiastic review of a book of verse by an unknown poet that one's eyes run along the lines of eulogy for established authors by established critics with, I confess, a certain spirit of resigned anticipation to what has become inevitable. There is a fashion in England today among literary circles to exchange praise. This seems rather sordid and there has recently been a burst of uncomplimentary correspondence over the matter. The layman is burnishing his sword to pierce the armour of this conventionally disgusting parvenu of literary habit. And well he might, for if Mr. A will review Mr. Z's latest book of verse enthusiastically because he has enjoyed a similar treatment at the hands of Mr. Z, what is criticism coming to? If the reader must get an insight into this unbalanced state of affairs let him go to the opening chapters of Mr. Harold Monro's *Some Contemporary Poets*. He will there see for himself how the "oracle is worked."

Imagine my surprise then on seeing in bold headlines in the space reserved for important reviews "A Negro Poet." My hair almost stood on end, for surprise has some of the elements of fear in it. They are psychologically allied. I put the paper down. I dared not proceed. Here was something as far from being in the nature of a platitude as it was possible to be. "A Negro Poet?" I whispered to myself questioningly. I was not exactly incredulous for I had heard of such before; but, what is more, I was astounded. The fact is I had never for a moment thought there were poets of Negro blood living; and to see a new name given a place of prominence in the *Times Literary Supplement* completed my amazement. Having collected myself, I proceeded with my reading of the column, and was not slow in observing beneath a surface of restrained appreciation a deeper current of awe and respect for the author of this new book of verse, called appropriately *Color*. (Drat that American spelling!) Anxiously I peeped into other journals and there, sure enough, were other such porcelained pieces of praise. I immediately cast my mind back (or was it unconsciously done?) to see when last such a reception was given a first publication of poetry. Roy Campbell came to mind with his *Flaming Terrapin*,[2] that long poem that prompted A.E. (George Russell) to exclaim that it contained more promise in it than any other poem he had read by an unknown author. And, by Jove! that Negro musical genius, Samuel Coleridge-Taylor,[3] leapt into memory like a flash of lightning. Here, said I to myself, is the poetic prototype of the great musician. His name? Countee Cullen. Alliterative and soothly sounding with its soft vowels. I decided there and then to send for the book. It came just a few weeks ago and if I have not read it a dozen times over, then – to indulge in a cliché – I have not read it once. And I am writing about him now because I know there are thirsty members of his great race in this Island waiting anxiously to drink one drop of dew that might fall from a heaven of their own making. And who can deny that Countee Cullen has made a heaven of his own whereunder spread primeval forests of darkness that Conrad[4] could write so beautifully about? And the wonder of it all! – this poet is but a mere boy – twenty-two years old when his volume was issued from the press.

Little is known of his life just now. Of course, he is just beginning to live. A man who stands on the threshold of twenty- two has very much more travel to make than he has done so far. Mr. Cullen was born in May 1903, and we are told that every poem in his book was written before his twenty-second birthday. He then, like Keats and Chatterton, is a youthful prodigy; and if, unlike Keats and Chatterton,[5] long life is granted him, may we not safely foresee great things for him, may we not [*sic*] the spirit of Poetry is lodged in a boy's soul and makes itself manifest in poems like "The Shroud of Color" and "Heritage" there is bound to bloom therefrom a perfect blossoming of beauty. Although Mr. Cullen has been called "the Roland Hayes of Poetry"[6] his achievement against odds leads one to suspect him capable of more than the great Negro singer.

We learn that Mr. Cullen's father is a Methodist Minister in Harlem, which implies that the poet was born in New York. He won his first recognition while in High School and has gone on since from victory to victory, winning the coveted election to Phi Beta Kappa (whatever that may mean). He took second prize in the Witten Bynner intercollegiate poetry contest. In his junior year he again won second prize and in his senior year he carried off the first prize. He was recently awarded the Amy Spingarn prize for poetry in the competition conducted by the *Crisis*. Since then his verse has found its way into the columns of the most exclusive papers of America, as anyone may see by the list of editors to whom he tenders thanks for permission to reprint. He was barely twenty-one when "The Shroud of Color" appeared in the *American Mercury,* creating a sensation "analogous to that created by the appearance of Edna St. Vincent Millay's *Renascence* in 1912, lifting its author at once to a position in the front rank of contemporary poets, white or black," writes Mr. Carl Van Vechten in *Vanity Fair*. Coming from such a critic this carries weight.

In all the cosmopolitan realm of literature Mr. Cullen's poetry adds a new language to it; a language whose symbol is the bitter conflict of colour. This is entirely new, and what makes it of greater importance is the fact that Mr. Cullen's medium is the English language. That vast, throbbing, dark heart of Africa he lays bare to the English-speaking world, a world whose unconcern for it has been there for centuries because there was no voice to rise up like Mr. Cullen's and bring home to the civilized conscience the pressing truth of Christ's teaching. With such an impulse prompting anyone into verse-composition there can be little wonder that we find in Mr. Cullen's volume a passion that is at times so barbarically fierce that he loses his intellectual control, and is seduced into such lines as: "The steaming crimson vintage of my youth / Incarnadine the altar-slab of Truth" and "I raised my burning eyes, beheld a field / All multitudinous with carnal yield. "[7]

But we cannot quarrel with him for that if it is just this very savagery that gives to his poetry its victory over a seething controversy between the mind and the heart, and which makes him cry out: "Not yet has my heart or hand / In the least way realized / They and I are civilized."[8] And yet Mr. Cullen's head is civilized; and if his heart can feel for his brothers as it does, in spite of the "note of jungles, primitive and subtle" and the monotonous, maddening beat of tom-toms, then it too has the essentials of organised sentiment.

The cry of the book is one of pain. We cannot read such a poem as the following without compunction of spirit:

Once riding in Old Baltimore,
Heart-filled, head-filled with glee,
I saw a Baltimorean
Keep looking straight at me.

Now I was eight and very small
And he was no whit bigger,
And so I smiled, and he poked out
His tongue and called me "Nigger."

I saw the whole of Baltimore
From May until December;
Of all the things that happened there
That's all that I remember.9

Although this poem shows how simply and well Mr. Cullen can write – and that is more than can be said of most of the living lyrists when it comes to use of monosyllabic words – it does not convey the poignant vigour of his insulted, outraged pride and the scandalous wealth of his imagery and powers of expression. That is left to be found in poems like "The Shroud of Color" and "Heritage".

If anything in the volume marks Mr. Cullen as a poet of remarkable talent if not genius, it is his "Shroud of Color". His bitterness, his hate, his forgivingness, his final victory in lighting the way for the armies of his dark brethren – these things are all found in the poem. And the theme – what a theme for the pen of a Negro poet to work around! – the persecuted patience of millions of people whose God-given land has been entered by quasi-pious men with the Bible in one hand and the sword in the other! His control breaks away occasionally, as is only natural, for it must be remembered that this boy-poet is bringing to birth through expression a new consciousness and perhaps a new religion that shall embrace all men as brothers and give to the Negro the patrimony of his land.

In "The Shroud of Color" the poet calls on God to take him away from the unjust world:

Across the earth's warm, palpitating crust
I flung my body in embrace; I thrust
My mouth into the grass and sucked the dew,
Then gave it back in tears my anguish drew;
So hard I pressed against the ground I felt
The smallest sandgrain like a knife and smelt
The next year's flowering; all this to speed
My body's dissolution, fain to feed

The worms. And so I groaned and spent my strength
Until, all passion spent, I lay full length
And quivered like a flayed and bleeding thing.[10]

The bleeding poet is then lifted from the slough of his despair on a black wing (the black wing is significant) and taken to heights which lend the power of vision to his eyes. He sees the earth as it really is – in the throes of an eternal fight for life wherein there is only the survival of the fittest. But nothing seems to want to die, not even the flower that challenges: "Coward", and man is pitted against man, not for the sake of death, but life. And still the poet cannot revoke his call on God. Death is for him in a world where his colour is his curse until the vision is granted him of his race in the power of

... bitterness and death,
The cry the lash extorts, the broken breath
Of liberty enchained ...

It is then that the old passion of atavistic memories courses through his veins, and, as he himself says:

Somehow it was born upon my brain
How being dark, and living through the pain
Of it, is courage more than angels have ...
The cries of all dark people near or far
Were billowed over me, a mighty surge
Of suffering in which my puny grief must merge
And lose itself; I had no further claim to urge
For death ...

and the poem closes on a quiet note of victory over himself, a victory that has brought his spirit home which "sailed the doubtful seas."

There is little wonder that the poem caused a sensation when it first appeared. Its imagery is startlingly in keeping with its justifiably savage outbursts of passion and its eloquence is undoubtedly on a very high level. There are conceptive faults, but these are overpowered by the overpowering sincerity of the poet.

Mr. Cullen can write too of themes that have no bearing on the colour conflict, and when this is possible in a poet with as equal a success as is to be discovered in his poems dealing with a matter that is to him his life-blood, then it is time we regarded that poet with a deep respect. Perhaps we can find in the following the dominant note of his message without the colour symbol – the dark heart of all humanity, in its striving upwards from inherent and vestigial instincts towards that spiritual goal which is the cause of all effort, cannot hope to win its way through by any petty subterfuge, but must first be crushed in the wine-press of experience and undergo a vital change:

> I fast and pray and go to church,
> And put my penny in,
> But God's not fooled by such slight tricks
> And I'm not saved from sin.
>
> I cannot hide from Him the gods
> That revel in my heart,
> Nor can I find an easy word
> To tell them to depart:
>
> God's alabaster turrets gleam
> Too high for me to win,
> Unless He turns his face and lets
> Me bring my own gods in.[11]

NOTES

1. Mendes subsequently shared an office with Countee Cullen in New York City, when both men worked for the Federal Writers' Project of the Roosevelt Works Progress Administration (Mendes, *Autobiography*, 91, 92). He had previously written to Cullen enclosing a copy of his review, and had received a letter from the poet dated 20 September 1926, expressing his appreciation.
2. 1924.
3. Samuel Coleridge-Taylor (1875–1912), composer of the cantata *Hiawatha's Wedding Feast*.
4. A reference to the novella *Heart of Darkness* (1902) by Joseph Conrad (1857–1924).
5. John Keats (1795–1821) died of consumption. His greatest poetry is generally reckoned to have been written in the year before his death. Thomas Chatterton (1752–70) swallowed arsenic at the age of eighteen apparently in a fit of depression.

Though clearly possessed of extraordinary ability, he gave himself little time to develop his gift.

6. The celebrated African-American tenor (1887–1977).
7. These couplets are from "Shroud of Color".
8. "Heritage".
9. "Incident".
10. This passage, and the two extracts which follow, are from "Shroud of Color".
11. "Pagan Prayer".

A COMMENTARY

As everyone knows, when *Trinidad* appeared in December last, there was a
hullabaloo over what a section of the press and public thought obscene in it.
We are at present concerned with expressing our own views, since everybody
at that time said what he thought – both in and out of print.

To start with, we have only to be acquainted with contemporary literature
to find ourselves face to face with the fact that the *Zeitgeist* is one of revolt
against established customs and organic loyalties. Since the War, this revolt
has been directed not so much against the Puritanism of the sixteenth century
as against a degenerate form of it popularly known as Victorianism. This Victorianism, as exposed in the writings of most of the novelists of the period,
insisted that maidens should be prim and proper, that the contours and lines
of objects should be concealed by laces and embroideries, that philosophies
should deny the reality of evil, that children should be spoon-fed with a thick
soup of lies, and that the good life was conditioned by expurgated speech, going
to church, and in nine cases out of ten smiling when you should frown and
frowning when you should smile. That meant that insofar as a man was concerning himself with abstractions and detaching himself from the obvious evils
of his environment, he was advancing in his conquest of the life eternal; and,
as in all the teachings of the great religious teachers, prejudices against the
human body, and tendencies to be disgusted with its habits, are to be found.
It is not surprising that human beings, like the ostrich that buries its head in
the sand, and supposes that because it cannot see, every seeing object around
it has been suddenly struck blind, should have believed that by covering their
passions with fig leaves (today it is tweed suits and flowered frocks) they are
conquering them, forgetting in their haste (fig leaves, we think, are evidence
of haste) that the tongue and eyes and nose can be as offensive as any covered
member of the body. In consequence of all this, men and women have failed

to see that an act is sinful only because of the relative position it occupies on the bench of traditional antiquated morality. In other words, it is we who animate a happening with quality; of itself it is as empty of quality as a blown beetle.

But the creative artist is primarily concerned with the weaving of patterns: the material that he uses is so much grist to his mill, for he who is sincere about his literary work (or any other art-work for that matter) cannot stop to consider how much ugliness there is in the matter that comes his way. It would be silly to tell the architect not to build in stone because stone is rough and amorphous; to warn the sculptor to leave bronze alone because bronze is brown and blatant is like warning the priest and parson against heathens because they have no regard for *our* anthropomorphic god; even so it is futile and puerile to ask the writer of fiction to leave bodies and barrack-yards alone because they are obscene in the popular sense. It all depends on what literary treatment they receive, though it does not necessarily mean that, so treated, they shall be no longer obscenities; it simply means that they shall be obscenities presented for reasons other than raising the disgust or sexual desires of the reader. Surely "it is because obscenity, with all its superficial repulsiveness, has a peculiar power of heightening the higher imaginative values in its neighbourhood," as Mr. Leonard Woolf once said, that we have it in almost all the world's great literature: in the Bible, in Aristophanes, Plato, Lucretius, Catullus, Juvenal, Petronius, Chaucer, Shakespeare's Comedies, the Restoration Drama, Ben Jonson, Swift, Sterne, Fielding, Byron, Boccaccio, Rabelais, Voltaire, Rousseau, Balzac, and Proust. Things might, perhaps, be better otherwise (though we doubt that very much), but the perfectly natural fact is that both Life and Art are very much less pretty than the Victorian novelists would have us believe. Vermin and vice will come creeping in.

Furthermore, the idealization of the fair face of the Coin of Life[1] indubitably tends to encourage the smug complacency of the idle rich; the unjust persecution of the prostitute, who is after all only a necessary factor in the scheme of our social organization; the legal measures against the thief who is a thief simply because an infinitesimal minority is allowed to control the world's wealth. Stevenson[2] said: "The most influential books and the truest in their influence are works of fiction. They do not pin their reader to a dogma, which he must afterwards discover to be inexact; they do not teach a lesson, which he must afterwards unlearn. They repeat, they re-arrange, they clarify the lessons of Life." For these and other reasons which should be obvious, the literature of fiction brings to the doors of people who otherwise would have known little or nothing of these things, the burden of this truth: our social organization is not what it ought to be; it is diseased. We have heard people murmur glibly: "Oh, we know that these things exist, but why talk about them in books?" Exactly because there are so many people who make this kind of remark, there are a few who think it their duty to present to their readers the other side of the Coin of Life in all its stark realism of vermin and vice, especially when it is remembered that sex is the spring-board from which leap most of our desires. That way lies a readjustment (or should we say adjustment?) of the disordered condition of present-day society, for most of the literary artists, instead of acquiescing in the taken-for-granted expediency of a divinely revealed decalogue, are endeavouring to discover a more apt decalogue from the experience of human life; in short, they are looking within themselves for salvation instead of waiting for it to fall from heaven: they have waited now for centuries – in vain. The divorce law, companionate marriage, birth control and the gradual closing in of the tentacles of Socialism are unequivocal signs of this.

Now what of *Trinidad* and the obscenities it was accused of harbouring? One, knowing nothing of the magazine and reading the remarks made against it in a certain section of the press, and overhearing the tittle-tattle about it at tea-parties (it is usually tea parties that damn or deify books as well as other things), would have been led to the conclusion that the magazine simply stank from cover to cover. But is that the case? We are sure it is generally agreed that to decide what is obscene and what not is an extremely difficult problem, for the minds approaching the precincts of the problem do so, because of their dissimilar composition, from entirely different points of the compass. For instance, there is a certain type of mind that would recoil shuddering from the sight of some bathing-suited female dolls we saw in the windows of a certain store recently, and yet gaze with no show of revulsion at the living female dolls on Macqueripe Beach³ of a Sunday morning. For ourselves popular airs like *Sonny Boy* and *Ramona*⁴ are not only vulgar, but obscene: not because of the words, which are banal enough to mean nothing, but because of the *tunes*. There is the person too, who, though admitting to himself that the Motion Picture magazines and even the Motion Pictures themselves can be very obscene at times, will give no voice to his inward misgivings, and yet shout out from the housetops (and the hilltops if you gave him a chance) that *Trinidad* should be banned. And why? It all depends on our orientation, for we are all the slaves of fashion and custom: because such and such is being said or done by everybody with a show of inevitability, then there can be nothing wrong with it; or, to put it more truthfully, because the herd sanctions the innovation, it is tolerated; which leads us to the conclusion that if we are to be good citizens we must constantly be practising the art of hypocrisy.

But what has been the reaction of the public (the public, in this case, being probably about four hundred *readers* of the magazine) towards *Trinidad*? Here we are faced with an exceedingly interesting psychological situation. The personal observation of one of our contributors to the first issue can, we think, be recounted as an illustration of what, in nine cases out of ten, this reaction has been. Here is a young man whose activities are centred in an office employing many young men and young women. "Oh," they say to him as soon as it is generally agreed that the magazine is obscene, "you ought to be ashamed of yourself. You are dirty, you are filthy. Look at the company you've mixed yourself up with!" – all this in shocked and indignant tones. Throughout the day they scowl at him, they abuse him, they think they are causing him much spiritual discomfort. One of his employers, with a wise air (we have always observed what wise airs directors of businesses wear for the most futile occasions) says to him: "There's going to be trouble over this thing." One girl, with a deeply wounded expression, flings her copy of the magazine through the open window, into the street. "You are sowing bad seed," our contributor remarks with a wicked wink, whereupon the girl throws more fire and contempt at him through her glare. And then, at odd moments of the day, sounds of suppressed giggling come to his ears, At first he takes no notice of them. Then he begins to take notice. Soon he realizes that there is something up, for they do not want to let him see that they are giggling, forgetting (poor innocent things!) that he can *hear*. He catches one girl, then another and another. "They are giggling over the spicy portions of the stories," he says to himself. And he was right.

Now what does this all mean? It means that these young women failed to see the vast difference between secrecy and modesty. In trying to keep secret what they considered should be kept secret, i.e. their salacious enjoyment, they imagined that they were being modest; but secrecy is informed by fear, whereas modesty is gentle and reserved. The preposterous mistake is that organised religion has identified the one with the other, and as organised religion is the law for most people, it necessarily follows that they cannot distinguish between the two, or pretend not to be able to. Modesty never seeks to insult sex. Secrecy does, and as long as you insult sex in literature, as long as you want "to stink and filth it" as the "proper" Victorian novelists did with their secrecy, you become pornographic. For ourselves, Thackeray is decidedly more obscene and pornographic than James Joyce or Aldous Huxley. It is the insult that shows up the dirt in a man; it is the insult that makes sex dirty. But if only for the reason (strong enough, we think) that the sexual act is both pleasurable and procreative, sex can be nothing but wholesome, clean, beautiful. Then why be secret about it? Why try to relegate it to the jakes? Why not come out into the open and talk about it? Indeed, try using the perfectly respectable word *rape* in a local drawing-room and see what happens. People will squirm in their chairs as if you had flung cow-dung at them. Now this is all nonsense, all canting hypocrisy.

But the point is: where is your standard of obscenity? Who is to be proclaimed the pundit whose pronouncement shall be final? – for we are faced with this difficulty, that we thus have in any community two distinct opinions, one accusing a certain work of being obscene, the other denying the accusation. Recall to mind the recent case in England of *The Well of Loneliness*.[5] It was agreed by all the responsible periodicals that the book was not a work of art, that it was "dull, badly written, hysterical, with an unpleasant strain of religiosity," as the *Criterion* characterised it; and yet in spite of the fact that it was banned they did not consider it an obscene book. As we see the situation in this island, we can give no serious thought to the recent outcry against *Trinidad* in a section of the press. The late Mr. D.H. Lawrence not long ago said that when people begin to identify the excrementory flow, which is death, with the sex flow, which is life, it is then that obscenity and pornography rise up like a cloud to darken the perspective.[6] That, we think, is going to the root of the matter. When Mr. James Belmont[7] satisfies us of his competency to declare that "*Faux Pas* is the most revolting thing I have ever come across," then, and not till then would we be inclined to give him the attention that we should pay the average school-boy. Anyone can have traditional literary principles; it takes the responsible person to apply them correctly. Who in this island knows anything at all about the relation of Art and Morals and what part the printed word plays in the corrupting of human souls? This is a problem that has proven so difficult for some men that they have not had time to think about anything else in life.

Finally, nobody was more surprised than were we at the objections raised against *Trinidad. Épater les bourgeois*[8] is not a desire of ours; and after all, even as one loves according to one's capacity for loving, so is one shocked according to one's capacity for being shocked. Our aim in writing at all is only to attempt to create artistic forms, irrespective of whatever material might clamour for shape; and we are sure our reading public will believe us when we say that the intention informing our efforts is a perfectly honest and sincere one; and though our work might not be what we [*sic*] want it to be, still, that's not *our* fault.

Trinidad 1, no. 2 (Easter 1930)

NOTES

1. This seems to be a memory of a saying by the American writer Carl Sandburg (1878–1967): "Time is the coin of your life. It is the only coin you have, and only you can determine how it will be spent. Be careful lest you let other people spend it for you."
2. Robert Louis Stevenson (1850–94) wrote extensively on the art of fiction.
3. On the northwest coast of Trinidad.
4. "Sonny Boy" was written by Ray Henderson, Bud de Sylva and Lew Brown. It was featured in the 1928 "talkie" film *The Singing Fool*. "Ramona" was written by L. Wolfe Gilbert and Mabel Wayne. It was the title song for the 1927 film *Ramona*.
5. A sympathetic study of the lesbian experience (1928) by the novelist Radclyffe Hall (1886–1943).
6. In an essay entitled "Pornography and Obscenity", *This Quarter* (Paris) 2, no. 1 (July–September 1929), ed. Edward W. Titus.
7. James Belmont, *Trinidad Guardian*, 22 December 1929. See note 3 to the introduction to the section Short Stories.
8. Shock the middle class.

FROM ST. LUCIA BY AIR

You take your early morning coffee in Castries and your ten o'clock breakfast in Port of Spain; soon it will be: you put your socks on in Castries and your shoes on in Port of Spain. But why this hankering after haste? Is it that we are, with our rapid means of moving from one place to another, more content than were our forefathers who found time always for taking thought of the morrow? For myself, I must admit that I like speed. I can remember the time when I was a little boy and my father used to have a smart gig which was drawn by what he considered to be the most spirited chestnut mare in the city in those days. With what a keen sense of elation I used to sit near to the groom as the gig sped around the Savannah of a Sunday afternoon! But alas, I am afraid that I have become so accustomed to the faster modes of travel that I should be fearfully fidgety if I were made to travel in a gig once more. The relative, after all, is what informs our judgements. The gig's speed would be to me what the snail's speed must be to the birds of the air. Indeed, nowadays like the late Poet Laureate:[1] "I would be a bird and straight on wings I arise / And carry purpose up to the ends of the air." Signs are not wanting that speed is a fashion of the age.

There was heavy cloud brooding over Castries as I was rowed out to the landing-stage of the *São Paolo,* but outside of the bay, in spite of the threatening look of the skies, I could see the taut sails of fishing boats dotting the sea here and there like large white birds resting on the water. And then, as we arrived at our spot, the large maroon bird of the NYRBA line[2] sailed over a shoulder of the land and gracefully landed in the bay. We were soon alongside, and I was glad to see "Mac" (as he is popularly called) once again. I could not forget the fun I had had with his little boy on the northward flight some two weeks before. How delightful it was to watch his childish antics in the belly of an airliner fifteen hundred feet up!

Standing on the deck of the *São Paolo* before taking to the air, it was great fun throwing cents and pennies into the dark-blue deeps of the sea and watching little boys, who had come out to us in their naïve baby-boats, dive down after them, boring deeper and deeper down until their bodies were brown shadows grooving passages like sharks perhaps twenty feet below; but always they would rise to the surface with the coins between their teeth; and once again would start the chorus of their shrill voices calling for more pennies to be thrown. An old American gentleman, travelling from New York to Buenos Ayres [*sic*] by air, asked me all sorts of questions about the people and the place, some of which I could answer, most of which I could not. I liked the old man's face: it was pleasant and open.

We took off at about a quarter to eight. We took off running towards the town, rose facing north-east, then curved round and over that same shoulder of the land across which the *São Paolo* had sailed in arriving. We just skimmed the tops of the trees and I could see astounded people gazing up at us, open-mouthed with wonder. In a minute or so we were well past the mouth of the bay and were speeding along the coast at a height of fifty feet from the water. It was beautiful to see the frail fishing-boats ploughing the choppy seas. The black fishermen stood up in their craft to watch us disappearing. I could see one man's face distinctly as we whizzed past him. It said, plainly: "Well, this is a funny world."

I walked across to the speedometer and saw ninety-five miles per hour registered. The ship was steady, with now and then just a dip to remind you that you were not exactly travelling on a billiard table. Looking across at the land about a mile or so distant you did not get such a sensation of speed as looking down on the water. I remember thinking at the time: "Well, yes, at last I have an adequate demonstration of the earth spinning round on its axis once in every twenty-four hours."

The puissant hum of the engines was not an unharmonious noise: it was rather a vibrant song, like the song of a million birds singing on one unending note. And that is where, I think, you get the impression of tremendous power from; for there is no doubt about it: the air-liner is a thing alive, possessed of power such as we give in our imaginations to monsters of the primeval mud. And as you remember that you are travelling in this fashion because of the ingenuity of man, you are awed into silence and would almost fall down on your knees, whether you are religious or not, and worship the divinity that flames within each and every one of us.

As we got past the last toe of St. Lucia, the two peaks called Piton rising sheer into the sky like the noses of two giants seeking the scents of heaven, our 'plane began to rise very steadily, so that when we were abreast of St. Vincent we were a thousand feet up. The mechanic came along then and adjusted the ventilator above my head, so the wind, cool and clean, poured down my neck in one unceasing flow. The higher peaks of the Island's mountains were covered in dark cloud, and in some parts you could see the sheets of rain stretched from heaven to earth. Looking down on the sea you would have thought that there was no movement in it, that it no longer knew the treacherous current or the swallowing wave or the angry crests of foam, that it had found peace at last from its everlasting tumult and tumble. But it was only our height lending calm to the view.

We could see Kingstown in the distance, a light mist mantling it and making it look (I don't know why the simile leapt into my mind) like a weeping bride. Here were we a thousand feet in the air, and there down below: "The weariness, the fever and the fret / Here, where men sit and hear each other groan. "3

What palsied man had gone out to his office that morning knowing that he had come to the end of his tether? What youth had grown pale and spectre-thin and would die in that small town that day? What weeping maiden had lost her lover because man is forever a deceiver? Up here, in the blue, the fret and fever of terrestrial life seemed very remote, or rather seemed like the dream of another and baser life left behind. We were in a pure element now, or, if you prefer it, an unhuman element, cut off from the madness of men and the hollow nature of our social intercourse. We were facing a new life, feeling only the great universal pulse of existence, unwarped, uncontorted, untrammelled by those creeds and contacts which futilely attempt to smother what wisdom, like a god, would be content to animate. That at least, was worth risking a great deal for, though not quite as much as the mythical Icarus.4

And now, with the last point of St. Vincent left behind, we are fifteen hundred feet up. I rise, take off my coat, and stretch my cramped limbs. The speedometer tells me that we are hurtling through space at a hundred miles an hour. (And I know men who get scared when you accelerate your car to thirty miles on a straight stretch of asphalted road!) Just at this minute I see "Mac" worming his six-foot of body through the aperture leading from one of the pilots' seats into the belly of the 'plane in which we sit and move about at will. His face is as red as the morning sun, his hair tousled, his neck bandaged because of a recent carbuncle-attack. Earlier in the morning, in Castries harbour, he had said to my inquiry: "carbuncles," with a broad smile on his sunny face. He approaches me now and stops to have a chat. "Enjoying the trip?" he shouts. "Magnificent!" I shout back. "Must have enjoyed your north-trip to be returning with us," he suggests lustily, and I agree as lustily. "Had a good time in St. Lucia?" I poke my thumbs up and he laughs, shaking a finger at me. "Quiet place though, I should have thought," he bellows. "A place is what you make it," I bellow back. He nods, smiling mischievously. "How's your little boy?" I ask, pretty loudly. "Fine, and dying to fly again," he replies, pretty loudly too. We exchange a few more words, and he moves on to the wireless operator.

A sudden and unexpected swerve sends me to my window, full of curiosity. We are flying over the Grenadines, eighteen hundred feet above them. They are beautiful dark-green jewels on the grey-green ocean with grey-brown embroideries of reefs encircling them; and on the reefs the seething white foam breaks. I can see two reefs, curving from the crab-like body of an island like two gargantuan claws. Our engines sing their song, and I imagine the pounding indignant speech of the waves on the reefs eighteen hundred feet below. The sky is a blue savannah with no white sheep wandering across it. The sun rides high, darting arrows of light everywhere, cracking the scintillant mirror of the sea and piercing the shadowed vales of the verdured rocks sliding slowly past immediately beneath us. One island is arid, as naked as it was heaved up from the womb of the ocean, and, shocked into parturition by the high hum of our singing airplane, pullulates innumerable goats that scamper to and fro across the surface of it like so many lice seeking shelter from the unhomely heat of the sun. And now we are to the windward of Grenada, nine o' clock, and at least five miles out from the land. It sprawls along the horizon, a dark amorphous mass, like a huge thesaurus of ancient lore, or better still, like Satan who:

> Prone on the flood, extending long and large,
> Lay floating many a rood, in bulk as huge
> As whom the fables name of monstrous size.[5]

It seemed that we were rising slowly as we spanned the sixty-mile chain of islands connecting St. Vincent with Grenada, because when I next looked at the altimeter I found that we were two thousand two hundred feet up. The ship had no motion as far as you were concerned. You walked the length of it and it was just as though you walked across the floor of your drawing-room. Only the vibration you sensed more than felt. As Grenada was already far behind and the hundred-mile stretch to Trinidad was yet to be traversed, I settled myself comfortably on my air-cushioned seat with a copy of the "Geographical Magazine." I was reading an article by ex-President Taft,[6] when, without any warning, I lost the thread of what I was reading and began to think my own thoughts. "Suppose," I thought, "the 'plane were suddenly to catch fire?" But no: I looked out at the red sun, now like a great forge in the heavens, and considered it just as probable that it would set fire to the old earth, as that our 'plane would catch fire. "Suppose one wing were to fly off?" I then thought. But birds do not lose their wings when in flight. "Then supposing both motors should cease at this height?" was my next thought. But who has ever seen a bird die in the air?

I was interrupted in my thoughts by the old American gentleman with the pleasant face coming and sitting near to me with paper and pencil in hand. "How many days did you save on this trip?" he asked as best as his failing voice would allow. I could see that he thought that I had gone to St. Lucia on business. "Oh", I said, "I was there on holiday." He appeared to be taken aback, but only for a moment, for he asked: "But how many days would you have saved if you had gone on business?" I smiled in my heart, made a mental calculation, and told him. "Yes, I thought so," he said, "I met a travelling-agent between St. Thomas and Antigua who saved four most valuable days by travelling like this. The business man: he it is who will enjoy the benefits of this air- service, I guess. Time is precious these days when a man has to have a part of his brain in New York and another part of it in Buenos Ayres [sic] if he would be successful in his million- dollar deals." He paused to catch his breath, his face red, and at the same time jotted down a few notes. "I am writing a book, see," he continued. I was immediately interested. "From what point of view?" I asked. "Oh, from the business point of view, of course," he replied quickly. To change the topic of conversation, I put the immemorial question to him: "Ever been in these parts before?" "Dominica, once," he said, with a meditative air. "Oh, Dominica," I said. "It is a beautiful island, isn't it?" He looked at me in a sort of surprise. "Beautiful? I guess so. It was during the war that I was there. We had reports up in New York that there were huge tin-mines going a-begging in Dominica. Down I went, sir, to make a fortune. All's fair in love and war, you know," he excused himself with, rather needlessly, I thought. "And the fortune?" I asked. "Oh, there was no damn tin there. I lost a fortune instead." Really, I wasn't sorry for the old American gentleman with the pleasant face.

We leapt into the Diego Martin Valley at a height of fifteen hundred feet, and then the fun started. Our 'plane dipped and swerved, pirouetted and fox-trotted, shivered and dipped again, all because we were over the land where the air-pockets and currents are numerous and tricky. I could have laughed aloud with the fun of the game. I leant over with my eyes against the glass of the window, holding on to the arms of my chair so that I should not lose balance, and saw far below ribands of road serpentining over the hills and down the dales; saw a tiny stream running a zig-zag course down to the sea; saw the islands of the Gulf over the forehead of Point Gourde: saw little colonies of houses and, distinctly, the poor-houses recently put up in St. James. And then we were over the mud-ugly Gulf of Paria with three or four steamers and clusters of sloops riding at anchor on its placid dun surface. Rapidly we fell seawards, and "Mac," long since at the controls with his co-pilot, made a perfect landing at a quarter past ten just off the English steamers' Warehouses.

When I got ashore the smell of the earth, the proximity of my fellowmen, the familiar noises of the land and the taste of the earthy breezes pulled me down with a shock from the height of my sky-dream to the level of earth-reality. Life had once again assumed its mundane character and I was genuinely sorry to have left the clouds.

Trinidad Sunday Guardian, 22 June 1930

NOTES

1. Robert Seymour-Bridges (1844–1930). He was succeeded as poet laureate of England by John Masefield. The quotation is from a poem entitled "I would be a bird".

2. NYRBA, the New York, Rio and Buenos Aires Line, operated a seaplane service from New York City to Rio and Buenos Aires, and other points on the east coast of South America in the 1920s. It was merged with Pan American World Airways in 1930.

3. The quotation is from John Keats's "Ode to the Nightingale". Words and images from the poem are continued in the prose of the following paragraph.

4. Icarus was the son of the architect Daedalus, who designed the Labyrinth for King Minos of Crete. Wishing to escape from Minos, the father designed wings made from feathers and wax for himself and the boy. During the flight from Crete Icarus flew too close to the sun. The wax in his wings melted, he fell into the sea and was drowned.

5. From John Milton, *Paradise Lost*, bk. 1, 195–97.

6. William Howard Taft, a member of the Republican Party, was president of the United States from 1909 to 1913.

DIVORCE IS NOT A TAX

To the Editor of the *Trinidad Guardian*

Dear Sir, – Capt. Longridge, I am afraid, is a religious fanatic. The world has from time immemorial regarded such men with grave suspicion. It is unfortunate for the Catholics that he was chosen as their mouthpiece: his fulminations in the public newspaper Press have amused some people, irritated others and advanced his cause not one inch with all decent-thinking people living both outside and inside the pale of the Church of Rome.[1] I do not understand revelation, I do not understand faith (in the senses in which he uses the words). For me and for a vast number of other civilised people these words are synonyms for the bogey called Humbug.

It is unlikely that the members of the Legislative Council will be influenced by the sound and fury of the Catholics into believing that there is not a large section of the community wanting the Divorce Bill passed. Even within the congregations of the Catholic Churches in the city, there are large numbers wanting the measure.

All the Catholic countries (if that means anything at all) in the world have it. One would think, to judge by the hullabaloo kicked up by the Catholics here, that this island is their stronghold, the hub, of their religious ramifications. It is not. It simply is not. It is only a small island off the coast of South America, unimportant both to God and man, with 400-odd thousand people differing in pigmentation and religious convictions as widely as it is possible for these differences to be.

Why all this infernal din? The Divorce Law is not a tax: it is a measure evolved by changing circumstances for the protection of those who want it.

Let the Catholics show a little more Christian charity by keeping their mouths shut. If they are so superhuman that they do not need the Divorce bill, let them remember that there are others in their midst, humbly human, who want it.

Poison, though dangerous, has its admirable uses, and if there were not poison then men, desiring to end this dream, would cut their throats or blow their brains out or dive deep down into the fathomless sea.

If the Catholics want to destroy the necessity for Divorce, they must change the constitution of lots of other things they are just now fostering. They must stop teaching people to be humble in this world and stop promising them a reward for humility in the next: that teaching is the bedrock upon which stands the structure of Capitalism, a most iniquitous brothel. They must stop glibly talking about "What God hath joined together . . . " and etc. and etc. God isn't a sort of patent cement.

But to do all these things they will cease to be Catholics: and then, Watchman, what of the night?[2]

ALFRED H. MENDES
45 Richmond Street
Port-of-Spain
March 4.

Trinidad Guardian, 5 March 1931

NOTES

1. The battle in Trinidad's press over proposed divorce legislation raged from 1930 until the bill became law on 1 January 1933. Mendes threw himself into the war of words with tremendous gusto, causing considerable offence to Trinidad's Catholics, who were united in opposition to the legislation. The part he played in the letter and poster war is described in his autobiography (77–80). Captain Longridge sided with the Catholics' position in the Port of Spain city council.

2. Isaiah 21.11.

REVOLT!

Mr. O'Reilly's motion for the introduction of a Divorce Bill into the island has been brilliantly moved, wittily seconded and effectively carried. And in full realization of the fears of *Mr. Ambard's newspaper*,[1] God should by now have gathered up His skirts and glanced about Him shyly, preparatory to flight. In the dilemma of deciding (like Mr. Melpomenus Jones)[2] what course it were best to pursue, something of the sigh of Mr. Squire's lines must have escaped Him: "Good God," said God, "I've got my work cut out."

All the civilized countries have thought fit to have the law, and as the East is pagan (God hates Paganism and especially the people who practise it), and Africa savage (God has fashioned a bright burning place called Hell for savages, both civilized and otherwise), He perhaps will have to shift the exercise of His energies to some other planet of our system.

He must long ago have come to the conclusion that it was all so hopeless with the Earth, except that spot on it called Trinidad, so He stuck to it to the end like the true Sticker that He is.

How uncomfortable He must have felt when He realized His impotency against the fervent prayers of the innocent little schoolchildren and the good, pious adults telling their beads, all importuning Him to hypnotise the Official Members of the Legislature into voting against their wishes! However, He succeeded nicely with Mr. Grier. Not so bad, but the Seance, didn't you think Sir, could have been more successful? Especially as Svengali[3] was the Almighty Himself.

And still Mr. Ambard's newspaper, like an irate prophet in the wilderness, with its four staunch henchmen – Asceticism, Bigotry, Ignorance and Conceit – sends its wailing voice to the dark, merciless heavens, calling day by day upon the God who has flown away. Will He return?

They all gaze to heaven with rapt attention, mistaking a sun-edged cloud for the Almighty, hearing in a distant cloud – voice His familiar tones, waiting patiently from dawn to dewey [*sic*] eve4 the pyrotechnic burst of His bright wrath.

Alas! God is very vexed with Trinidad and, incidentally, the rest of the Earth, so why trouble Him now? In my early days, one always waited until Papa's ire had abated before asking any favour. He was more approachable then. In the case of God, the only trouble is that it might be difficult to find Him when the solitary prophet with his four staunch henchmen decides upon calling once again.

Papa could only run from the house to the office: and even as a child one knew where the office was. God can fly on and on, seated on a ray of light, and the lonely prophet will have to wait, if Einstein's theory be correct, until that curved ray of light returns God into his hearing. As that might take a few million years to accomplish, I need not tell the prophet and his henchmen that they will not be here to receive Him then. I can only hope that they will not be in that place they themselves have asked God to create for Pagans and Savages.

Adhuc sub judice lis est:5 I had forgotten that.

Of the Unofficial members of Council born in the West Indies, five voted for the motion and six against. Had Mr. Teelucksingh been there, it would have been six for and six against. On the Official side, four were born in the West Indies – and all four voted for the motion. From this emerges the fact that of the total number in the Council of West Indian birth, ten voted for the motion while six opposed it.

There are grounds for believing that Mr. Grier with the very best intention sacrificed his inclinations to what he conceived to be the popular call. It must have surprised him not a little to view the fateful telling amidst the acclamations of the crowded Chamber.

Mr. dos Santos, I know, was honest in his support of the motion; and I think that those who are acquainted with our Acting Colonial Treasurer will agree that nothing on earth can force him into doing what he doesn't want to do. That is a characteristic which he shares with all men of honour.

This has been a struggle between the local Government and Roman Catholicism; and the Government has won. It is really time that the Catholics were made to realize that they cannot have everything their own way. With the standard of education rising, the superstition of all forms of organized religion is bound to pass away, even the Roman superstition. What a fine pass it is for any community to have to build up its social fabric upon the notions of a group of men who profess to have nothing to do with women in a particular way and who must be blatantly ignorant of conditions of family life! In elucidation of this, let us examine for a moment in company here and there with Miss Naomi Mitchison,[6] the recent encyclical *Casti Connubii.*[7]

That there is an ideal of monogamous union among western peoples, nobody doubts. Unfortunately, it is quite impossible to enjoy this kind of union with permanency. Furthermore, very few couples are so successfully mated as to enjoy it at all. The Christians call this kind of union sacramental: it is the rebirth of the *kataleptike fantasia*[8] of the Stoics. Upon this beautiful and often fleeting relationship, a whole system of rules and taboos has been built up, which absurdly presupposes the sacramental nature of marriage to be permanent between Roman Catholics. In order to make this a premise, there is, in the encyclical, an utter denial of all pre-Christian anthropological and documentary history, with the exception of the Bible, of course. In short, our authority is *Genesis*, our lawgiver the tribal God of Israel – and this in the twentieth century.

The section dealing with children and women will shock most sensible mothers. The two old theories creep in once again: first, that the wife and child are the property of the man; and secondly, that the wife shall be chaste and even chilly. This last is a wicked social idea, for it is one of the causes of the existence of the prostitute. Both Paul and Augustine are copiously quoted, and no wonder. Paul had a curious bias about women and Augustine entertained the reformed rake's usual views of women, so that they both twisted the perfectly sane sayings of Jesus to suit their purposes.

Next comes the section on False Notions concerning Marriage. Companionate Marriage is condemned without a word said for its historical foundation. And the lightnings flash at Contraception and God's voice thunders. To quote a lull in the storm: "Nor are those considered as acting against nature who in the married state use their rights in the proper manner although on account of natural reasons, either of time or certain defects, new life cannot be brought forth."

All this very tortuous and serpent – subtle cant after a severe condemnation of "deliberate frustration" of conception. Is the "safe-period" method of birth control (and this must be counted among the meanings of the above passage) not considered a "deliberate frustration"? Dust is all right in the road, not in the eyes of the people.

And so on through Abortion and Eugenic Sterilisation of the Feeble-minded and a return to the status of women in society. Woman, His Holiness tells us, must sit upon her truly regal throne as wife and mother; if she descends she will become the slave of man once more. Here one doesn't know whether to laugh or howl. What should men who profess celibacy know about women and family-life? At least, I prefer to consider seriously Westermarck, Fraser, Ellis and Kraft-Ebbing [*sic*].9

The poison has settled to the bottom of the vial containing the encyclical. Here it is: the Canon Law should be made the Law of the Land. Now this is deliberate incitement to interference with the State. We have only to remember Brazil as an example. In this island, we have recently had and are still having ample evidence of the Catholics' desire to frustrate the duties of the Government. Outside of the island, Malta is a recent case in point. Had they succeeded here with the Divorce motion, it would have meant more pressure at other points.10

The Divorce motion should not have been interfered with by any religious body and for a very simple and clear reason: marriage is legalized by the State, not the Church, and the State should reserve to itself the right of dissolving a bond it has itself created. That is axiomatic.

The motion has been carried: it remains now to frame the Bill. I know perfectly well that the suggestion I am about to make will fall on barren ground, for Trinidad soil has only been turned up; it has yet to be manured. I insist, however, on making it because I am convinced of its validity.

I do not think adultery as strong a reason for divorce as incompatibility of temperament. The Church stresses the spiritual part of the union, and that, to any intelligent person, is what really matters in marriage.

I am open to correction, but I believe that the Church considers adultery a mortal sin. This is where it is so inconsistent, for while enthroning the spirit on the one hand, it crowns the flesh on the other.

One thing emerges from the controversy: the tendency of religious bodies to give Sex its Christian significance of filth and stink.

Trinidad Sunday Guardian, 15 March 1931

NOTES

1. The *Port-of-Spain Gazette*, which favoured the Catholics' position in the divorce debate. André Ambard, the owner, was himself a devout Catholic.

2. The unfortunate curate in Stephen Leacock's "Nonsense" poem "The Awful Fate of Melpomenus Jones", *Literary Lapses* (1910). Mr Jones was unable to extricate himself gracefully from a visit, and ended up dying of old age in his acquaintances' house, resented by all.

3. In George DuMaurier's novel *Trilby* (1894) the musician Svengali hypnotized the eponymous heroine into believing that she could sing. During a concert her voice cracked and failed her at the moment of Svengali's death.

4. A memory of Mulciber, one of the rebel angels in *Paradise Lost*, bk. 1, 742–44: "From Morn / To Noon he fell, from Noon to dewy Eve, / A Summer's day".

5. The matter is still under judicial consideration. (Comment in the newspapers is therefore prohibited.)

6. Naomi May Margaret Mitchison (1897–1999) was a Scottish novelist and poet. She was a committed Socialist, campaigner for women's rights, and advocate for birth control. She was also a Life Fellow of the Eugenics Society. It is unlikely that Mendes knew of this last aberration. He would certainly not have felt comfortable in her company, even on the printed page.

7. Pope Pius XI's Encyclical *On Christian Marriage* (31 December 1930), which condemned birth control, divorce, and "companionate marriage".

8. The term, used by the Stoic philosopher Epictetus in discussing how to apprehend reality, is probably best translated in this context as " a criterion for truth".

9. Writers on human sexuality. Richard Freiherr von Krafft-Ebing (1840–1902) was an Austro-German sexologist and psychiatrist, whose best-known work is *Psychopathia Sexualis*. He coined the terms "sadism" and "masochism". Edvard Alexander Westermarck (1862–1939), Finnish philosopher and sociologist, specialized in the history of marriage, morality, and religious institutions. Henry Havelock Ellis (1859–1939) was a British sexologist, physician, and social reformer, with an interest in the causes of homosexuality.

    Fraser: either Alexander Campbell Fraser (1819–1914), the Scottish rationalist philosopher, or Sir James G. Frazer (1854–1941), the social anthropologist and author of *The Golden Bough,* a monumental study of magic and religion (Editor's note: I incline towards the second option, despite the difference in spelling. *The Golden Bough,* published in 1906–15 in 12 volumes, and in 1922 in an abridged version, had a profound influence on writers and artists of the first half of the twentieth century. T.S. Eliot's *The Waste Land* owed a considerable debt to Frazer, as the poet himself acknowledged in a note to his work).

10. In the 1930s both Brazil and Malta experienced power struggles between the Catholic Church and the state. As in Trinidad, the Church in Malta mounted a crusade against divorce.

FLYING INKPOTS

To the Editor of the *Trinidad Guardian*

Dear Sir, – Since my return from the U.S.A. I have heard a lot of talk about the behaviour of our City Council, all of it abusive. The press too has joined in the mudslinging. I am amazed.[1]

While in America I was present at meetings during which inkpots flew like mad about the room, harsh and obscene words were spat around, men used their fists freely. On occasion the police had to be fetched in. I have read reports of sessions of Congress that were not one jot less rowdy and vulgar than recent meetings in our City Council chamber. And always in retrospect, when tempers had cooled and reason was restored, there was rejoicing over the fact that there were countries left in the world where men were sufficiently free to express their views and struggle constitutionally for the physical shape and form of their ideas.

Democracy as it is economically constituted today is at its healthiest when it is most rowdy and vulgar. To speak of a free community of men without clashes and animosities is a contradiction in terms. The moment men cease to disagree among themselves, at that very moment they cease to be free. For me, one of the few evidences left over from our peacetime democracy is our City Council with its boisterous aliveness, its noisy antics. And let it not be forgotten that only those men who have been prepared to suffer the indignity of bodily ejection from the meeting hall have ever succeeded in bringing about reforms for which their posterity has blessed them.

As I see it, Mr. Gomes seeks to destroy what he considers to be a vicious political machine; Capt. Cipriani on the other hand is determined to preserve and perpetuate it. Fine! Let the two fighters go to it and may the man with the better cause win. At least, it gives us assurance that our democracy is still alive and kicking.

A.H. Mendes
14 November 1940

NOTE

1. The incident behind this letter is a confrontation between the mayor of Port of Spain, Captain Arthur Andrew Cipriani (1875–1945) and Albert Maria "Bertie" Gomes (1911–78) in the chamber of the Port of Spain city council on 31 October 1940. The labour leader Quintin O'Connor had requested permission to hold a meeting in Woodford Square, and Cipriani had ruled that it was against the constitution to hold political meetings in public places like Woodford Square. Gomes had objected strenuously and at length to the ruling, and upon the Mayor's summoning a number of policemen to escort him from the Chamber, he had lain down on the floor, forcing the unfortunate policemen to carry him out. At that time, he weighed 240 pounds. Michael Anthony, *The Making of Port-of-Spain*, vol. 2, *Port-of-Spain in a World at War, 1939–1945* (Cascade, Trinidad: Paria, 2008), 47.

Although both men championed the cause of Trinidad's poor – Cipriani was known as "the champion of the barefoot man" – Mendes's sympathies are clearly with Gomes. He and Gomes had been friends and colleagues since *Beacon* days, and Cipriani had earned his ire by supporting Trinidad's Catholics in their attempts to block the divorce law.

CALYPSONIANS PRAISED

To the Editor of the *Trinidad Guardian*

Dear Sir, – I believe I'm in a better position than Mr. de Boissière to pass judgment on the present condition of the calypso.[1] The other evening I visited a tent for the first time in ten years. Of even greater advantage is the fact that during most of that period I was absent from the island: so that renewing friendship the other evening with the calypso, I could look upon it with fresh eyes, listen to it with young ears.

Usually an experience of this kind is rewarding: in my case it was.

Let me say that I was immediately struck by the high level of the songs sung and the sustained excellence of their execution. I'm not so sure that the quality of either composition or rendition has improved, for after all talent and the creative instinct in the arts are not things that are heightened by accumulated knowledge.

What I must, however, admit is that range of subject has widened to embrace a keen awareness of what is wrong with our island – and, for that matter, with the world. I mean our calypsonians have grown politically conscious: in consequence their wit and satire, two qualities that are the very lungs of the calypso, have muscled to meet the new demand.

Of the twenty or so pieces offered the other evening, there were at least ten that commended themselves to me as gems, in all conscience a high enough percentage of goodness in any eveningful of stuff.

And what variety of mood they evoked! Brilliant nonsense, Rabelaisian wit, Voltairean satire, pure poetry – all these weapons were used in restrained measure and with consummate skill.

All in all, the performance convinced me that our contemporary calypsos are as good as ever the best have been, and can stand as peers in company with the folk-song of any other land.

Alfred H. Mendes
Port of Spain

Trinidad Guardian, 5 February 1944

NOTE

1.   Ralph de Boissière had written a letter to the *Trinidad Guardian* praising the calypso form on 3 February 1944.

IF CALYPSO IS FOLKSONG IT SHOULD BE ENCOURAGED

Those of us who are attuned to the genre and do not permit our judgment to be influenced by the bourgeois proprieties are agreed that our calypso singers, when they are good, produce pieces that satisfy the aesthetic sense as effectively as does a good lyric.

From any season's crop a choice governed by the most exacting standards will show a surprising proportion of successes, and it is significant that to this lot of winners almost every chansonnier has contributed at least a song or two. It would, therefore, seem that the calypsonians we now have with us are those who have survived the competition on the improvised boards: they are there because they are good.

I am willing to concede that it is possible for there to be many among my own people who do not like calypso, and for reasons other than their acceptance of the conventions. On the other hand, I cannot agree that it is impossible for them honestly to acknowledge merit in a thing they do not like.

I sometimes suspect, however, that in a number of cases the rejection is a pose, a pose informed by snobbery. It's a pity. Snobbery is like a mouse that gnaws at the hearts and minds of those who afford it hospitality, and at length the humanity is gnawed out of them. It's a pity.

You see, I am taking it for granted that the calypso is not only not a mediocre form of song writing, but that, within its strict limitations, it is an exercise that has found practitioners measuring up to its needs.

But this is not the subject of my article. The truth is that I can never satisfy my own *amour propre* unless and until I am able to say with conviction that the calypso possesses a quality that identifies it with the island, or, at least, with the West Indies.

My subject is then contained in the question: has the calypso a local habitation and a name? Is it folksong?

My answer is: yes. Allow me to present my case.

Unfortunately, I must at the outset confess myself incompetent technically to discuss its music. From a nodding acquaintance with the Latin-American rhythms, I know that the calypso has some affinity with them. Too, I know that the syncopations we have inherited from the old Negro slaves, who in turn brought them across the waters in the dark days before emancipation, have left their mark upon the melodies.

For that matter, I have a sneaking suspicion that the tempo of the tunes from Latin-America has itself been borrowed from the African jungle-settlements; so that, by and large, the beat of the melodies now wedded to the calypso is probably African, while the melodies themselves are obviously European.

If this be so – and I have yet to discover someone more learned in the lore than I to refute it – then we possess something that is composed of the blending of two parts having their birthplaces in spots far distant from each other, travelling long journeys across the ocean, meeting, mating, and producing the calypso music.

This by itself is something. But it may be equally true that these same two parts, fusing in the Latin-American countries, have forged a music that is structurally akin to the calypso.

What then is it that gives me the right to assert that the calypso melodies are folk tunes, and, at that, folk tunes peculiar to but a few of the West Indian islands? My reply is: the same half-dozen or so melodies, with but slight variations from time to time, have for generations been sung as calypsos. The melodies remain; only the words change.

I find myself on even firmer ground when I come to consider the other aspects of this inquiry. They are, for my purposes, three in number:

1. The verses.
2. The singers.
3. The *mise-en-scène* or décor.

What, you ask, about subject-matter? Frankly, I find it difficult to perceive how there can be anything indigenous to any country in the content of an art form. Birth, death, love, hate, joy, sadness – these are universal things, the things that tell us all men are brothers under the skin.

What gives them their distinction, what invests them with a special flavour, a special colour so that we can say: "That's Spanish, that's Chinese", is treatment, the manner in which the matter is expressed.

By verses I mean, of course, the words of the songs. And here it is possible on the one hand for the island-bred-and-born to sense at once the flavour and colour of his home, and on the other for the stranger to feel himself in the presence of something utterly alien. From this it is but a step to understanding why it is so difficult for the average individual in a community to see any good or beauty in a folklore not his own.

The next time you are in a tent listen to the odd intermingling of the single and many-syllabled words, how the Latinisms and the simple Anglo-Saxon sounds pounce upon the heels of each other.

True, English writers have time and again used short and long words in the same way. Our calypsonian, however, strikes them anew upon the island-anvil and gives them a pronunciation all his own, an inflexion often startling in its effects.

But words by themselves add little to the evidence I seek. How they are composed, welded together in sentences, marshalled in paragraphs – this can mean a great deal. It does in the calypso.

Nothing can be more delightful to the connoisseur than the quaint manner in which the chansonnier integrates his clauses, thrusts a patois phrase into the context slyly to illuminate a half-hidden meaning, sneaks in a colloquialism to sharpen the satire, inserts solecisms that make his speech as much of a dialect as any, mispronounces words to mouth the most fantastic rhymes, strings unfamiliar sounds together to heighten the effect.

I submit that the manner in which these tricks are performed is unequivocally Trinidadian. Each by itself may have little weight; together, overwhelmingly they prove my case.

And finally, consider for a moment the sobriquets: Lord Executor, The Lord Invader, The Roaring Lion, The Growling Growler, Atilla the Hun – where also are such grandiloquent pseudonyms heard?

The singers. Well, there can be no room for opinion here, for what our eyes see our hearts understand. I make no bones about it: our calypsonian, the physical man I mean, is, judged by the rules of the middle-class, a vulgar-looking fellow.

He is dressed either too flashily or lacks the little touches that are said to make gentlemen. I accept the gibe. But tell me, why should you reject vulgarity that is honest because it is just being human, and accept respectability that is hypocritical because it is trying to be other than human?

Indeed, without this brand of crudity upon his person his songs would lose much of their local tang. I once saw a band of calypsonians, Trinidadians all, perhaps, in a New York night club. You'd never believe it: they wore dinner jackets! There and then I realised how much a part of the calypso is the rude appearance of the calypsonian. Can you imagine a folk dancer dancing without costume native to the dance?

Even more important, the local chansonnier comes from that economic stratum of our society that is largely responsible for folk-stuff the world over. The approach to his themes is invariably from the angle of his class-consciousness: every weapon he uses he wields in the fashion of a man who has known exploitation and oppression.

And significantly enough, as a group they show a surprisingly ethnic homogeneity; so that here also we have a striking reminder of the calypso's locale: is not Trinidad's population predominantly Negroid? Can you fit a European, a Chinese, an East Indian into the picture? I can't.

There remains the décor in the midst of which the calypsonian does his stuff. The "tent" – whence the word? In what other country, for that matter in what other Caribbean island, is the word ever used to describe a shelter that cannot by any stretch of the imagination be identified with a tent? And while at this point, let me say how much I deplore the passing of the bamboo poles to support the rough roof. They created atmosphere and lent the structure an intimacy that is gone.

Too, I regret the disappearance of the female chorus: voices swinging and swaying, bottles and sticks aggravating the gusto of the refrain, faces agitated with the neurotic pulse of the music. Nowhere else could you possibly have seen the likes of it in a similar setting.

I appeal to those responsible for the performances to restore the touches that serve to intensify the folk-quality of the songs.

My case is closed. Before I leave you, I ask you to reflect for a moment upon the points I have presented and I'm sure you'll perceive how they fit into a pattern. They are all of a piece. Each informs the other, each helps to amplify the folk-nature of the calypso. And as folk traditions are potent signs of the maturing of a people, and the calypso the fullest we have, it is up to us to nurture it and not attempt to snuff it out with an approach that is sanctimonious and false.

Trinidad Guardian Weekly, 13 February 1944

CARNIVAL PIECE

In the life of every human being there are childhood experiences that bind him to the land in which he was born or in which he was nurtured from babyhood. In later years the memories of these experiences are a reservoir from which he draws for sweetening whatever is bitter in the present and lending enchantment to the past. Particularly is this the case where indigenous customs are concerned, for not only do they flavour the place that has fathered them, but they also make it possible for a man to push down roots into the soil and to enjoy in consequence a sense of being a small part of an infinitely larger and more powerful whole.

Now this intimate relationship between the human being and his birthplace is of paramount importance to all men, for it is this that above everything else inspires confidence and security. He who has cut himself adrift from fellowship with his brothers is indeed a lonely person; and this loneliness breeds growing fear of the unknown. Such a man is like a child who has lost its parents.

I contend that carnival is one of the very few customs, peculiar to Trinidad, that give us the opportunity for identifying ourselves with our island. One proof of this lies in the fact that our people as a whole, although a hodgepodge of innumerable racial stocks, regard the fête as a genetical legacy, as something that is the very warp and woof of their spirits. I go so far as to say that if we allow any ethnic group to renew and multiply itself for the span of but two generations in our island, you will find that almost without exception the offspring are devotees of the pre-Lenten celebrations, worshippers at a shrine that despite its noise, its pagan abandon, its vulgarity, or perhaps because of these very attributes, is nonetheless sacred and dear to them all.

During the two days of last carnival I wandered, in the company of Wenzell

Brown, an American writer of some distinction,[1] about the bedlamised streets of Port of Spain. As evening drew down upon the second day and the riot of revelry rose in a crescendo, Wenzell turned to me and remarked: "This is about the only democratising thing I have discovered in Trinidad." So true was the observation that I was for a moment startled. It so often happens that the obvious passes us by, unrecognised. It so often happens too, that the stranger in our home, bringing to it a fresh vision, will apprehend truths that have escaped us. And this was a case in point. When I reflected upon the matter, it amazed me that I had failed to perceive how close a relationship exists between our folklore and customs on the one hand, and on the other their levelling and equalising influences upon our people: Negro, Indian, European, Chinese, and the fantastic mixtures amongst them all.

How admirably do mask and costumes conceal colour and class and at the same time reveal the instinct in us all to mix freely with our fellowmen and be one of the common herd! I have given some thought to the problem of our social organisation and I have long since come to the conclusion that the class structure of our society is a symptom of the disease weakening all hope of the human family living in peace and comfort. Unfortunately, in our island the problem is complicated by the race question. There can be no advance for us until this obstacle has been swept away. That much should be clear to those of us who think.

But before we can begin to stand on our feet and behave like a mature people, we must create a culture of our own; and the historical development of all peoples teaches us that before we can set out on the road to a culture, race distinctions must be put behind us as vehemently and decisively as Christ put Satan behind him.

I believe carnival can help us here. At least, very early in my own life, it was responsible for teaching me a lesson that I shall never forget.

I couldn't have been more than seven years old when the incident occurred. The carnival season was approaching and, because of my father's objections, I had conspired with my mother to have a clown suit made for the occasion. My father's groom was always about the yard. With him, at every chance, I held secret sessions as to what colour the cloth should be, what shape the hat (he finally fashioned it for me himself), how to cut the balloon-trouser legs, and so on.

At last the glorious day arrived (the glory of that bright, sunny day is with me now as I write) and, shaking with excitement and child-like trepidation, I donned the flaming thing and took to the streets as fast as my little legs could do the job. Down Frederick Street I skipped, my costume's bells merrily tinkling, the spangles and miniature mirrors on my breast sparkling in the sunlight.

Behind the wire-mask on my face a strange sensation of freedom, unfettered and complete, seized me, and after a few minutes my heart was emptied of all timidity. Every syncopating band that came my way I joined, cavorting in front of each like a faun gone mad. I sang, I shouted, I screeched. Hoarseness mattered not. Henry Street, Charlotte Street, Prince Street, all the streets where the poor exist were caught up in a miracle of metamorphosis: drabness had given way to jubilation, the ugly chrysalis had changed into the butterfly.

And then it happened. Although more than forty years ago, my memory is precise upon the incident: even now I see the towering "devil," the massive mask leering at me through baleful eyes, hideous nostrils and murderous mouth, the towering "devil" armed *cap-à-pie* with all the infernal forks. There he stood, magnificently malevolent, the cynosure of all the packed bystanders.

Suddenly I realised, how I cannot tell, that the monster's gaze was fixed on me. I stopped in my tracks. The joy and sense of safety behind my mask deserted me in that instant. In an alien tongue the great "devil" hurled an imprecation at me and took two strides towards me. I recoiled. Horror suffused my limbs, petrifying them. It seemed that only a few steps separated me from the end of my days on earth. And then, with a howl never heard on land or sea, the evil thing leapt towards me. Panic released me and I fled . . .

When I arrived home I was put to bed by a scared old nurse and that night a high fever shook my little frame. The next morning an anxious mother squeezed the story out of me. She tried to comfort and reassure me, but it was not until months later that I could look back upon the incident with calm, for then I learned that the great "devil" was after all only my father's harmless groom!

And I learned much else. I learned that my father's groom could, in changed conditions, exercise authority over me. I learned that he was not only a groom but a human being. And because of this, I learned to respect him. The child-like arrogance that had been taught me by the surrounding class-colour distinctions underwent a change: I was inclined to be humble before my father's groom ever afterwards. He is long since dead. It grieves me that I was never able to thank him for helping to teach me the virtues of humility before all human beings, black, white, or brown. I know now that the skin and the dress are no criteria for the spirit behind them.

Trinidad Guardian Weekly, 16 February 1947

NOTE

1.   Wenzell Brown (1911–81) subsequently wrote to Mendes thanking him for hospitality, and mentioning two books which he had been writing. The first, *Angry Men – Laughing Men: The Caribbean Caldron*, was about his travels through the West Indies, with four chapters devoted to Trinidad, and including "quite a bit about Bertie and you". The other, a mystery, *The Rum and Coco-Cola Murders* (the title obviously owes it origins to Lord Invader's calypso "Rum and Coco-Cola"), he was dedicating to Bertie Gomes and to Mendes. Brown explains apologetically in the letter that he has had to resort to "Southern States Negro" dialect rather than Trinidadian speech in the novel, as American readers would be unable to comprehend the latter.

ART SOCIETY EXHIBITION RICH
IN HIGH QUALITY PAINTINGS

Had I the power, I would compel every member of the committee set up by Government to advise upon the proposed constitutional reform for our island and every person planning to give evidence before that committee, to attend the annual exhibition of the Trinidad Art Society now being held in the Prince's Building. This I would do because I am convinced that a people who can create the crop of paintings I saw on Saturday afternoon last can without the shadow of a doubt manage their own political and economic affairs.

The past teaches us that most human communities have moved forward in a more or less uniform pattern and that before culture can take root and grow, a people must have taken on the responsibilities of nationhood.

Here in Trinidad it seems as if we have been so impatient of waiting upon natural development from phase to phase that we have hurdled the obstacle and, still champing at the bit of alien domination, gone on [to] the exercise of the creative urge lodged in our racially heterogeneous community.

In literature, we have made a promising start that swung into stride with my own generation. Twenty years ago some of us, observing the rich human and nature material in our island, grasped its significance and wove it into stories and novels that were perhaps crude and immature, but which were, nonetheless, honest and original because Trinidadian. At least we helped put the generation that followed ours upon the right road; and if I am to judge from the stories I have recently seen in our newspapers and magazines, then I shall be surprised if one or two of our younger writers fail to win reputations reaching far beyond our shores.

In music we have the calypso and the steel band – the former an art-form that has gained recognition in metropolitan centres of the North American continent. There is something in both that stems from the earliest awareness of the possibilities of our congealing into a West Indian type, physically and spiritually.

Miss Beryl McBurnie,[1] whose efforts have fructified in occasional dance-festivals, is trying to snatch from a tragic oblivion the choreographic expressions of our people. She has brought to her task a conviction and ardour without which the creative instinct cannot keep alive, and her troupe of young men and women have caught the infection. To watch their bodies sublimated by the frenzy and grace of recreating a West Indian folk dance is to be lifted above earthly horizons and yet be made one with the land of our birth. She is a challenge to those who would turn their backs upon native forms of expression.

All these people – our painters, our writers, our music-makers, our dancers, those who have sought salvation in the island heritage of immortelle and poui, of sweetman and "barrackyarder," of combite and canboulay, of bèlè and bongo, – they are all, I submit, more effective ambassadors of our fitness for, and certainly more telling advocates of our interest in, responsible government than our local politicians.

Leaving alone allusive reflections on art, I now come to the exhibition itself. Three parts of it deserve attention: the finger paintings, the water colours, and the oils. Under the first category the sole exhibitors are the Kellman sisters, Phyllis and Coral. In the water colour section the most successful pieces are contributed by Eric Cameron and McDavid. The oils yield richest accomplishment and promise, and I do not hesitate to name Leo Basso and Alladin as two of the most significant West Indian artists in any medium.[2]

Of the works, my pick in each division is: Finger Paintings – Phyllis Kellman's "The Variety of Mood", and Coral Kellman's "Flowers". Water Colours: Eric Cameron's "St. Ann's River", and McDavid's uncatalogued group of huts on a hillside. Oils: Alladin's "The Pound of Rice" (the picture with the biggest spiritual content in the collection), "The Mourners", and "The Gravediggers"; Leo Basso's "Through a Window", "Indian Women Preparing for a Fete", and three large still-lifes – "Mango and Mammy Apple", "Banana Leaf", and "Sapodilla and Peame".

Finger painting is novel to Trinidad and I know nothing of its history. I understand that an American woman taught its technique to the Kellman girls about a year ago. The paint is applied to damp paper with finger and nail, and because of a rapidly drying process plasticity lasts a short time and the picture must be completed before hardening sets in. This imposes speed in execution. The fact that does emerge from this group is that the Kellman sisters are highly talented. Where Coral is lyrical and timid, Phyllis is robust and bold. "Flowers", for instance, is a decorative burst of loveliness in half tones, whereas Phyllis' "Variety of Mood" is a symbol of flaming phalluses exploding into dark orgasms. In both young women, the sense of design is highly developed. They are worth watching.

"St. Ann's River" is the best Cameron water colour I have seen. Its tranquil greens and rippling browns, cocooned in an atmosphere of spontaneity, fuse to make it a thing of beauty.

Although McDavid uses the medium unconventionally in that his opaque application of the pigment robs the surface of luminosity, one of the prime essentials of a water colour, I thought his sense of composition so good that I discounted the tendency in nearly all of his pictures to accept more than was necessary for his effects. Why, for instance, the human figures in his painting of the huts?

In my pick of oil canvases, Pierre Lelong's[3] uncatalogued portrait of a semi-nude girl was deliberately omitted. It is indeed the most efficiently executed canvas in the exhibition. His style is the thin coat with the glazed effect, and he uses impasto for his highlights with éclat; but he will forgive me, I trust, when I tell him that although he has identified himself with our island and done our young painters an incalculable service through his classes, I am at this moment concerned with the work of the West Indian born and bred.

Boscoe Holder jumps to mind immediately. Why have I given the cold shoulder to the one young artist who, up to a year or so ago, seemed certainly destined to grow into as noteworthy a creative person as any born to these islands? The answer is that he has stopped growing: his repetitions are not even as good as his originals. It is a pity and I hope the phase is temporary.

There is also Alfred Codallo. He appears to have struck a barren patch and I for one would deplore any weakening of the urge in one so gifted as he. In this exhibition he has among others two water scapes in oil and an odd little gem called "The Dwens". The first two are gentle in mood, "The Dwens" pure phantasy.

There remain Alladin and Leo Basso. They both use oil and they both paint the island that is theirs and the people with whom they have played and sorrowed. But here the resemblance ceases.

Basso's spirit is tender, sensitive, and everything he does is imbued with a touch of other-worldliness – like a Walter de la Mare poem. The truth is that Basso is a primitive, and on top of that he sees life through the eyes of a child.

For me his canvases listed above are things of joy – fresh, pure. Examine the colours: they are all cool pastel shades that merge into each other like the moods of young men and women in love. He possesses the rare gift of endowing his stills with a quality that negates the meaning of the still life: the quality of movement. This is in turn related to his child-like wonder at seeing the world for the first time: mammy apples are on the point of rising into the air, a banana leaf poises for flight on a tilted yellow plane, sapodillas' shadows are the only indication that the fruit are resting on a solid base, and so on. Again like Walter de la Mare, his whole work is suffused with an air of magic.

Alladin, on the other hand, is a naturalist who looks at life through mature eyes and with gusto. He is even more than that: his work, in which the human figure is seldom absent, is crammed with sociological content. His colours are vivid, his compositions superb. Look at "The Pound of Rice" and observe the rhythm of the movement rising to a crescendo of violence in the outstretched hands framed by the doorway. The remarkable balance of the large group of 31 figures all anchored to the imperturbable Indian squatting on his hams in the foreground, is nothing less than a tour-de-force. "The Mourners" reveals the same qualities of draughtsmanship and composition – and power.

This then is the contrast between our two best painters: one a child, the other an adult.

Trinidad Guardian, 13 March 1947

NOTES

1. Beryl McBurnie (1915–2000) was a close friend of Mendes. She was a renowned dancer and choreographer, and was responsible for rescuing many melodies and folk dances that would otherwise have been lost to Trinidad and Tobago. She founded the "Little Carib" theatre in 1948.

2. For anyone interested in Trinidad's art scene in the decade of the 1940s, Mendes's canvas of names provides an important record. Of all of those listed in this and the following article, four are well known today: Leo Basso (1901–82); M.P. Alladin (1919–80); Alfred Codallo (1915–70); and Boscoe Holder (1921–2007). Mendes devotes an entire article to Leo Basso ("Basso Holds a Place with Best W.I. Artists", this volume) and another to Boscoe Holder in his capacity as dancer/choreographer ("Holder's Creole Extravaganza", this volume).

3. The French artist Pierre Lelong began to teach classes at the Art Society at the beginning of 1945.

ART SOCIETY'S SHOW PRODUCES FIVE
PAINTERS WORTH WATCHING

Lest I be misinterpreted, and so misunderstood, allow me to define my attitude towards art exhibitions held in the island. Obviously I am interested in art in all its modes of expression mainly because it is the one immortal language and as such the one hope mankind possesses for a better understanding of the problems of all races and all national communities.

Indeed, it seems to me that art denies the validity in moral terms of the division of the human family into national and class groups. I believe that pride and prejudice when brought under the disinfecting force of an art object can be like cloud-clusters before a powerful wind.

For this is exactly what art does do: it cleanses, it purifies, it sublimates. Uglinesses like race-prejudice, avarice for money, the inequalities imposed by our economic dispensation would surely die for want of nourishment in a world of men and women gifted with the creative urge and using it to fashion things of beauty.

But in the island to which I am native my attitude condenses to a more special, more narrow, more topical approach. Whenever I visit a local exhibition of paintings the tendency is to search out the stuff that, so to speak, smells of the frangipani, tastes like callaloo, looks like the immortelle, and sounds like the keskidee.

I suppose the truth is that I am unwilling to accept the suggestion that there is a Trinidadian culture until I am persuaded by eye, ear, tongue and nostril that its matter and manner are of the island's life and scene.

I do not, and cannot deny that the fundamentals are the same everywhere; but I am equally convinced that before a people can claim the right to call themselves cultured, they must first have absorbed into their creative expressions the texture and spirit of their immediate environment.

I am led into attempting to make a further point. In any work of art the synthesis of form and content is more often than not complete, the exceptions being only those huge canvases like Tolstoy's *War and Peace*; Beethoven's *Choral Symphony*, and so on, where the spiritual content is so vast as to transcend infelicities of form.

This means that for the reader, the listener, or the observer, it is impossible to conceive of a mould more suited to the subject-matter, than is to be found in any work of art. Just as the Chinese, the East Indians, the Africans and the Europeans have made vehicles that can best carry ideas and emotions to their fellowmen; and in turn, just as the English, the French, the Germans and the Italians among the Europeans have invented modes of artistic articulation that have characteristics peculiar to each and quite different from each other because of the compulsion, under the creative impulse, of wedding manner to matter – so I feel must the West Indian artist discover as by instinct, accompanied with sweat, the dress that will best clothe the native things that inspire him.

This is why I have always been suspicious of the wisdom of sending our gifted children abroad to study technique; for let there be no mistake about it: the really big vision has no choice but to make its own rules, be they ever so iconoclastic. I contend that the spirit and scene of our island can produce a style of expression that future critics and art-lovers will recognize as being typically West Indian.

To our own people who are trying to express themselves in any of the art-forms I say: discover the things that make Trinidad and the West Indies what they are, and by incessant work the idiom best suited to both your temperament and your background will come to you.

Turning to the Trinidad Art Society Exhibition now being held in the Royal Victoria Institute, I am compelled to observe that although the average standard of the paintings is as good as last year's, and execution in many cases improved, the highlights are not there except for a magnificent portrait by a famous foreign artist, Kurt Schwitters.[1]

This is only another way of saying that I lament the absence of exhibits by Alladin, Cameron, the Kellman sisters, and Basso (who has only one not-so-good canvas, but still an unmistakable Basso). Alladin is "studying" in England: I wish him luck – with my fingers crossed. Cameron and Basso are apparently too busy making their livings. One of the Kellman sisters has got married and has presumably diverted her energies to the domestic field, while the other is perhaps in a mood of creative laziness.

As I wandered around the panels of pictures, observing the broad influence of the Lelong style in Cicely Forde, K.A. Ogier, Joseph Augustus, Mildred Almandoz and others, I concluded that there are five of our younger painters whose careers are worth watching: Louis Agostini, K.A. Ogier, Claire Bowring, Cicely Forde, and Henri Telfer.

Louis Agostini must be dealt with separately: his is an adventurous spirit seeking to assert itself in the experimental genres.

Of the other four, by far the most significant is Henri Telfer. An extremely young man, perhaps 19 or 20, already his work is stamped with a remarkable maturity. His number 14, ineptly titled as are all his canvases, is a portrait of the Society's maid in coloured chalks, with brick-brown predominating. The thing has character and the draughtsmanship is good.

But before passing on to Louis Agostini, a word must be said about Sheila Myer.

Her free and easy style, unhampered by any restraint is best illustrated in "The Carpenters", a semi-monochrome in brown with two beautifully balanced figures occupying most of the canvas area. Its one flaw is the patch of green foliage between the men: it fails to deepen the perspective.

I have left Louis Agostini for the last because he is that rare Trinidadian artist whose work is radically experimental.

When Braque, Picasso, and Schwitters around 1911 became Merzists[2] *épater les bourgeois* [sic], Agostini was born. A few years ago he became Schwitters' friend in England and was then introduced to the startling idiom called Collage. No finer exponent could he have met; for was it not Herbert Read,[3] the famous English art-critic, who pronounced Schwitters the greatest practitioner in collage abstractions?

Collage is abstractionism with waste. The artist, feeling his impotence to reproduce the texture and colour about him, takes the actual objects – a piece of confectionery paper, a bus-ticket, sand, anything – and fits them into a pattern aided by the accepted ingredients of ink, pencil or paint.

Agostini integrates his designs, his colours, his textures in dramatic motifs. I am curious to see if he will ever succeed in stamping upon his abstractions the West Indian timbre and tone.

Pure form: I have said on another occasion that it exalts to ecstasy. I say now that it is the quality that invests visual art with the power to evoke the aesthetic thrill.

Trinidad Guardian, 9 November 1947

NOTES

1. Kurt Schwitters (1887–1948) was a German experimental artist and poet, and inventor of MERZ activity, a method of painting by using collages. He was considered decadent by the authorities in Nazi Germany, and was forced to flee to the United Kingdom, which, after a period of internship there as an enemy alien, became his home.

2. Merzism or MERZ – activity was invented by Kurt Schwitters. He called his collages "Merz Pictures", and published a periodical, *Merz*, from 1923 to 1932. He explained the derivation of the term as follows: "This name was born out of one of my pictures: an image on which one reads the word MERZ, cut out of the KOMMERZ AND PRIVATBANK advertisement and stuck among abstract shapes."

3. Sir Herbert Edward Read (1893–1968) was a prolific and influential art historian and critic.

BASSO HOLDS A PLACE WITH BEST W.I. ARTISTS

Ever since the Trinidad Art Society's last exhibition at the Royal Victoria Institute, Leo Basso's single exhibit has been haunting me.

I recall the manner in which I came upon it. Shuffling around the room with my friend, Eric Cameron, I asked him after a while: "Is there nothing by Basso?" – when presto! There on the panel before us was a picture the identity of whose maker I at once recognised.

The exhibit in question was, as I have remarked in another article, not one of Basso's best. Its composition of cashew nuts and fish was far too symmetrical and obvious to merit much attention *qua* composition; but there, on the canvas, caught unmistakably in lines and colours, was the Basso style and quality.

His magical treatment of the objects, the askew plane of the canvas, the just-so-much distortion as to deprive the fish and cashew nuts of their cognitive element – in short, the picture's significant form bore his identifying touch as no other painting in the room indicated its author.

The question has kept flinging itself at me: what is there in Leo Basso's work that so uplifts me? Why does a Basso canvas move me to ecstasy while all the others, even though I admire excellent craftsmanship in so many of them, leave me standing on the wooden floor?

Now I know the answer. Now I know that Basso is the real McCoy, as our American friends say, a genuine artist. Although I have seen little of the work now being produced in Haiti and San Domingo, I'm sure that Basso is amongst the two or three greatest West Indian painters living today.

Unquestionably he is the finest artist Trinidad has ever created.

It now becomes imperative that I should attempt to define what I mean by a work of art, for upon that definition hinges my case for Leo Basso. My theory has matured only after many years of browsing around picture galleries, reading copiously on the subject, and practising one of the art forms over a period of time longer than half my life. But – and this is important – I am not alone in holding it.

Now a thing like a picture or a statue makes its impact upon the emotions as an object complete in itself: each can be seen as a whole and the reaction may be immediate. Not so with a novel or a symphony.

In the case of the picture the effect is instinctive, in the case of the novel deliberate and ratiocinative.

In the visual arts, it is the emotion and the emotion alone that counts. In literature certainly, and music not so certainly, the intellect is fused with the emotion in any evaluation.

If I delve a little more deeply, the evidence in support of my theory appears to strengthen. Is it possible for a novel to be called a work of art in the sense used in the expression's application to a painting? I say no, for a picture is a work of art when it moves the spectator to an aesthetic thrill, a wholly emotional experience, whereas great thinking without great feeling will often make great literature. It seems to me that our accepted nomenclature is not precise enough in its efforts to label manifestations of the creative urge, for I should prefer to confine the use of the expression "work of art" only to that congeries of things that evokes the aesthetic thrill.

I have often spoken of significant form or pure form, and I mean by that the synthesis of lines and colours, their relations and quantities and qualities, that is an end in itself, the essential reality, the God in everything. Speaking for myself, it is only in contemplation of pure form that I am transported into that state of exaltation that completely cuts me off from the concerns of life, and this I consider the quintessence of all human experience, far more profound and sublime than any that can be won from descriptions of facts and ideas.

I have said before that Basso is a primitive, and most people who know anything about art have been persuaded that primitive works move them most. The hypothesis is that the representative or cognitive element in any canvas is apt to divert the focus of the spectator from that quality in a work of art, its formal significance, that makes it such. In any case, the fact is that absence of representation and technical swagger, and the Post- Impressionists had little of the former and none of the latter, are of immense help to pure appreciation.

I do not suggest for a moment that the representative element, which has absolutely nothing to do with art, cannot be endowed with aesthetic significance; but what I do insist upon is that in a work of art we are concerned only with its aesthetic and not its cognitive value.

Now the Post-Impressionists – and to that family of rare human beings I unhesitatingly assign Basso – have invented a short-cut to our aesthetic emotions by employing distortions in order to frustrate human curiosity, and at the same time orient the spectator to the design. This is why the Cézanne-Matisse-Van Gogh method is more rewarding than abstractionism. In the use of this device Basso is as sensitive as instinct itself. Recall his three large still-lifes in the 1946 Exhibition: "Mango and Mammy Apple", "Banana Leaf", and "Sapodilla and Peame". All three are works of art and all three are Post-Impressionist in treatment.

I rest my case for Basso. As there are no hard-and-fast rules, no measuring rod by which a picture may be judged, the verdict must be a personal one. The essential is that the spectator must possess sensibility, for without it there can be no aesthetic experience.

He lives up Bank Hill, off the St. Francois Valley Road in Belmont. His shack, unpainted and dilapidated, looks across a valley to higher hills beyond. He does not need to see the higher hills for he has long since risen above them.

Trinidad Guardian Weekly, 30 November 1947

MASQUERADE

On Monday morning, February 9th, I shall wake to sounds that will take me back to the days when I was a boy. They'll be nostalgic sounds, sounds that will give me the excitement of reliving a quality of experience that is all of a piece with the child-like state.

It will be Carnival on that Monday morning and the sounds of "jouvert" will come like so many Peter Pans merrily tripping into my bedroom.

Many years have gone by since I was a boy, a number of them spent in foreign lands, but not all the influences of these sojourns abroad have in the slightest impaired the vital and tender memories of my early carnivals.

Now that I have arrived at a middle age that insists on keeping young, I know something of the history and composition of Carnival. This reminds me of Keats's lines in which the poet suggests that scientific knowledge of the rainbow tends to destroy for one the beauty of the rainbow.[1] Maybe that tragedy has fallen upon some of my fellowmen, though I strongly suspect that such men may never in the first place have been blessed with the gift of being spiritually uplifted at the sight of a rainbow. Speaking for myself, I must confess that whenever a thing moves me I am restless until I have, so to say, vivisected it and discovered how it works. True, this does not in any way affect its quality for stirring me, but it does help to appease my *amour propre*.

In these days of Freud, Jung and Adler,[2] I suppose it is only natural for me to say that Carnival for the Trinidadian is a sort of catharsis – and I fancy I know the reasons why.

We are a crown colony, and throughout our history we have been afforded no opportunity for running our own affairs. This has generated within us an inferiority complex, with its attendant frustrations and inhibitions. But if you have ever worn a mask you will at once understand the extravagant sense of freedom it can give to the timidest soul in Christendom. Why, I have seen a most sensitive man, bedevilled by a neurosis of abject inferiority, behave when masked like the boldest and brazenest of God's creatures on the streets of Port of Spain. Observing him in that mood, you would swear he was one of the town's hooligans.

Moreover, because the vast bulk of our people is pathetically poor, as the "natives" in most of the world's crown colonies are, the pomp and colour of Carnival grant them two glorious days of escape from the slime and sewers of their slums. Stick in hand, powder on face, any old pair of pants turned inside-out and festooned from the waist with strings of coloured ribbon, the porter forgets for forty-eight hours his malnourished child, and prances himself into believing that he is the happiest of mortals on earth.

What can be more stimulating to the out-of-work stevedore than to lead an army of Ju-Ju Warriors down Frederick Street to the pulsating, frenzied rhythm of a steelband? Carried back to atavistic days, he is once again the headman of his tribe, the rags of his real life cast aside. Instead, he plunges forward with dignity and power, revelling for once in a fleeting sense of authority and responsibility.

Watch that "doctor" with tailcoat verdigris'd from age and tall hat snatched from some rich man's garbage can playing and, what is more, believing himself to be a medical practitioner. Out roll the words, an amusing jargon of polysyl-lables with more meaning in them than the real man's existence as a street scavenger. At least, the miracle of Carnival has given him and the thousands of others disguised as tailors, sailors, constables and clowns a status and a stature they will never know this side the grave.

Why is it that only Venezuelans play the delightful role of "buroquite?" A friend of mine who has lived in the Basque country tells me that she once saw there at a festival dramatising indigenous dances the same type of hobby-horse dance. It is therefore obvious that the "buroquite" is of Spanish origin, as indeed is the word itself.

Alas, gone underground is "Dame Loraine!" I say alas because although, judged by bourgeois standards, an obscene barrackyard performance parodying the manners of the Courts of Louis Fourteenth and Fifteenth in the style of the Hogarth satires, it nevertheless bore traces of Negro improvisations that gave it value.

The "calinda," happily, is still with us in a modified form. Not danced as frequently as in the past, it can still occasionally be seen on the streets of Port of Spain during the two days of Carnival. A relic of stick-playing times when rival bands from Belmont and Newtown roamed the dark, deserted quarters of the city and fought it out against each other with "bois," bottles and stones, terrifying the populace, it has now become something respectable enough to suit the taste of the not-too-squeamish.

In those days, when "cannes bruilles" had already been put down by law and the authorities had decided that stick-playing was a menace to peaceful citizens, every band of whatever disguise had its "king" and "queen," both resplendent in feathers, beads, silks and satins. At least on the Monday and Tuesday of Carnival the washerwoman, who all the year round scrubbed and bleached her drab life away, could with head held high and eyes aflame with pride be a "queen" at the front of her band. And the carterman who week in, week out, month in, month out had sweated himself to a condition of muscle and bone with the lifting and handling of bags, boxes and bales, could on Carnival days be "king" to his "queen" and wear a crown on his head.

Speaking of stick-fighting, I am reminded of a good story my father is fond of telling. During a Carnival night in 1881 a bloody battle between two bands exploded immediately in front of his father's house. The police, with the intrepid Captain Baker in the forefront, were making desperate but losing attempts to subdue the law-breakers. My grandfather, from all accounts a handy man in an emergency, stood anxiously peering out through jalousies at the furious men thudding each other's skulls with poui sticks. Suddenly a bright idea seized him. Rushing to a drawer, he extracted from it a small round object encased in coloured paper, stole into the front garden, hid in a bush and, applying a lighted match to the object, hurled it into the air above the murderous mêlée of men. A terrific detonation cracked in the midst of the stick warriors and, before you could say "mocojumby", stick-fighters and police had vanished into the enveloping darkness.

Not so Captain Baker. He alone stood his ground, his frightened horse cavorting under him.

The next thing my grandfather saw was the Captain himself striding up to the bush in which he stooped concealed – as he thought. "Mr. Mendes," said the Captain in his brusque way, "I saw you throw that thing. I want to congratulate you for doing what the police couldn't do. Thanks!" – and off he strode to his horse tethered to a lamp-post in the street.

My grandfather had used an innocuous Madeira-made "torpedo" to quell an incipient riot!

The mere sound of the word "mocojumby" rekindles within me memories of the most celebrated stiltwalker of his day. We called him "Castlerose," why, I never knew. I was only six years old, but in my mind's eye I can see him now: a small black man, perhaps five foot three, a bald head. He may have been fifty. I knew him well because he was our neighbour's groom. Never have I seen stilts so tall, hat so decorated, stockings so bright, pants and jacket so bespattered with spangles. And dance! Why, "Castlerose" could play such choreographic tricks with his sticks that I blamed no one for believing that they were born with him – as I believed at the time. He once said to me: "I'se a small man, but mocojumby does make me feel jes' like a giant."

And there, in a nutshell, is one of the points I have been trying to make about Carnival in this piece.

Trinidad Guardian Weekly, 1 February 1948

NOTES

1.   "Lamia", pt. 2, 229–38.
2.   Sigmund Freud (1856–1939), Alfred Adler (1870–1937) and Carl Gustav Jung (1875–1961) conducted important research into the human unconscious self. Their differing approaches loom largely over twentieth-century thought, as well as literary and artistic practices.

HOLDER'S CREOLE EXTRAVAGANZA

Boscoe Holder is our wonder-boy, a sort of local Billy Rose.[1] Had he been born in the United States of America, he would undoubtedly have blossomed into a maker of stage or film spectacles, for his is the flair that needs for its amplest expression the large place, the large purse, the large population.

Think of it: his 1948 *Coloqué* (from the Spanish *collocar* meaning to mix) is the third in the series – and the first was produced in 1945 when Boscoe was only 22 years old!

I remember reading in one of the American slick magazines that Billy Rose had made his first fortune by the age of 25.

As it is, Boscoe lives with his parents in a small house on drab Richmond Street, but even into this limited space he manages to spill splashes of his flamboyant colours.

On the walls of the little drawing-room hang a few of his paintings – landscapes, seascapes, portraits, – and before you know how it has happened, you are transported to wooded hills and wide sea, and at one breathless moment find yourself gazing at the burnished beauty of creole coquette, all done in decorative patterns of colour.

It is obvious that the source of Boscoe's interest in the dance is his creative instinct, inherited from his maternal grandfather, who was of pure French descent. But his gift for expressing it in stylised colour-form undoubtedly stems, not only from his urge to create, but also from his sense of showmanship.

As Boscoe's extravaganza unevenly pirouetted and pranced its way on the Empire stage last Wednesday evening, you can imagine with what delight I perceived that a miracle was being performed, perhaps a small one, but nonetheless authentic.

Have you ever seen a particular artist's paintings come to life and begin to dance before your very eyes? Well, in a special sense this is exactly what happened last Wednesday evening. I know that Walt Disney, in his "Fantasia" and films in a similar genre, has done this time and again, but Boscoe took live human beings, put them upon a stage, and presto! The trick was turned.

Remember, of course, that his canvases, although related to things within our experience, are essentially dependent for their aesthetic evocations on colour forms. In them we recognise the tree, the hill, the valley, the man, the woman, but what makes them syntheses is the manner in which the canvas areas have been filled with colours, and the quantity and quality of each colour.

Specifically I mean that Boscoe has taken the colour-pattern from his pictures, placed them upon a stage, and animated them into thematic variations. In short, Boscoe's paintings and dance-expressions are of a piece. This is where he differs from our other dance-enthusiast, Beryl McBurnie, whose accent is on choreography above all else.

You will observe my use of the word "unevenly" in the opening sentence two or three paragraphs back. Taking the pot-pourri as a whole, I am sorry to say that it failed to come off. The irony is that it possessed all the nuances for crystallisation; but the show, from opening foot-beat to final colour flash, lacked coherence, lacked time-continuity, lacked form.

Form there was in each item of colour-dance, in some instances exquisite changes in colour-form, but this piecemeal approach aborted the embryonic whole. I must at once confess, however, that Boscoe Holder cannot be entirely blamed for fashioning an extravaganza out of material that could have been woven into a pattern of counterpoint and fugal responses, and the reason is obvious.

One of the most laborious and complicated jobs in stage experience is the production of a show similar in kind to the *Coloqué* of 1948. A large part of the burden of its success rests upon spectacle, the expression of colour and movement on a scale that can only be supported by a large place, a large purse, a large population.

Costumes are costly. Casting must be correct, décor daring, music mesmeric, lighting luscious. Moreover, the organisation needed to bring off the thing with éclat is fantastic, involving more managers than you can shake a stick at.

And think of the kind of stage that is a "must" in a production of this sort. Acoustics at the Empire just don't exist. Sitting near the front [as I was], it was pitiful watching the impish Gloria Jennings trying to put across the words of the ravishing "De Maroons da come here." Where the facilities lay at hand they were woefully inadequate – and in so many instances they were no nearer than New York.

What could you expect? Perhaps Boscoe could have improved on the pacing of the turns. An accelerated tempo would certainly have lent the show a suspicion of unity, of oneness. That he failed even here can be accounted for by his having to do, alone, more than was humanly possible.

I do not wonder that he gave the impression of being a frustrated Billy Rose all through his *Coloqué* of 1948.

Trinidad Guardian, 19 September 1948

NOTE

1.   William "Billy" Rose (1899–1966) was a celebrated American songwriter, impresario, and theatrical showman.

BERYL McBURNIE'S DANCE GROUP ARE
BALLERINAS OF THE CARIBBEAN

Of all creative West Indians, I can think of none who gives me greater pleasure to write about than Beryl McBurnie. For me there is something heroic about a young woman who put behind her the possibility of building up a lucrative reputation as a dancer in the Colossus of the North, to return to her native land in order to found a school whose purpose would be primarily to snatch from the grave our Caribbean folk dances.[1]

Against the heat of odds before which most of us would have melted like candle wax, Beryl has succeeded in gathering together a group of young men and women, inspiring them with her passion for the dance, synthesising them choreographically, and presenting them upon the boards in ballets forged on the anvil of her own flaming imagination.

Moreover, in an island where poverty is the lot of the vast majority of the inhabitants, and indifference and even hostility their attitude to most local artistic endeavours, Beryl has not only built her "Little Carib" theatre, but actually converted a large number of people to the belief that the task she has undertaken to perform is a worthy one.

I cannot help remembering that not so very long ago there were only a few of us who perceived the value of her work and honoured her for it. Today you have only to attend one of her shows at the "Little Carib" to observe the change that has taken place.

Now what is Beryl after in her ballets? Belaire, Bongo, Calenda, Limbo, Shango – all these dances and many others she has taken from their native habitat and given them form and substance on the local stage. But as I see it, her vocabulary of movement is a re-interpretation of the folk dance-steps of our islands, and a revolt against what has now jelled into the clichés of traditional ballet.

She has fused the many idioms of Caribbean folk dances in every one of her ballets so amply that it is possible to detect in each the Limbo, the Calenda, the Bongo, the Belaire. In short, Beryl has completely restated the purpose of our dances by sewing them together in patterns of her own.

Now I maintain that it takes talent of the highest order to perform the miracle of blending dance-dialects in such a fashion as to give the illusion that they were born that way. Even where she attempts to tell a story in the Maupassant[2] genre – beginning, middle, end – using the folk manner in her matter, the emphasis is on the purity of the dancing: *ars gratia artis*.[3]

I recognise, of course, the sociological content in many of her ballets, and I know Beryl well enough to feel that the conscious direction of her effort is towards this emphasis, but in spite of herself, she is first of all an artist – and then a commentator on the politics of our age.

Trinidad Sunday Guardian, 31 October 1948

NOTES

1. Beryl McBurnie had made a career as a dancer for herself in New York, under the name of "La Belle Rosette". See note 1 to "Art Society Exhibition Rich in High Quality Paintings", this volume.
2. The French author Guy de Maupassant (1850–93) was a prolific writer of short stories, not all of them as cut and dried as Mendes suggests here.
3. Art for Art's sake.

BERYL McBURNIE'S "TALKING DRUMS" A CARIB CLASSIC

Beryl McBurnie's dance show to celebrate the opening of her "Little Carib" last Thursday evening[1] set up a train of thoughts within me that I must express before coming to grips with the recital itself. Obviously, all these thoughts circled around the dance, and specifically the West Indian dance.

I remember Lincoln Kirstein, the famous American choreography critic,[2] once remarking to me that the American folk dances, and particularly the aboriginal Indian, had all but died out. As I sat in the "Little Carib" last Thursday evening watching the programme unfold, Kirstein's tragic comment came back to me.

It struck me as being ironical that while in a big, boisterous and creative country like the Unites States of America the native dance was passing into oblivion, here in a small island like Trinidad, just ripening to creative adolescence, a brilliant and successful effort was being made, not only to revive our folk dances, but to recreate them in new patterns and startling combinations.

Let us be frank and admit that up till Beryl's return to her native land a few years ago, the Belaire, the Bongo, the Calenda, and the Limbo, four of the most characteristic of the Trinidad folk dances, were on their last shaky legs.

As far as my own experience went, it was seldom that I could find young people performing any of them – and certainly the best and truest interpretations were being given by older folk in behind-God's-back spots of the island.

I see, of course, all the reasons why our dances were limping towards the grave, and would certainly have tumbled in and been buried, were it not for Beryl or someone else with her nervous energy and imagination.

Whereas in the years before the motor car and aeroplane young folk stayed at home, went to church, and settled themselves into tight communities that could do nothing but perpetuate the folk activities of their forefathers, today swift travel has shattered the old loyalties and created new ones.

Whereas in the days before the gramophone and radio the simple folk tunes, made at a time when sugar was king and the slaves sang in the hot fields to lighten their tasks, were passed from generation to generation, today we have become familiar with alien melodies and strange rhythms brought to us from the remotest corners of the earth.

To cap it all, we have only to recall the last two world wars, when men of all races were flung together in a holocaust of destruction that sent the survivors back to their homes with changed hearts and a clearer understanding of why the old order was giving place to the new.

But while a politico-economic dispensation which had tortured the human family since the end of feudal days on the twin racks of slum and war was undergoing violent change, it was necessary that men and women everywhere should hold on to those group activities that gave them a sense of security, a sense of belonging in a chaotic world.

Among these were the folk activities, the very substance of all art-expression, the reservoir from which the creative members of a people draw for giving an idiom to their art-forms. Particularly was it necessary to rescue the folk dances in our island, for always let it be borne in mind that the African spirit is best expressed in the dance.

I have said here and elsewhere that Beryl is restating the folk dances of the Caribbean area. Certainly this was brilliantly demonstrated on Thursday evening, in one instance with such éclat that on the spot I vowed it the finest piece of choreography she had so far composed. "Talking Drums"[3] she called it.

I am aware that many of those who attended the recital will be prepared to argue with me that "The Three Peasants" was even better. In a certain sense, yes. Let me explain.

In every art-expression there are two factors to consider: the manner and the matter, or how a work of art says what it has to say. In my view the emphasis in "The Three Peasants" lay upon the manner rather than the matter, whereas in "Talking Drums" Beryl accentuated the matter.

Now it is a habit of mine, where both are of the best, to regard matter as being more important to the needs of men and women – and this is why I choose "Talking Drums" as being the biggest dance-creation for which Beryl has so far been responsible.

In the case of "The Three Peasants" the choreography has been built around Ravel's "Pavane pour une infante défunte," a composition that is temperamentally foreign to the West Indian. Perhaps this is why the ballet emerges as pure patterns of movement, unrelated to our land or any other for that matter, though it does at fleeting moments articulate the lot of the West Indian peasant in idiosyncratic gesture.

The two Ector sisters and Cecile Maurice, three superb ballerinas who should hold their own in any part of the world, were as good as they could be.

On the other hand, the disparate parts of "Talking Drums" are held together by a recitative, uttered with impeccable taste by Melvina Scott, the beating of drums, and the singing by the dancers themselves of patois ditties.

The ballet opens with the slow Awasa, slides into the fast Seccate, maddens with the Pancou, slows down suddenly into the Limbo, speeds up again to the Bongo, rumbles with the staccato Macumba, swings gracefully with the Belaire, and finally exhausts itself in Shouters' convulsions.

For me the matter of the ballet embraced a large part of the history of our people in these parts – and in this fact lay its significance.

I cannot close without a word of praise for "Massala," a tour de force if ever there was one. Satirising an old theme, Ivan Harban gave a clever interpretation of an aged East Indian massala beater, and Barney Maurice, another of Beryl's most gifted ballerinas, a seductive performance of an East Indian girl dancing.

Alas, that I have no space left for writing of other excellences.

Trinidad Sunday Guardian, 28 November 1948

NOTES

1.   The official opening of the "Little Carib" took place on 25 November 1948. Paul Robeson (see following article) laid the corner-stone of the building.

2.   Lincoln Kirstein (1907–66) was a highly influential critic and writer on the Arts. With George Balanchine the choreographer, he founded The School of American Ballet, and subsequently, the New York City Ballet.

3.   A full description and explanation of "Talking Drums" is to be found in Molly Ahye, *Cradle of Caribbean Dance: Beryl McBurnie and the Little Carib Theatre* (Port of Spain: Heritage Cultures, 1983), 33.

ROBESON'S INNOCENT SIMPLICITY
WON HIM NUMEROUS FRIENDS

Paul Robeson, a great artist and a great man,[1] has come to our island and has gone.

For years we had been reading and hearing about him, about his singing in all the large cities of the world, about the throngs waiting to greet him everywhere he went, about his command performances before Royalty, about his concern over the sufferings of the poor and the work he was doing to change their lot, about his crusade against prejudice of every kind in his native land.

Over and over again we had listened to the sonorous organ of his voice on the gramophone and over the radio. We remember the stir of his Othello on the metropolitan stage.[2] And when, finally, we saw and heard him on the screen, the legend of the man had grown so massive that it seemed fantastic to hope that the man himself would ever step on our soil.

During the six short days of his stay with us he gave two formal recitals, sang spontaneously before a number of groups, rendered an open-air concert in Woodford Square for those who could not pay to hear him, attended a bewildering succession of parties, dinners, luncheons and civic receptions in his honour – but through them all he never forgot to smile, never lost his child-like simplicity, never failed to make ordinary folk comfortable and happy in his presence, and above all, never for a moment ceased to wonder at the adulation being given him by our people.

Burning with convictions, he could express them in undertones. Endowed with a body of majestic proportions, he could walk with humility and unaffected dignity. Possessing a huge head topped by a forehead of an Old Testament prophet, his eyes could light up with boyish joy. And what other man of his artistic stature have I ever met, who was more innocently generous with the priceless gifts of his labour and suffering?

Never shall I forget the evening of his first recital in Port-of-Spain.

I had met Paul Robeson while I lived in his country. I had heard him sing in Carnegie Hall and myself joined in the acclamations. But last Thursday evening was special for me.

His first group, sung with exquisite artistry, was received quietly, almost apathetically. It seemed as if the overcrowded house was expecting the giant on the stage to slip into the role of "Emperor Jones"[3] and roar and gesticulate. He did nothing of the kind. With his amazing restraint, the hallmark of the artist, with his outpouring of just so much as would precisely brim the vessel of each song, he disappointed them.

As he swung into the folk group, the voice mellowing as it warmed to the heart of effort, the audience lost its listlessness. Awake now, they were aware that something big was happening in their lives. Onwards from the "Hammer Song",[4] Robeson, with such control of his voice that he could modulate it to a bass diminuendo of pure tonal quality, dominated them and proceeded to touch the gamut of their emotions in Negro spiritual after Negro spiritual.

Then, having his listeners where he wanted them, the tense and taut state to which he had in a sort of crescendo brought them, the booming voice burst into Othello's soliloquy over Desdemona's murdered body.

That was something to remember. It left me limp with ecstasy, and the feeling that any man who can perform the miracle of generating in a vast audience of people mixed in race and beliefs a mood of oneness, of togetherness, can help lead the West Indian family into a better world.

Trinidad Guardian, 1 December 1948

NOTES

1.   The great black singer, actor and activist (1898–1976) travelled through the West Indies in 1948. See note 1 to "Beryl McBurnie's Talking Drums".
2.   Robeson had played Othello to Peggy Ashcroft's Desdemona in 1930, in England. He later reprised the role on Broadway from 1943 to 1945.
3.   The eponymous hero of Eugene O'Neill's play (1920).
4.   A gospel song.

McBURNIE'S ART SAID HONOURED WITH STAMP OF PUBLIC APPROVAL

It is many years now since I first saw a Beryl McBurnie dance recital, and I recall with some degree of pride the fact that my earliest impressions convinced me that the island possessed in Beryl McBurnie a creative creature of the rarest quality.

When so many others of the middle-class, persons who perhaps knew better, but who nonetheless timidly capitulated to the pressure of the herd's perverted sense of values, raised their eyes in horror at what they felt they must consider vulgar because it was native, a few of us stood up and stoutly defended the ethics and aesthetics of the movement labouring to be born in Beryl.

At that distant time, it seemed to us that the road ahead of this fiery young woman would sooner or later trip her into abandoning the hope of ever realising her dream. Did not the odds appear to be too heavily stacked against her?

Everywhere I went among my own people in those days, my task seemed to be to make them see that the only material that could be alchemised into West Indian art forms was the material indigenous to our islands: the folk songs, the folk stories, the folk tunes, the folk dances.

But they, alas, conditioned to accept the imported article as genuine and the local as spurious, could only look upon me as a queer, misguided fellow.

Now the wheel has turned full circle and what those of us, who from the commencement supported Beryl, said in and out of print, has been more than vindicated: it has been honoured with the stamp of respectability.

You have only to attend one of her shows to perceive how true this is, for in the audience – as racially and socially mixed an audience as you will find in any spot on earth – will be businessmen both big and small, Civil Service officials of high rank, lawyers, doctors, administrators, judges, editors, and even the "intellectuals" – although I must confess that I do not regard the last named as true representatives of the respectable classes.

Moreover, they go not only to see but to applaud, and more often than not to applaud enthusiastically. When the curtain rises in the "Little Carib", the theatre with the fantastic story and more than fantastic founder, and the Maurice sisters, the Ector twins, Harban and Borde swing into Confriari or Parang, and slide into Shango or Voodoo, you will observe Mr. and Mrs. Babbitt[1] clap as they have seldom clapped before.

I know that this is not what Beryl has struggled for, but it is significant. And more significant still is that on Saturday next His Majesty's representative in our island, Sir John Shaw, and his Lady, will be present at the "Little Carib".

Our Governor is known to be a man of understanding and sensibility. He will, I'm sure, wonder why Beryl's cultural movement was for so long ostracised by folk who ought by all the rules of the game to have acquired a taste for the decent and good things of our West Indian life.

Trinidad Sunday Guardian, 14 August 1949

NOTE

1.   From Sinclair Lewis's novel *Babbitt* (1922), here intended as an example of middle-class complacency.

GOVERNOR, LADY SHAW AT McBURNIE
SHOW FOR FIRST TIME

Dr. Eric Williams has given it as his opinion that the one apparent weakness in any McBurnie dance-recital is its episodic characteristic. I have myself thought so for a considerable time now, but recently, and particularly since last night's show, the idea has taken possession of me – and I pass it on for what it is worth – that the ballets performed in any single evening are to be viewed as parts of a whole, if a pattern of any kind is to be perceived.

It is obvious to me that Beryl has herself sensed this incompleteness in the forms of her individual pieces of choreography and is making a desperate attempt at remedying this by shifting the emphasis from the fragment to the whole, i.e. from the single ballet to the ballet-group, the device used being the narrator.

Let us for a moment consider an example from another mode of artistic expression – music. Take for instance the symphony. Such a work is usually divided into three or four main movements, each movement itself subdivided into clearly distinguishable motifs, each motif into phrases, and so on down the line to even smaller units. The movements are invariably differentiated by changes in tempo, which is only another way of saying: by emotion.

As the *élan vital*[1] of all art expression is almost entirely emotional in nature, it seems to me that the matching of moods is the synthesising agent in this context.

The paramount fact is that most of Beryl's dances are fundamentally of a piece in that they have their roots in the folk dances of the Caribbean islands. The dialect, the idiom, even the vocabulary of their movements are indisputably West Indian, and the manner in which Beryl has fused anecdote with dance tends to fortify their nativeness.

I am therefore convinced that it is possible to take any collection of McBurnie ballets staged in an evening and so arrange their sequence as to invest them with a façade of continuity and, what is so much more important, an aesthetic crystallisation.

If only she would alter the perspective of her approach, the task of building them up into a mature ballet composed of three or four "movements" should be simple for the founder of the "Little Carib". I know that she is fully aware of their homogeneity and how helpful this can be in the making of a work of art, but to attempt to give them continuity without form is not enough.

I applaud the idea of a narrator. My only wish is that all commentary and narration be done backstage and in as dispassionate a fashion as possible. As to form, I commend the structure of the symphony to her, and its reliance upon the matching of moods through tempo-changes for conferring upon it the distinction of being, though inexorably episodic, a work of art.

Trinidad Sunday Guardian, 21 August 1949

NOTE

1.   Vital impulse.

CRITIC ENTHUSIASTIC ABOUT
PERFORMANCE OF WHITEHALL PLAYERS

Seldom have I sat down to a task of reviewing with more enthusiasm than I now do, for last Wednesday evening I witnessed the Whitehall Players' two curtain-raisers, one competently presented and the other as finished and artistic a piece of work as I have come upon in travels abroad. In addition the "Romeo and Juliet" balcony scene was done with such finesse and tenderness as to confound the most exacting critic.

Indeed, this Shakespearean gem provided one of the surprises of the evening. I refer, of course, to Miss Barbara Assoon's Juliet. Errol John, who played Romeo with marvellous restraint and charm, we now know to be not only the island's finest actor, but a creature gifted amply enough to touch the sky of his profession. And mark my words, he will one day.

On the other hand, this was Miss Assoon's first appearance and, believe me, from the moment she uttered the opening exclamation: "Ah me!" I for one fell victim to her art and her physical loveliness.

Her voice and movements, tuned to the essential tones of some of the most beautiful lines in all poetry, cast a spell upon me, and by the sheer grace of her personality, she captured the ecstasy of the thing.

Heightening my enthusiasm for "The Tout" is the fact that it was composed by a Trinidadian, produced by the author, and acted by a cast of West Indians. All in all the half-hour play was so wholly satisfying that I am proud to share culture-patrimony with Errol John,[1] the young playwright and producer, and Stella Armorer, Leo Bennett, and Clayton Headley, the cast.

Between them, they deepened for me the meaning of the famous line about "A thing of beauty" written by the apothecary's boy.[2]

Make no mistake about it, "The Tout" as acted and produced last Wednesday evening would inspire any metropolitan audience and disarm the most vicious of critics. In other words, my claim for it is in the absolute, not the comparative sense.

Now, how can I best state my case with a thimbleful of words? I believe I effectively express what is paramount in my mind when I say that the quality of the production and acting was primitive. The very absence of tradition and technical training in the producer and the cast proved to be of immense advantage in this instance.

The play, let us remember, is a slum play about uncomplicated "uncivilised" folk. It is spoken in a dialect with a severely limited vocabulary, pivots around a chair-ridden character, and is pitted with long silences. Annie has no mind, Percy no conscience, old Muley only his deep, inarticulate love for Annie.

With an amazing economy of means and an understatement that was at moments skeletal, the actors stepped into their roles, and presto! "The Tout" burst into a living thing, burning with the conviction that Annie and Percy and Muley were caught up like flies in a web of tragedy.

Although one was aware all the time of the laborious work Miss Armorer must have crammed into the making of her interpretation, her simplicity gave the impression of a performance born painlessly. Her monotone, the way she moved, her rare gesticulations – all conspired to bring to each moment of her part a sense of fully experienced truth.

I shall not soon forget the penetrating pathos of the tunes she so plaintively hummed as she walked to what was, for "Gran' pa," her doom.

As I glance back, it seems a miracle that Mr. Bennett did not for even a split-second slip into the pit of melodrama. Muley was one of those odd roles most difficult to do well because so easy to over-act, but Mr. Bennett's taste was impeccable, his licence pitched in just the right range.

Finally, I doubt that Mr. Headley's Percy could have been played better.

Trinidad Sunday Guardian, 4 September 1949

NOTES

1.   Errol John's (1924–88) play *The Tout* was not published until 1966, when it was brought out by the University of the West Indies Extra-Mural Department, Port of Spain, Trinidad.
2.   John Keats, in "Endymion".

ART IS ABSTRACTION NOT REPRESENTATION

The sixth annual exhibition of the Trinidad Art Society opened yesterday afternoon at the Royal Victoria Institute, and I believe I am now given the right to say that the society has come of age. A life span of six years for an institution of this kind is a long one. Had the society never come into being it would have been impossible for us to have realised what talent, for the need of communal support, was running to waste in the island.

Now we know what we have gained, and it is my conviction that the ferment stirring our folk so feverishly of recent years in the field of painting has largely been generated by the influence of the Trinidad Art Society.

To herald the importance of the Society attaining its majority, the current exhibition is one of the largest ever presented and, as far as I am concerned, one of the two most exciting.

Many favourites are here again: Geoffrey Holder,[1] Carlisle Chang,[2] Louis Agostini, Coral Kellman, Sybil Atteck,[3] Mildred Almandoz, Claire Bowring, Althea McNish, Grace Collens, the American émigré [Vivian Lush] Piccirilli, Alladin, and Cicely Forde.

Notable absentees are Leo Basso, Boscoe Holder, Eric Cameron and Codallo. Sheila Myer, the English painter domiciled in Tobago, is at present exhibiting in a London gallery. Among the new contributors are Marguerite Wyke and Joseph Cromwell.

It is because of Cromwell that I consider this exhibition one of the two most exciting seen in Trinidad – the other being, of course, the occasion of the first presentation of Basso's work to the public. But of Cromwell more anon.

By and large I should say that the current show reveals a technical advance over previous ones, but this is saying very little indeed when I must hasten to add that from the creative point of view, most of the pictures are dull. As a rule where craftsmanship is good, you'll find uninspiring confusions [*sic*] of Nature's many forms presented with ardent fidelity to what the eye has seen.

In the painting sense, however, Art is abstraction, not representation. The individual born with the afflatus will take the unrelated and unaesthetically synthesised forms in Nature, sift and select them, and finally, with line, composition and colour, rearrange the selections and build them into a work that may come off. And even if it doesn't, then at least the imagination has been used in choosing the parts and fashioning them into a whole.

In other words, whether a work of art or not, the canvas has been *created*, not just painted.

Let me remind you of what Max Beckmann[4] wrote in one of his letters to a friend: "Learn the forms of nature by heart so you can use them like the musical notes of a composition . . . Nature is a wonderful chaos to be put into order and completed . . . The will to form carries in itself one part of the salvation for which you are seeking."

The very best craftsmanship without imagination is as nothing to me when hung beside a canvas born of vision but clothed in ragged technique. As an experiment, I should like to see an exhibition of gifted children's paintings in our town just now. It would be interesting to compare them with the canvases in the Royal Victoria Institute, for it is part of my creed that the artist's vision is intimately related to the child's.

Fortunately for my own beliefs, the exhibition illustrates the extreme of abstractionism at one end, the extreme of academism at the other end, and in the middle the impressionist's conception of the world of reality – and I use all the technical words in the loosest manner possible.

Louis Agostini is, of course, the iconoclast, Mildred Almandoz and Grace Collens apt representatives of the traditional type, and Joseph Cromwell and Geoffrey Holder exciting exponents of the style that can move me most profoundly.

I have come to the conclusion that I am more often than not insensitive to abstractionism because its forms can seldom be associated with anything in my experience. I cannot recognise them as belonging to the familiar, so I reject them as strange and even alien.

Agostini's *Bird* and *Glass*, however, are charming examples of his less esoteric work. I vaguely apprehend the bird and as vaguely the glass – and the forms in both pictures are immediately revealed as being no less pure than if there were nothing with which to identify them. One touch of nature . . .

When it comes to the conventional canvas, examples of which are everywhere in the Institute, the less I say the better. Perhaps the fault is mine, so I'll leave it at that.

Joseph Cromwell is only 20 years old, and this is his first public appearance. He started painting in earnest one year ago and has so far done few things, but if you are at all blessed with the instinct for perceiving beauty, then you will at once recognise in three of his canvases the quality that puts me on tiptoe.

His technique is naturally crude, but how bold his imagination, how sure his sense of form. There is much in him that reminds me of Basso: both are primitives and both *create*.

It is a happy augury for Trinidad that a few of her citizens paint not only with their hands, but also with their instincts.

Trinidad Sunday Guardian, 6 November 1949

NOTES

1. Geoffrey Holder, brother of Boscoe, was born in 1930. Multi-talented, he has been actor, dancer, choreographer and painter.

2. Carlisle Chang (1921–2001), was also a man of many talents. He painted in water colours, designed theatre sets and costumes for Carnival, and was sculptor and photographer. He received his early training from Sybil Atteck and Mendes's friend Amy Leong Pang of the Society of Trinidad's Independents.

3. Sybil Atteck (1911–75) is today regarded as one of Trinidad's most important early-twentieth-century artists. She studied in the United States under Max Beckmann, the German expressionist painter, and helped to found the Trinidad Art Society, established in 1943.

4. Max Beckmann (1884–1950), a German artist, was considered degenerate by the Nazi authorities, and like Kurt Schwitters had to leave Germany, ending up in the United States, where he wielded considerable influence over young American painters. In addition to painting, he was draftsman, printmaker, sculptor, and writer. The letter which Mendes cites may have been from a 1948 collection *Letters to a Woman Painter*.

ON THE PRE-ATOMIC GENTLEMAN

I should hate to be a gentleman in the Victorian sense: surely this is only another way of saying I should hate to be a gentleman in the middle class sense. Perhaps my readers will at once accuse me of not wanting to be a gentleman of any kind. It all depends.

The question that arises is obviously one of definition: what do we mean by the word "gentleman"? I am not now thinking of what the dictionaries say. I am thinking of what custom and usage have ordained; I am thinking of the spirit with which the word has been animated.

That until recently it possessed an aura that was vague and amorphous few can deny. It is only now that we have descended one peak of human history, traversed a wide and riven valley, and climbed some distance up the slope of a new peak, that we are in a position to obtain, so to speak, a panoramic view of the word and its meaning. It so often happens that the backward glance illuminates what was dark before, as it does in this case. I am sorry to say that what is revealed is not pretty. To the contrary: it might be a picture painted by Salvador Dali[1] in one of his most percipient moods.

Who, for instance, will have the temerity to doubt that of all the ingredients that went into the making of the pre-atomic gentleman, hypocrisy was as important as any? It just couldn't be helped. During the period of the last peak scaled by the human family, the "free enterprise" idea enjoyed its heyday and men devoted themselves to its exploitation. Hand in hand with this free-for-all-and-the-devil-take-the-hindmost went the opening up of unexplored lands which could supply raw materials extracted at slum-wages, and the creating of colonial markets that could re-absorb these materials in the shape of finished goods at prices amply profitable to the distant manufacturer. Further, as time passed, the machinery of imperialist rule was so perfected as to make it extremely difficult for the process of manufacture to be practised in the raw-material colonies.

Looked at from any point of view, this set-up was alien to the decalogue upon which, it was averred, western civilisation was founded. That the ruling classes were aware of this becomes evident when we remember the invention of two things for concealing from the subject races the immoral nature of a dispensation that gave unbridled economic power to the few over the many. I refer, of course, to the missionary and the gentleman.

The success of this twin invention was fantastic – while it lasted. True, although neither the mission of the one nor the gentleness of the other could ameliorate the physical anguish of human beings toiling in a state of servitude, nonetheless it was simple for the craft of both, practised as it was over ignorant and unsuspecting children of nature, to persuade them into believing that the author of all their woes and misfortunes was none other than that notorious gentleman popularly known as the devil. This soothed the Rhodes[2] conscience and threw dust into Uncle Tom's[3] eyes.

The point I am trying to make is that hypocrisy and dishonesty are absolutes and cannot be changed by appearances. On the other hand, our middle class values are based largely on things like dress, manners, speech, and so on. It thus became imperative for a man, no matter what quality of spirit was lodged in his frame, to conform to the outward pattern before he could hope to be accepted as a gentleman. And the frequent result of this was that men who believed in adding to the sum of their own comfort by denying it to as many of their fellowmen as possible, were not only taken for gentlemen, but treated as gentlemen. As the system was responsible for this, a change in the evaluation of the gentleman had to wait upon a change in the system itself.

I consider Mr. Winston Churchill[4] a classic example of the pre-atomic gentleman. Mr. Churchill is an avowed believer in the imperialist idea. The freedom that he so vociferously and mellifluously demands for himself and his class abroad and for himself and his own people at home, he is constitutionally incapable of according the subjects of his empire. In fact, that he regards them as a lesser breed is confirmed by many of his utterances. For instance, he once referred to Gandhi,[5] the spiritual shepherd of ten times the millions of souls crowding Mr. Churchill's "moated isle",[6] as "an Indian fakir." On another occasion, in fierce argument with Mr. Henry Wallace[7] over the British Empire, he angrily turned on the ex-Vice President of the United States with: "I am a painter and I know if you mix the colours all you get is a dirty brown." Against this, spoken in private debate, recall Mr. Churchill's public speeches with their rolling periods and resounding rhetoric that do nothing but wrap in purple any meaning he deems it indiscreet to express clearly and unequivocally. The language is the quintessence of the pre-atomic gentleman's mind and spirit.

By chance recently I read two books of speeches one after the other, the first by Mr. Churchill, the second by Mr. Stalin.[8] It was a most enlightening experience and I recommend it as an experiment. You may think what you like about Lenin's[9] successor, but in this collection of his public utterances I discovered a simple and direct style that stated facts and opinions with no ambiguity, no fumbling. The language is the quintessence of the atomic-age gentleman's mind and spirit.

Unfortunately for tragic and dangerous anachronisms like Mr. Winston Churchill, and most happily for the rest of mankind, time has changed, and with it ideas and values. Recently Mr. Henry Wallace, whom I regard as one of the best examples of the atomic-age gentleman, said that this was the common man's century. Scorched in the fires of two world wars, ravaged by the cancer of a world depression, and all within the span of a single generation, human beings have emerged with a clearer understanding of the causes of their misery. And among the things they have learnt is that, in some subtle way or the other, the pre-atomic gentleman was in part accountable.

And so as always the old is giving way to the new. Dress and manners and speech are no longer the hallmarks of the gentleman. Instead they have become the discredited symbols of an age that used them largely for base purposes. They are now seen for what they were: sweet means to vile ends. Now we demand something more solid, even in poor dress; something more vital, even with rude manners; above all, something more Christ-like, even in crude speech. Surging up from the bottom, as they were bound to sooner or later, is a vast mass of human beings who have for too long borne the burden of the world's work without terrestrial reward. One by one these millions of awakened citizens are knocking down, like ninepins, the Victorian gentlemen and the gentlemen of all the other Victorias. For them a new dawn is rolling up from the east, a dawn that promises, in brightening the lives of the great majority of men, women and children everywhere, to brighten in the end the life of the whole human family. In this apocalypse I have my faith.

Now you know why I should hate to be a gentleman in the Victorian or middle-class sense. On second thoughts, I am not so sure that I like the sound of the word wedded to any qualification, and I am fast drawing to the conclusion that it would be wisest and best after all to be just simply a man who believes that the wealthy few and the poor many can coexist only in a world of slums, ignorance and war. It is up to those of us who so believe to use every weapon in our armoury to abolish these abominations, and to build in their place a society that shall own everything collectively and yet be individually rich in the fruits of the earth. It can be done.

NOTES

1.   The Spanish Catalan Surrealist painter (1904–89). The "percipient mood" here is probably one of nightmare.

2.   Cecil Rhodes (1853–1902) was born in England, but is particularly associated with colonial expansion in Southern Africa. He was both businessman and politician, and believed firmly in the ideal of empire. He is especially famous for establishing the Rhodes Trust, which sends deserving students from former British colonies to Oxford University every year.

3.   The original Uncle Tom was the gentle, decent and heroic slave, hero of Harriet Beecher Stowe's anti-slavery novel *Uncle Tom's Cabin* (1852). As a term used pejoratively by Mendes, and even today, it implies passivity bordering on compliance on the part of a black man towards a white oppressor.

4.   Sir Winston Leonard Spencer Churchill (1874–1965), noted statesman and orator, and prime minister of Britain during the war years of 1939–45. Mendes's revisionist perception is particularly interesting, coming as it does within two or three years of the end of the Second World War.

5.   Mohandas Karamchand Gandhi (1869–1948), the revered "Mahatma", who led India to independence from Britain in 1947. He pioneered resistance to tyranny through civil disobedience, and was an advocate of non-violence.

6.   "moated isle". Mendes may have had in mind "this scepter'd isle" from John of Gaunt's patriotic speech in Shakespeare's *Richard II*, 2.1.

7.   Henry Agard Wallace (1888–1965) was the thirty-third vice president of the United States (1941–45). He was secretary of agriculture from 1933 to 1940 during F.D. Roosevelt's tenure as president, the period when Alfred Mendes was living in New York City. His liberal views, attempts to improve the lot of the "common man", and campaign against segregation in the South, certainly qualify him for Mendes's ideal "atomic-age gentleman".

8.   Joseph Stalin (1878–1953), general secretary of the Communist Party of the Soviet

Union's Central Committee from 1922 until his death in 1953. After the death of Lenin (n9, below) he became leader of the Soviet Union.

9.   Vladimir Ilyich Lenin (1870–1924) was the leader of the Bolsheviks in the October Revolution of 1917, and first head of state of the Soviet Union. He gave his name to Leninism, the Russian application of the tenets of Karl Marx.

THE MAN, HIS LAND AND HIS CULTURE

The Man, his Land, and his Culture – yes, this is indeed the subject of this evening's discussion. Having regard to the fact that my good friend Beryl is responsible for it, I am not surprised that we have been set a task that requires a year instead of an hour if it is to be adequately performed. However, we all know our Beryl. We all know that because she possesses a measure of energy that is rarely given any one mortal, she assumes that we too have been similarly endowed. I for one have not been; and if it were anyone else who had asked me to join in undertaking this impossible task I would certainly have declined.

But what could I do with Beryl but consent? I must confess that even against the average woman, as my wife so well knows, my weapons of resistance are few and futile; where then am I against an irresistible woman? And I am sure that my canonical friend, Max Farquhar, my extremely timid brother, Charles Espinet, my dashing compatriot, Jack Kelshall, and my nimble-minded confrère, Hugh Wooding,[1] will all agree with me when I say that Beryl is indeed an irresistible woman. Obviously they already know it to their cost, for are they not on the same platform with me this evening to discuss the same mighty subject in such mouse time?

I can only hope that Beryl will not at any time approach any of us with a request different in nature from the one resulting in this evening's function, for let her bear in mind that Max is a parson and as such fearful of the hereafter; Charles a properly married man and as such intent upon preserving his domestic bliss; Jack a politician and as such pure in spirit; Hugh a brilliant lawyer and as such respectful of respectability; and I a weak little man with not enough principle to resist the irresistible.

I mean, as you have no doubt guessed, that I hope Beryl will never request any or all of us to return to this platform of the "Little Carib" for the purpose of preaching any subversive doctrine like socialism or communism, even though they be firmly built upon the Sermon on the Mount.

Here then are we all – Hugh, Jack, Max, Charles and I, and the first item in the title of this evening's discussion is The Man. Although I pride myself upon knowing Beryl well, I am not so sure that I know what she means by The Man. Does she mean *Ecce Homo* – the ideal man – or does she just simply mean The West Indian Man? If the former, then outside of Marx, Christ, and Lenin – you will observe the order in which I mention them – she will find him in no city, town, village or hamlet of this earth – unless it be the jungle where it is said only savages live. If, however, she means the latter, that is, The West Indian Man, then make your choice amongst us five specimens of the species. Here we are: the confused Canon, the loquacious Lawyer, the peripatetic Politician, the jousting Journalist, and the retired Writer.

I warn you, however, that Beryl is playing a trick upon you by limiting you from a certain angle in your choice of The West Indian Man. Why has she not filed alongside of us on this platform an Edward Lai Fook and a Chanka Maharaj – or, if you prefer it, a Ranjit Kumar?[2] How truly West Indian can we possibly be without the Far East? For what we must remember is that our racial destiny is a mixture from all points of the compass and all degrees of the thermometer – not to speak of the whole gamut of moral qualities from saint to sinner, as is so amply and magnificently represented by us five on this platform at this moment. Which the saint? You ask. By his collar shall ye know him! Which the sinner? Here I hesitate, and in my hesitation I leave the lawyer with his nimble mind to judge, realising well that if even he must pass sentence upon himself, he will do so without squirm or squint.

So far, so good – with the good only so far true. For though we five are as representative as can be of certain West Indian men, and if the Far East had been included, as honest and full a racial representation as may be demanded by The West Indian Man, yet I submit that the parson, the journalist, the barrister, the politician and the author are woefully unrepresentative of The West Indian Man in his class architecture.

Look well at us, and you will see what there is for all to see. You will see that although we vary in ethnic appearance, and so far partially represent the West Indian Man, yet we are indubitably of one class. Of the group here, in respect of occupation, which is a facet of the class structure of our society, it is possible for only one of us five to be a member of that vast majority class, and that one is the politician.

But I ask you, is Jack a member of the working class? On the contrary, we know him to be in his appetites, habits and personal standards as bourgeois as any parson, as respectable as any lawyer, as domesticated (within limits) as any journalist, and only in ideas as radical as any writer – who is in turn, in this instance, radical in comfortably cushioned seats.

Well then, although I will not go so far as to suggest that we are all five of us gentlemen, I do aver that we are all five of the bourgeois stratum of society. And in saying this, although it may appear to you to be a contradiction in terms, I hasten to assure you that it is not at all necessary for the West Indian Man, or for that matter any man in the civilised world, to be a gentleman before he can be regarded as belonging to the bourgeois class. Indeed, there is no class in our society that can boast a lesser number of gentlemen, in my definition of the word, than the middle or bourgeois class. So that if we agree to assume that two of the five of us are gentlemen, in my meaning of the word, of course, then the proportion of gentlemen represented in this little bourgeois colony of five, that is in turn supposed to be representative of the West Indian Man, on this platform at this moment, is most appreciably high, and should satisfy the *amour propre* of the most exacting Victorian lady or Edwardian gentleman in this audience. But satisfying such anachronisms has never been the business of science and truth, so again we see how unrepresentative we are in a most important respect.

We have admitted that the working class man, and in that phrase I include both town worker and peasant, is not represented on this platform. I believe I am on fairly safe ground when I say that The West Indian Man is at least ninety-five per cent worker and certainly no more than one per cent parson, lawyer, journalist, politician and writer all rolled into one. So that, in a most vital sense, we five are as representative of The West Indian Man as most of the organised religions are of Christ's basic teachings. That is, one per cent.

Not a happy thought.

There is, I feel, no necessity for me to tell you that our peasants and town workers are as poor as church mice, as are the natives in all Crown Colonies, but I tell it this evening because our subject for discussion is The West Indian Man, his Land, and his Culture. This is where I must refer you back to the remark I made a little earlier about the preaching of subversive doctrines.

I know how difficult it has always been, I know how difficult it is, I know how difficult it will always be, for the parson, the politician, the lawyer, the journalist and the writer, privileged professions all in our dispensation, to accept the teachings of Christ where those teachings, if put into practice, will have to destroy privilege and discrimination before making us brothers in the best and wisest sense of the word: brothers in food, brothers in clothes, brothers in shelter, brothers in education, brothers in opportunity, yea, and even brothers in liberty and freedom. I know how difficult it is for the human being to accept change where change means a sacrifice of his luxuries and even his surplus necessities. I know how difficult it is for the vast majority of us to accept, not only as the most healthy and ideal of all arrangements of human affairs, but also as a practicable dispensation, the brotherhood of man in all the physical and spiritual needs of men, and this in full recognition of the fact that the good and bad genes are unequally divided up amongst the member of the human family. I know all this, but it does not alter the fact that we are, through blood and sweat and tears, implacably and inexorably moving towards change simply because what we have is all too imperfect and unchristian, and the bad must give place to the better, and finally, the better to the best. It is the law of God that a system that gives lavishly to the few without rhyme or reason and heaps misery and suffering upon countless millions, dooming them even before birth to the filth and squalor of civilised slums, is a system that is itself doomed.

For months now through press and radio we have been told again and again and again and again *ad nauseam* about democracy in the United States, about democracy in Britain, democracy in France and Italy, and all the rest of the democracies. Methinks they do protest too much. All that I know is that where there is poverty, where there are slums in which babies are born and bred to be gangsters, thieves and prostitutes later in life, where there is the monstrous thing called race prejudice, where depression follows boom in cyclic repetition, where fear and insecurity dog the miserable steps of millions of human beings – all that I know is that where there are these things, there is indeed no democracy.

The West Indian Man and his Land. What part of the land can Adolphus the carterman have any interest in, let alone own? The West Indian Man and his Culture. What can Mamitz, the washerwoman, living in the barrack-yard with her malnourished children, know of her culture when she is probably illiterate, and if not, then made incapable by her slum upbringing to understand anything of her culture? And bear this in mind, for it is important to you in the saving of your own soul: the Adolphuses and Mamitzes make up the vast bulk of The West Indian Man.

It cannot be otherwise, and never will be otherwise, until my friend Max loses his dread of the hereafter. Until my friend Charles ceases to be so intent upon preserving his domestic bliss. Until my friend Jack changes his habits and personal standards. Until my friend Hugh refuses to have any respect for middle class respectability. And finally, until I am willing to walk hand in hand down the flaming streets with my radical ideas.

NOTES

1. Canon Max Farquhar wrote a column for the *Sunday Guardian:* "Candid Comments". Charles Espinet, also a journalist, had an interest in Trinidad's music. Jack Kelshall founded the West Indian National Party in 1942. He later led the United Front, a merger of the West Indian National Party, the Indian National Council, and the Negro Welfare Association when it contested the first general election in 1946. Hugh Wooding, later Sir Hugh Wooding, was to have an illustrious career as a distinguished barrister, mayor of Port of Spain, chief justice, and privy councillor. He became chancellor of the University of the West Indies in 1971, and gave his name to the Hugh Wooding Law School in Trinidad.

2. Politicians of the 1940s. Edward Lai Fook was a successful solicitor and Port of Spain city councillor. Chandericker "Chanka" Maharaj, a former wrestling champion, won a seat on the Road Board of St Ann's and Diego Martin Ward Union in 1940. Ranjit Kumar was a civil engineer who ran as an independent candidate in the City Council election in 1943, and won.

ALL MY SONS

Parents Can Be People, by Dorothy Baruch,[1] although not well known, is a good book. It flatters me to say so because many of the ideas expressed in this talk, which was written before reading *Parents Can Be People,* appear in the book. In any case, I confess that books of all kinds have played a part in shaping my attitude towards my fellowmen, and certainly towards children.

I have been married three times. I have had three children, all boys. My first child was born when I was twenty years old, my other two after I had passed forty. I say this because I wish to convince you, if not myself, that not only have I had sufficient experience to talk about children, but also that my two qualities of experience in fatherhood, first as a young father, then as a middle-aged father, should have helped in deepening my understanding of children.

I ask you to forgive me if I make this talk a very personal one. "The child is father to the man"[2] said the poet Wordsworth, and I can assure you that just as my own childhood helped to fashion, in both good and evil, the man I now am, so have my children in turn added to the substance of my own adulthood. In other words, genes are not the whole story.

In the matter of bringing up one's children, it is ridiculous to judge of success or failure until one defines what one means by these words in the present context. The matter grows more complicated when we remind ourselves that standards of value differ amongst races, classes, and even individuals.

Perhaps I can best give my own definition by telling you what I most wished my children to be. Please bear in mind, however, that the kind men I hoped my children to be has been closely associated with the fact that they were first of all born into a world of violent change, and secondly, in an island of sharply contrasting races and cultures. If they were destined to live the greater part of their lives in Trinidad, and this I accepted as the strongest of all probabilities

– then how best could they be conditioned for a proper adjustment when the time came for making that adjustment?

But even in the larger world of men the same question arises in regard to the training of children, for surely we have come to the point in our development as a human family where we are world citizens, with obligations and responsibilities, not alone to our fellow-islanders, but, just as importantly, our human brothers everywhere. In deciding then that my first duty to my children resided in teaching them, as best I could, how to live in an island in the throes of change and inhabited by folk of all colours, classes and creeds, I was indeed attempting to prepare them for that *One World* of which Wendell Wilkie[3] speaks in his book, and that Commonwealth of Nations advocated By Clarence Streit in his book *Union Now*.[4]

Now in applying myself to this task I disregarded, perhaps involuntarily, any question of a future for my children that would ensure their economic security. I suppose this is so because in me the acquisitive instinct is weak. Instead, I have sought to make them good brothers, not in the narrow sense of good brothers to each other (for they fight like the very devil) but in the broad sense of good brothers to all men everywhere. This means that I should like to see them grow into men who will put public service before private gain; men who will recognise that the states of contentment and well-being are, like peace, indivisible; men who will perceive that where so many babies are born in slums, it is wise and right to make personal sacrifices in order to help in creating a truly democratic world.

It makes me happy to know that my first son, now a man, is like this. In the popular meaning of the word, I have not been successful with him. He is poor, he does not respect respectability, he refuses to conform – and all because he has dedicated his life, in his small way, to making this unhappy world a more decent home for the whole human family.

I sometimes think that the greatest stumbling block to peace is by nature economic. After all, in the last analysis a peaceful world is founded upon good and friendly relations between nation and nation, race and race, person and person. Anything that tends to harm these relationships will sooner or later generate fear, suspicion and hate. And often in the past, all too often, war has ensued.

Now it seems to me that the economic structure of our society is not conducive to peace, and without peace human beings cease to have been made in the image of God. I do not say that economics tells the whole story amongst men, but I do suggest that marauding capital, uncontrolled world markets, cartels and big business are harmful to the cause of peace. And I say with conviction that the fact that a man who owns land or factory is in a position to make unhappy so many other men by exploitation of their energies, is a grave danger to the cause of peace. You may not like Communism, but certainly Karl Marx in his book *Das Kapital*[5] exposed all these flaws in our system a long time ago. And I know of dozens of books written by men who harboured no sympathy for Socialism that have pointed accusing fingers at these same defects.

Ever since I became a man I have tested my fellowmen by the manner in which they behave towards those over whom they hold economic control. I have time and again observed women of the best local families, in the presence of their children, treat domestic servants as they would hesitate to treat a dog that had strayed into the yard. For years the psychologists have been telling us of how much happens to the child that later expresses itself in the man. Read Sigmund Freud's popular exposition of the subject in his book called *Psycho-Analysis*[6] and you will understand. In the home the behaviour of parents towards their servants is of profound importance in shaping the child's future. If we believe in the concept of democracy and the teachings of Jesus Christ, we must know that being vicious, in the presence of our children, towards fellow human beings who are in our employ, is to ensure sowing the seed for the growth of future fascist gauleiters[7] in our own children.

Another of my concerns as a father is that my children should grow into men with no race prejudice. It is a truism to say that the world is contracting. More and more we are becoming inter and intra dependent. Our world family is composed of many races, many skin colours. The imperative need is to learn now, at this very moment, that if we do not live together in friendliness and understanding we shall, as sure as God made little apples, continue to die together in wars of ever-increasing savagery. As Henry Wallace says in his book: "Life in One World or Death in many compartments."

The monstrous thing called race prejudice is more often than not put into the child's heart by the parents in the home. In turn, these infected children go into the schools and inject the virus into others who happen to be uncontaminated.

I am not in the least interested in the complexion of any of my children's friends, nor in the class from which they come. All are welcome to my home as long as my children wish to bring them in. And believe me, just as I have found some very fine slum boys amongst my children's friends, so have I found some very vicious middle-class ones.

> I was at Franklin Roosevelt's side
> Just a while before he died.
> He said: One world must come out of World War II
> Yankee, Russian, white or tan
> Lord, a man is just a man
> We're all brothers and we are only passing through.[8]

There has just been published in America an important book called *Sexual Behaviour in the Human Male* written by Kinsey, Pomeroy and Martin.[9] Much of the volume is devoted to the sex habits of pre-adolescents, and the revelations have upset many old wives' tales. I am aware that most parents look upon this secret aspect of their children's lives with deep concern and neurotic fear. Kinsey and his co-authors reveal that the number of sex-outlets used by children, their frequencies and incidences, are much higher than was previously thought, and that it is all perfectly normal and healthy. Speaking for myself, I have always been honest with my children on this subject, for I know that their curiosity about it can be easily satisfied unhealthily outside the home. Let us always remember that the Hitlers and misfits have frequently been helped to develop as they have because of an inhibited sex environment in pre-adolescent years.

I have called this talk "All My Sons"[10] after the play of the same name. Those of you who saw the film adaptation will remember the moment when the father, in an attempt to defend himself against bitter accusations flung at him by the son, cries: "All my life has been spent for the benefit of my own little family." Therein lay his tragedy.

No man's family is wholly his own, and all men share in the fortunes of all families on earth. All men's sons are my sons, and my sons are all men's sons. The acceptance of this is necessary to the making of a better world. It is up to us parents so to teach our children that they in turn will be parents who perceive and embrace this Christ-like truth.

NOTES

1. Dorothy Baruch (1899–1962) was an American writer, educator and psychologist who worked hard to bring about greater understanding between parents and children of all backgrounds. *Parents Can Be People* was published in 1944.
2. In "The Rainbow".
3. Wendell Wilkie (1892–1944), a Democrat who crossed the floor, contested the 1940 presidential election on a Republican ticket, and lost to F.D. Roosevelt. His book, *One World* (1943), is a document of meetings with heads of state, commanding officers and ordinary citizens in Allied countries during the years of the Second World War. It discusses the need for some form of world government and pleads for an international peacekeeping force.
4. Clarence Streit, the New York Times correspondent at the League of Nations, published *Union Now* in 1939. It proposed a federal union of leading democracies to help promote democracy in totalitarian régimes, and thus forestall future conflicts.
5. Published in 1867.
6. *An Outline of Psycho-Analysis* was published in 1940.
7. A gauleiter was a district political leader in Nazi Germany.
8. The final verse of a song, "Passing Through", one of the songs used on Henry Wallace's campaign in the 1948 US presidential election, as a candidate for the Progressive Party. Wallace was unsuccessful.
9. The first of the two *Kinsey Reports* by Alfred C. Kinsey, Wardell B. Pomeroy and Clyde E. Martin (1948).
10. By Arthur Miller (1947). The film came out in 1948.

Section 4

~ LETTERS ~

ALFRED MENDES WAS IN THE HABIT of writing to other writers whose work he admired, as with Countee Cullen. Where possible, he made contact and socialized with them, and the Jamaican Claude McKay, to whom he had written in praise of his novel *Banana Bottom* (1933) was one of the many writers in New York City with whom he partied. There are not sufficient letters from McKay to offer any huge insights into his work, but they do give some indication of his writing activities and interests during the mid- to late 1930s as well as those of Mendes, and I hope may be of interest to scholars looking at McKay's life.

I have included the two letters to C.L.R. James and Mendes from Hulbert Footner, a Canadian novelist and publisher's agent because of the influence which they exerted over both writers at the time. James did go on to write a novel, *Minty Alley*, and Mendes did take Footner's advice over incorrect details in his stories. James also used Footner's letter to Mendes as the basis for his own advice to Mendes about the latter's writing. Mendes seems to have adopted the advice which Footner gave to James about writing a ghost story in the words of a cook or nursemaid. Certainly "La Soucouyante" (*Pablo's Fandango*) is written along the lines which Footner recommends.[1] And Mendes was certainly encouraged by Footner's enthusiasm for "Triumph" to write more barrack-yard stories of his own.

The letters of James to Mendes are particularly important in defining the kind of relationship that existed between the two young writers at a crucially formative period in their careers. Although each gave the other generous credit for initiating and fostering the growth of West Indian literature in the early twentieth century, there seems to have been a period of alienation in mid-century, when James was heavily involved with Eric Williams's political party, the People's National Movement, in Trinidad. An interview James gave to Reinhard Sander[2] is permeated by a kind of weary bitterness, with an element of racism when James refers to Mendes and other *Beacon* writers. Mendes obtained a copy of the interview, and judging from the plethora of question and exclamation marks which dot the pages, he did not think too highly of his old friend's insights. It is reassuring to read what each said of the other in old age,[3] in the light of James's early letters to Mendes, which are full of delight in the things of the mind and the warmth of shared intellectual experiences. Mendes's second son Peter met James who was then an old man, at a book launch at John La Rose's New Beacon Book Shop in London. Peter Mendes told me that James talked to him of Mendes on that occasion with great gentleness and affection.

Unfortunately, as writing letters on a daily basis was their chief method of communication, few of Mendes's correspondents at that time bothered to date their letters. The only letter which James dated before he left for Great Britain in 1932 is the one of 15 December 1925, which means that I have had to rely on sometimes sketchy internal evidence to attempt a chronological arrangement. The letters written in Trinidad end around the time of the appearance of *Trinidad* 1, no. 1, in December 1929. Then apart from the letter written from London to Mendes in New York following the publication of *Minty Alley*, which is dated 4 June 1936, the remaining few letters were written while James himself was in New York City in 1938, involved in political activity. It is clear from the later letters that James's focus had shifted by then from literature to politics.

The Trinidad letters, though, are full of information about James's views on writing and the arts, including his admiration for Thomas Hardy and the great European novelists of the nineteenth century. When they are read in conjunction with Hulbert Footner's letters to Mendes and himself, a picture forms of nights of stimulating and vociferous argument, reading their works aloud to each other, and listening to music along with other members of their circle. The letter in which he asks Mendes to facilitate his borrowing of one hundred dollars to cover his Christmas obligations, is moving in its suggestion of struggle against straitened circumstances. It led to the landmark publication of *Trinidad* 1, no. 1, in December 1929, and *Trinidad* 1, no. 2, in April 1930.

NOTES

1. See the *Journal of West Indian Literature* 9, no. 2 (April 2001) for a reprint of James's ghost story "La Diablesse".
2. "Interview with C.L.R. James" in *Kas-Kas: Interviews with Three Caribbean Writers in Texas*, ed. Ian Munro and Reinhard Sander (Austin: University of Texas, African and Afro-American Research Institute, 1972).
3. See note 5 to the introduction of this volume.

LETTERS OF C.L.R. JAMES TO ALFRED MENDES

Letter 1

> Trinidad New College
> 67 Dundonald
> 15. 12. 25

Dear Mendes,

I return the two books I borrowed last evening. I have read those three short stories. They have a most life-like atmosphere – even in a translation. I did a good deal of miscellaneous reading in the *Dynasts* and it is, I can see, a work of noble scope and, like Hardy's prose works (I know little of his poetry) of very fine workmanship. Unfortunately I have neither the time nor the energy just yet to give a book like that the attention it deserves. Reading such a book is a landmark in one's literary life, and I would like to see a few days clear before me.

I send a volume of H.F.[1] Last night, speaking of great poetry, you used the expression – the verdict of posterity. I used to have much faith in it myself; but now I am not so sure. Read pp 94–99 and you will see why.

I shall be glad if you could lend to me for a day or two "The Outline of Art".[2] I shall enjoy looking at those pictures.

Thanking you for the first 'literary' evening I have had for many a long day, with kind regards.

> Yours faithfully
> C.L.R. James

Letter 2

Wednesday a.m.

Dear Mendes,

I send you Coppard[3] and *The Outline of Art*. I must really apologise for keeping the latter book for so long. By the way if you are interested in that sort of thing I may be able to get a book for you, Randall Davies's *Six Centuries of Painting*,[4] very beautifully illustrated in colour.

How do you like my sketch? It is rather annoying of me I admit, but I like to hear your opinion on what I have written. You know how isolated you can feel in this God-forsaken hole. I wrote a story last night by the way – about 2500 words – a rather ambitious psychological study. But a story. When it is type-written – the first draft – I shall annoy you with it. I send you the best of the Volumes of Tchekov. They take some reading. But they are extraordinarily good.

I must off to school.

Yours,
James

Letter 3

Dear Mendes,

I send symphony and 3 sonatas. They are for you and Carpenter[5] to work on. When both of you are quite satisfied we will hear them together and compare notes. Will you send by bearer *all catalogues and Prospectuses* dealing with the Gramophone, and *The Gramophone* edited by Compton Mackenzie. Without them I will not be able to send for the records. As you have finished with Turner's *Music And Life*[6] will you send it along also?

Yours
James

I find the piano concerto lovely; the violin concerto also. But not so much content in either of them.

Letter 4

Dear Mendes,

I have a headache this a.m. and as I have to go to Oval this p.m. I think it wiser to stay at home.

I went to D and J. yesterday. I got a book by Schnitzler[7] – one of the most famous of Austrian writers. How did you miss it? One gets in the habit of using superlatives, but this is a piece of work that has me astonished – knowledge of life and artistry combined to make a perfect whole.

I hope I will see you at cricket later.

I send the book. Persuade your wife to read it, or any young lady you know. Will you send Lawrence's[8] *Short Stories*?

Yrs
James

Letter 5

Dear Mendes,

I am sorry about *Rhapsody.*[9] A lady borrowed it, but I shall tell Gomes's messenger where to pass for it and I am sure he will get it.

I do not know what story Evans[10] means exactly except it is *The Hopeless Truth*[11] which is one I showed you long ago and you said you did not like. I have rewritten it. Or it may be Alicia[12] which I do not think you have seen in typescript, though I have read it to you. I send both. Mrs. Woods[13] has been jotting down suggestions. I sent Alicia to Breckmann (?)[14] months ago. On Feb. 10th I received an acknowledgement and have heard nothing from the man since. I have an idea that he is trying to sell it. If not I must have heard something by now.

I fancy Alicia very much by the way.

Yours,
James

I am looking at this very minute on the long story I told you about. I had put it aside for a fortnight as I felt very lazy. I have had no news of anything but I expect a bunch of news during the next month or so. Yesterday was three months since my barrack-yard story went to J.E.S.[15] If he sends it back I shall be very annoyed. He is not entitled to keep my story over 9 weeks in his office. After all, there is a limit to these things.

Letter 6

Dear Mendes,

I have put José in order; also *The Rise and Collapse*.[16] I have cut out a page or two of irrelevant matter in *The Rise and Collapse*. I shall send the two of them to Footner.

I send you *The Rise and Collapse*. Some time this evening – around 8 I shall come round. If you will be busy let me know. I know you are keen on doing as much work as possible during the week-end.

I read the preface to Sitwell's play.[17] I found it very interesting, but the play itself I only glanced at.

I am working on the child story.[18] I shall bring it this evening if I am done with it.

If you are busy with your writing, don't let me interrupt you, as I have already done what I wanted to do.

Yours,
James

Letter 7

Dear M,

I send you F's[19] letter.

I wrote C. [Canon] Farquhar this a.m. I told him of what had happened; and I also told him that you had sent your kind regards – a lie which I am sure both Providence and you will forgive me.

What an impertinent youth that Evans is! "If James and Mendes can, I can." Does he not realize the vast gulf which divides "practising authors" like ourselves and insignificant aspirers like him?

Yet I forgive him, as I am sure you will. For firstly but one short story divides us from him; and secondly the boy is full of brains – astonishingly developed for his age. I wish to goodness he would write something.

Yrs

James

Letter 8

Dear Mendes,

Enclosed is letter. I am wondering if all these offers of publishers about novels are of any real value. Maybe of no more than the lies of editors about always wanting short stories. H.F's[20] advice is sound. Of course in a way I knew it before. But it is good to have it stated so clearly and with such emphasis by a man of H.F.'s knowledge and experience. It is what in essence, I in my own way am always telling Carpenter. Now I am going to committ an impertinence. Here goes. The way I translate H.F.'s message for A.H.M. is this.

Stop choking your own ideas and vision of things with that incessant stream of modern novels. I do not think anything else but confusion lies that way. Read the classic writers and any modern novelists or poets or historians who really appeal. But I am convinced that for a young writer this incessant tapping into the fashions of the day is bad. I have read it and I know it. Men whose minds and principles, psychological approach and actual technique are definitely formed, can afford to do that sort of thing. These things do not affect them. But the growing or rather the mind not yet mature cannot afford it.

Amen.

Yrs

James

Letter 9

Dear Mendes,

Congratulations.

Was the glad news unexpected? I think it must have been. How did you survive the shock? Survive it you did because when I heard from Evans you were still alive.

I would come down this afternoon, but I've had a heavy dose of fever etc during the week-end and am very weak. But I shall pass your way at a little after 7. I cannot stay so I would be glad to see you – and if possible get the magazine[21] for to-night. I think that after your immediate family circle the privilege should be mine.

If anything will make me feel brighter this will.

I have no envelope nor anything, but I send this by your brother.

Yours,
James

Letter 10

Dear Mendes,

I have sent to your house
Chopin.
The Delight of Great Books[22]
Vol xiii Tchekov
Psychology Vol 5

Vol VI will appear in due course. I send you Turner's articles in *The New Statesman*.[23]

Somewhere about 6.30 this evening I shall pass for my ms. I have to give a final revision tonight as I post tomorrow.

I'll probably be down your way this afternoon at about 1. If you could manage to have them there (there are two lots) I'll be glad. You will understand how anxious I am to work on them.

I hope you and your wife and the small person are well.

Tell Carreia (?)[24] I send him my ~~sympathy~~ regards.

Not a sign of records yet. It's a hell of a big bunch, so I suppose that's why.

Yrs.
James

Letter 11

Thursday Evening

Dear Mendes,

I am awfully sorry to trouble you but I want your assistance in an important matter – strictly between us.[25]

I am in straits for money – rather desperate straits, because a man who promised to lend me some put me off to-day at the last minute. What I want you to do for me is to put me on to someone who will be able to lend me $100, at a reasonable rate of interest. I think that you know a few people who do a lot of that sort of business on the quiet. My endorser will be Mrs. Bell, my landlady. She has a house which is mortgaged but I don't suppose the average person wants a whole unencumbered house to lend $100.

Please understand this clearly.

I don't want you to lend me any money nor to put yourself under any obligation for me. Not half-a-dollar for half-a-day. You see, I know, however sound friendship may be, the sense of money obligations will at once alter the relationship. It certainly will in my case.

But if you can introduce me to anyone and say "I know Mr. James. He is a master at the College etc etc" I shall be very greatful [*sic*]. It is Xmas time and although I don't care a straw about that, yet I have certain obligations around me to fulfil and people who are looking to me to fulfill [*sic*] them at this time and the idea that I wouldn't be able to is enough to make me feel to committ suicide. Believe me, it is only when I learnt of the disappointment this afternoon and had considered the matter that I reluctantly decided to send to you. I thought of coming, but wrote instead.

I shall see you in the morning.

Yrs James

Please read the letter carefully. The handwriting is hurried, but I have thought very carefully over what I have written.

Letter 12

My Dear Mendes,

Just a hurried note. I shall come for you to go to Greaves's[26] house about 1. It must be early because I know he has an engagement for later in the afternoon.

Silva[27] sings for H.M.V. and is in the English catalogue among Schipa[28] and Co. – Red Seal.[29] I'll bring it.

Letter 13

> 9, Heathcote Street,
> Gray's Inn Road,
> W.C.I.
>
> 4th June, 1936.

Dear Mendes,

Thanks for your note, and the kind cable that you and Toni[30] sent.

I was able to read your second book. I have not yet seen the first. The atmosphere of "Black Fauns" a friend and I thought good, but the book as a whole lacked a strong central drive. I have a belief that barring the extraordinary power of Joyce and people like that, some sort of plot, physical or spiritual, some sort of purpose is necessary. I may be wrong.

The play[31] I have re-written and there are people in New York who have copies and will tell me some time whether they want it. The reception here was mixed. The audience could not have been better; the "Times" and "Observer", Charles Morgan and Ivor Brown liked it, Ivor Brown being quite enthusiastic. The "Sunday Times" and one or two others abused it unmercifully. They can go to hell. I have used some of their suggestions and now it is quite allright. "2A, Minty Alley" will be published in the autumn by Martin Secker.[32]

I am almost entirely absorbed in politics nowadays. I have adopted the Marxist philosophy and am devoting myself to helping the advance of the international revolution. I believe that the official Communist Party, led by Stalin, is the greatest danger to the working-class movement. I am writing a book, which a publisher has commissioned – "The Decline and Fall of the Communist International".[33] I am also commissioned to write a book on the Revolution in

San Domingo and Toussaint Louverture,34 so you will understand I have plenty to do.

Let me hear from you again, although I am afraid my interests are now almost entirely political.

Yours as ever,
James

Did you make any money by the books? And how is your son getting on?

Letter 14

Oct. 31, 1938
125 W. 121
Mo. 2 – 1384

432 Fourth Ave.

Dear Mendes,

Heard of your whereabouts thro' Harold Jackman.35 Will you drop in to the above on next Monday evening? There will be people here. Meanwhile you could ring me and you, Jackman and I could lunch. I am looking forward to seeing you.

C.L.R.J.

Letter 15

WESTERN UNION

Received at: 11 WEST PARK AVE. LONG BEACH, N.Y.   NOV. 12 PM 4. 15

NT74 13=NEWYORK NY 12 400P
MENDES=
414 EAST OLIVE ST LB=

TONIGHT IMPORTANT LITERARY PARTY DOCTOR PAUL LUTTINGER36
5 WASHINGTON SQUARE NORTH PLEASE COME=
       JAMES.

Letter 16

My dear Mendes,

I expect the party[37] has notified you of the meeting. But in case not I send you these two complimentary tickets. I have a copy of *Minty Allen* [*sic*] which I could lend you also for a few days. I am sending to England for some and will then be able to give you one.

Now I am speaking at meetings in the intervals of preparing for the lecture on Nov 30. It is my first here and it takes up every moment of my time. When it is over we shall meet.

My regards to the carpenter[38] and your folks.

> Yrs
> James

Letter 17

> 125 W. 121
> M. y.

My dear Mendes,

I shall come – you willing – on Saturday a.m. sometime and shall be glad to stay until Sunday at about 8. I am speaking in Harlem on Sunday evening.

Carpenter goes to hear a recital on Saturday. He would like to come by the 5.21; says he must be met. I shall come any time you fix.

We shall then discuss the war[39] and many other questions.

> as Ever.
> J.

NOTES

1. Hulbert Footner? William Hulbert Footner (1879–1944) was a Canadian writer of non-fiction and detective novels, who visited Trinidad in 1928. His letters to Mendes and to C.L.R. James appear in this volume.

2. Edited by Sir William Orpen (1923).

3. A.E. (Alfred Edgar) Coppard (1878–1957), a British writer of poems and short stories.

4. 1914.

5. Henry McDonnell Carpenter, violinist, and friend of James and Mendes. A member of the *Beacon* group.

6. By W.J. (Walter James) Turner (1921).

7. Arthur Schnitzler (1862–1931), dramatist and novelist.

8. D.H. (David Herbert) Lawrence (1885–1930).

9. Possibly George Gershwin's "Rhapsody in Blue" (1924).

10. F.V.S. Evans, friend and fellow member of the *Beacon* group.

11. A "lost" story?

12. The timing of this letter, coupled with James's enthusiasm for his story, suggests that "Alicia" may refer to "La Divina Pastora", which was the first West Indian short story to be published in England (by the *Saturday Review*, 1927). If so, James changed the name of his protagonist to Anita for publication.

13. I have not been able to place Mrs Woods. Perhaps a family friend?

14. Possibly a publisher's agent.

15. Another publisher's agent?

16. See Hulbert Footner's letter to James, n2, this volume. These stories have not been discovered, as far as I can ascertain.

17. Possibly *Façade* by Edith Sitwell, a collection of verses written in collaboration with the composer William Walton as an entertainment for voice and orchestra (1922; performed before an audience in 1923).

18. C.L.R. James, "The Star That Would Not Shine", *Beacon* 1, no. 3 (1931): 15–17.

19. Hulbert Footner.

20. Hulbert Footner.

21. It seems clear that James is referring to "Lai John", a short story which Mendes wrote with Algernon "Pope" Wharton, which was published in the *London Mercury* of January 1929. A local publication would hardly have generated such excitement. "Lai John" was Mendes's first "foreign" publication.

22. By John Erskine (1928).

23. W.J. Turner was music critic for the *New Statesman*.

24. Unidentified.

25. I take this letter to be the genesis of *Trinidad*, Mendes's and James's joint publication, which came out in two issues in December 1929 and April 1930 (editor).

26. Unidentified.

27. Herminia Silva (1907–93), a celebrated Portuguese Fado singer.

28. Tito Schipa (1889–1965), Italian opera singer.

29. The Victor (later RCA Victor) Red Seal label was reserved for the finest classical artists of the time.

30. Jean "Toni" de Boissiére, who was in New York City at this time (Mendes, *Autobiography* 120–22).

31. "Toussaint L'Ouverture" (1936). (Published as *Toussaint Louverture: The Story of the Only Successful Slave Revolt in History; A Play in Three Acts*, ed. Christian Høgsbjerg [Durham, NC: Duke University Press, 2012].)

32. The novel was published as *Minty Alley* (London: Secker and Warburg, 1936).

33. 1937.

34. *The Black Jacobins: Toussaint L'Ouverture and the San Domingo Revolution* (New York: Dial Press, 1938).

35. Harold Jackman (1901–61) was a central figure of the Harlem Renaissance. He was a close friend of Countee Cullen, and edited *New Challenge* with Dorothy West in 1937.

36. A bacteriologist and researcher, with a strong interest in politics and the arts.

37. The American Communist Party.

38. Their mutual friend Henry McDonnell Carpenter.

39. The Spanish Civil War, 1936–39.

LETTERS OF CLAUDE McKAY TO ALFRED MENDES

Letter 1

December 12

Apartado 27
Correo Español
Tanger, Morocco

Dear Mr. Mendez [*sic*]

It was a pleasure, of course, to have your letter praising "Banana Bottom". It has been liked generally by thoughtful people and was favourably received by the Press, but the public did not support it. It was published at a bad time too.

I suppose your forthcoming book[1] is also about West Indian life. I shall be very interested to read it. I consider the West Indies a fine field for fiction, both historical and contemporary realism – plenty of ground for exploration and experimentation.

I am sending this letter through Mr. Trounstine[2] who writes that you are in New York. Forgive me not writing before. I have been very much occupied with pot-boiling work and under the anxiety my health has not been so very good.

My best regards
Sincerely
Claude McKay

Letter 2

April 25

> 168 West 135th Str
> New York City

Dear Alfred Mendes,

Thanks for your note and invitation, but I am afraid we can't get together this week – for it is half gone and I am dated up for Friday and Saturday. What about next Wednesday? That gives enough time for exchanging letters and I am free then.

> Cordially
>
> Claude McKay

Letter 3

April 30

> 168 West 135th Str
> New York City

Dear Alfred Mendez [*sic*]

I regret that I cannot keep our engagement for next Wednesday evening. I am booked for a date over May Day that takes in Wednesday also. Later we may be able to get together.

> Faithfully
> Claude McKay

Letter 4

Nov. 6   183 5–7th Ave
                                        1935 New York City

Dear Mendez [*sic*]

I gave your novel[3] to Harold Jackman who read and liked it – now Dorothy[4] has it – she said you told her to take it to read. I didn't get round to it because I am up to my neck rushing through work on my novel[5] for my agent who must have so many pages for a publisher by the end of this month.

                        Hope I see you soon.

                        Sincerely,
                        Claude McKay

Letter 5

May 18   205 West 115th St
1936   New York City

Dear Mendez [*sic*]: I have just discovered your address after asking Countee to write to tell you about Esther Hyman Chapman, the editor of The West Indian Review[6] in Kingston, Ja.

She was here to see me last week. She has read your books and specially likes the last and wants to meet you. Her address is 35 West 82nd St Apt. 3C Tel: Trafalgar 7–7730. You know she wrote a book about Jamaica mulatto life, called Study in Bronze.

Why don't you drop in some time. I wonder are you still in Long Island. Anyway I am sending this letter there. I am finishing at last the final pages of my book and hope soon I shall be free to see more friends and oftener.

                        Sincerely
                        Claude McKay

P.S. Couldn't you send us about two typewritten pages of your impressions of a party in Harlem or of a party downtown with Harlemites.

Letter 6

The African
JOURNAL OF AFRICAN AFFAIRS   10 WEST 117TH STREET NEW YORK, N.Y.
ORGAN OF UNIVERSAL ETHIOPIAN   Telephone: Monument 2—5992
STUDENTS ASS'N   May 28, 1938

Mr. Alfred Mendes
414 E. Olive Street
Long Beach, New York

Dear Mendes:

I was glad to hear from you again. A few times I wanted to ask you over but could not locate you. It is good to see you enthusiastic over the idea of a good group magazine; it is up to you to help make it worthwhile.

Countee and I and two or three more persons read White Man's Magic. It opens with good dialogue. But after the first two pages it doesn't seem to get anywhere, the talk becomes monotonous and it just peters out. I'm sure you can find something with more plot to it and yet peppery for us.

I may hold it till you come over, or if you need it in a hurry, I can mail it.

We had a nice meeting of a few of us last night. Hope we will soon get together.

Yours sincerely,
Claude McKay

P.S. Couldn't you send us about two typewritten pages of your impressions of a party in Harlem or of a party downtown with Harlemites.

NOTES

1. *Pitch Lake* (London: Gerald Duckworth, 1934).

2. John Trounstine was a publisher's agent in New York City, where Mendes had been living since November 1933.

3. Probably *Black Fauns* (London: Gerald Duckworth, 1935).

4. Dorothy West. She and Mendes had a brief affair 1934–35 (Mendes, *Autobiography*, 92–93).

5. This may be a reference to *Romance in Marseille*, published posthumously in 2008.

6. Esther Chapman subsequently published five of Mendes's stories in *West Indian Review*: "The Man Who Ran Away" in 2, no. 11 (July 1936); "Lulu Gets Married" in 3, no. 4 (December 1936) and 3, no. 5 (January 1937); and three chapters from *Black Fauns*: "Miriam" in 3, no. 6 (February 1937); "White Man's Magic" in 3, no. 7 (March 1937); and "Ethelrida and Some Others" in 3, no. 9 (1937).

LETTERS OF HULBERT FOOTNER TO C.L.R. JAMES AND ALFRED H. MENDES

Letter 1

Lusby, Maryland
U.S.A.

June 11th 1928

My dear James,

We have just got home, and utter confusion prevails. To make matters worse, it is raining heavily, an all-day affair, keeping the four children indoors under the feet of the work-women, scrub-women, carpenters etc. It is like chaos and old night.[1] I have been put out of my room bodily while it is cleaned.

I cannot write intelligently at such a moment. This is merely a bulletin to announce that I left the first four stories with Mr. Thomas Wells, editor of Harpers, on my way through New York, and I found your letter waiting for me here with 3 stories[2] enclosed, which I have read. I like the unnamed story very much indeed; it is thoroughly immoral, and delightful. What a magazine editor will say to it, I don't know. It is a bad length for a magazine. I adjure you to write a novel.

As to the Prescott story (and the same applies to all the stories in that genre) I respect the matter-of-fact method you have hit out for such tales; it is very clever, but personally the stories leave me cold. I would like to see them dramatized a little more. That is my idiosyncrazy (can't spell that word!) You must take this advice with reserve, especially as it was a story of that sort which won O'Brien's[3] notice. The child story is all right. I commend your observation, but I don't care much for the story because I hate to see little children exploited by their elders, made to do tricks and so on. Another idiosyncrazy.

I read the barrack-yard story to myself on ship-board, fearful that I might have been a little carried away by the *viva voce* rendering. But not at all. It afforded me a complete artistic pleasure. In that field I am sure lies your best material. At least for the present. After you have arrived you may write what you please. In the barrack-yard you are unique and unrivalled. Consider what an advantage that gives you. The barrack-yard is all your own artistically.

If you write another tale of superstition try it in the *words* of your cook or nursemaid and see if it is not more exciting. It will be much more difficult, but that is good for you!

Our association gives me a lot of pleasure. Having mismanaged my own artistic career, I have a passion for warning others. But you must not always take my advice, only examine it.

Ever sincerely

Hulbert Footner

P.S. Do not neglect to write Squire[4] about the barrack-yard story.

Letter 2

Lusby, Maryland
U.S.A.

June 11th [1928]

My dear Mendes,

I have received the two stories, and I congratulate you on your labors. They seem to me to be very good indeed; they always had good ideas, and now I think they have real quality. Do not however allow this to raise your hopes too high. These are good stories, I am willing to bank on it, but as to how an editor will react to their slightly exotic flavor (which I find delightful) I'm sure I don't know. I am cynical in respect to editors. They have reasons for turning down stories which would never occur to anybody – but an editor.

I have ventured to make two trifling alterations. "Slushy" with us always means snow, which is slightly out of place in Trinidad. And a drizzle never "patters", in fact it makes no sound at all.[5]

I do not think your titles are good enough for the stories. Alas! these titles. How I have agonized over my own! "Coals of Fire"[6] will never do; too hackneyed. "A Day of Sorrow" is not so bad, but I think you could do better. Would you be willing to use a title which suggested the idea of the story? It would help with stupid people. How about "Compassion"? "The Funeral" would be all right, lacking something better. There is a lovely gaunt landscape by Manet called "The Funeral". I have been racking my poor brains for suggestions for the other, but nothing comes except "Heat Lightning" which is not good enough.

Meanwhile be thinking about a novel. "Coals of Fire" contains the germs of a novel. The author takes full responsibility for a book, and nobody seeks to interfere with him.

I will be sending these stories around.

We have just returned to our home; the house is full of work-women, scrub-women, carpenters etc., and to add to our difficulties it is pouring rain. I will be able to write to more advantage at another time. It gives me great pleasure to think over our talks in Trinidad.

Ever sincerely
Hulbert Footner

NOTES

1. From Milton's *Paradise Lost*, bk. 1, 543.

2. In all, James sent seven stories to Footner: "José" and "The Rise and Collapse", the unnamed story, the Prescott story, and the three known to have been published. The "child story" is "The Star That Would Not Shine"; the barrack-yard story is "Triumph"; and the tale of superstition is "La Diablesse".

3. Edward J. O'Brien edited *Best Short Stories of 1929*, which listed James's "Triumph" (and Mendes's "Her Chinaman's Way") as among the best short stories of that year.

4. J.C. Squire was editor of the *London Mercury*.

5. "A Day of Sorrow" takes place against a back-cloth of rain. Mendes seems to have put Footner's suggested corrections into place.
6. No typescript for "Coals of Fire" has so far turned up, and Footner's suggestion for "Heat Lightning" as an improvement on the title gives no clue as to the subject-matter.

GLOSSARY OF TRINIDADIAN WORDS AND PHRASES

agouti Forest-dwelling rodent, rabbit-like and fleet of foot; hunted for its meat

ain', aint I ain' tired tell: I'm tired of telling; you ain' name man: No one can

balata A large evergreen tree used for timber, which bears a small edible fruit; bullet-wood

barrack-yard Tenement consisting of two rows of wooden buildings facing each other across a communal yard-space used for cooking and washing clothes

barrack-yarder One who lives in a barrack-yard

behind God's back Somewhere remote, far from towns and people

belaire, bèlè A folk-dance performed by women; a topical song (French *bel air*, of fine appearance)

bois Stick used by a stick fighter (French: wood)

bongo A dance of African origin performed to drumming especially by men, at wakes in honour of the dead

buckra A white person; person of authority

burroquite Burrokeet, a Carnival character dressed to resemble a woman on a donkey (Spanish *burriquito*, little donkey)

bus' Bust, break up, are destroyed

cacao Cocoa, either the tree which bears the pods, or the product, which is used to make chocolate

calenda, calinda A dance of African origin, performed to drumming and with chants, which accompanied stick-fighting

callaloo Soup made from dasheen leaves and coconut milk, which may include okras, dumplings and salt beef, and especially crab; the term is used by extension to mean a mixture of different ingredients

calypso A popular satirical song aimed at recognizable people or situations, and providing social commentary

calypso tent The venue for calypsonians preparing songs for Carnival; originally a structure made of bamboo

canboulay, cannes bruilles, cannes brûlées A procession with torches that marked the beginning of Carnival; derived from the custom of burning fields of sugar cane before harvest (French *cannes brûlées*, burnt canes)

capra Length of cloth used by East Indians in Trinidad to form garments

Carnival Huge annual street festival held in Trinidad during the last four days before Ash Wednesday, consisting of competing costumed bands and calypso singing, with road marches and street dancing (Latin *caro, carnis*, flesh, and *levare*, to take away, thus: remove the meat)

carry Carrying place; a portage between navigable rivers or channels (United States and Canada)

chansonnier Song writer (French)

chuck A jab or blow; as verb, to give same

confrère A fellow member of a profession or scientific body (French)

coolie Person of East Indian extraction. Though the term did not originally carry a stigma, it is now considered offensive

copra Dried kernels of coconut

crapeau Possibly a corruption of Venezuelan *carapo*, crabwood (Latin *carapa guianensis*), a semi-evergreen tree of 25–35 metres or higher; the wood is used in joinery and construction

cream Ice cream

Dame Loraine Carnival character, a man dressed as a woman with large bosoms and posterior, who danced with exaggerated vulgarity

devil Carnival character, a man dressed as the devil with mask and trident, who dances with bold, threatening gestures

doctor Carnival character, a man dressed as an old-fashioned doctor, with top hat and tail coat

dry goods store Shop selling cloth and articles of clothing

dwens Characters in Trinidadian folklore: a dwen or douen is the spirit of a child who died before baptism; it wears a large floppy hat, utters a soft hooting cry, and is instantly recognizable by its feet, which are pointed backwards

eat am Eat: the suffix "am" adds no meaning to the verb; it is used to help distinguish the speech of the East Indian labourer from that of the other creoles in "Gold Beans"

estate-side Into, or on the estate

fanega Measure of weight for cocoa and coffee beans, the equivalent of 110 pounds.

flamboyant Delonix regia or Poinciana, tall, spreading ornamental tree with masses of deep vermillion blossoms in June–August

frangipani Tree with fragrant star-shaped flowers of white, pink or red

hunh Opening word, approximate to "well", "so", "um" which distinguishes the speech of the East Indian labourer in "Gold Beans"

immortelle A tall shade tree with a thorny trunk and bright red or yellow blooms, used in Trinidad to shade the cocoa

jes' now Soon, shortly

jouvert The beginning of Carnival celebrations before dawn on the Monday before Ash Wednesday, with street dancing to steel bands, and costumed figures from folklore (French *jour ouvert*, daybreak)

Ju-Ju Warriors A traditional Carnival masquerade depicting spear- carrying African warriors

keskidee Bird of the family of Tyrant Flycatchers named for its cry of "Qu'est-ce qu'il dit?" (French: "What is he saying?")

lappe Large forest-dwelling rodent resembling a guinea-pig in appearance, brownish with white spots on its sides; originally hunted for its meat, but now protected by law

limbo A dance in which the dancer must bend backwards to pass under a stick held horizontally; the dancer's skill is determined by how low he or she is able to go

Macumba A belief system practised by the Bantu peoples of the Congo region and transported by slaves to the New World, especially to Brazil – the practitioners are traditionally wise women, herbalists, who use their knowledge and skills to help those who seek their aid; a folk-dance of Brazil

mammy apple Large fruit with firm yellow flesh around a hard seed, and a tough, reddish-brown skin

massala A mixture of spices, including coriander, cumin and turmeric, ground together on a flat massala stone to make a curry seasoning

merino A man's sleeveless white cotton undershirt or vest

mocojumby Male Carnival character dressed in rags, who dances on stilts which have been painted with stripes

morbleu A butterfly, the Cocoa Mort Bleu or Morbleu, Caligo teucer insulanus, which belongs to a South and Central American species; in Trinidad, it is often found in cocoa estates, hence the name.

ner Interrogatory word taking its meaning from the immediate context: "Whoa with, ner?", "who with, then?" (pronunciation peculiar to Barbados)

oranee, orhani, ohrni Veil or scarf draped over the head and allowed to hang down to the shoulders; worn by East Indian women

parang A Christmas custom originating in Venezuela: groups of musicians go from house to house singing religious songs, both traditional and improvised, in Trinidadian Spanish dialect (often traditional Spanish folk-dancing is included); when used as a verb, the word indicates performance of the above

parlour A small grocery shop selling cigarettes, snacks and non-alcoholic drinks

peame, paime, paimie, pémi A pudding made from ground or grated corn mixed with grated pumpkin and coconut, raisins and sugar, moistened with water and formed into parcels, wrapped in banana leaves, and steamed until cooked

pélau Traditional Trinidadian dish made with chicken, pigeon peas and rice, cooked with coconut milk and seasonings

Potegee Portuguese

poui A decorative shade tree flowering annually with masses of yellow or pink blossoms

provision Onions and potatoes

purpleheart Tall forest tree with dark purple wood used in building and to make furniture

roti Indian unleavened bread made of flour, salt, and water, served with or used to wrap curry

sabby Know (Spanish *usted sabe*, you know)

sapodilla Brown-skinned tropical fruit with sweet, sometimes gritty pulp and shiny black seeds; naseberry

The Savannah The Queen's Park Savannah in Port of Spain, Trinidad, a large park of about 232 acres known as "the lungs of Port of Spain"

Shango A Yoruba deity, god of thunder and lightning; the worship of the god celebrated with drumming, dancing and chanting, and animal sacrifice

Shouters Baptist sect characterized by loud shouting of prayers and praises

soul-case The body

spree Party (noun and verb)

stick-fighting Ritual combat between two men using sticks or "bois", and accompanied by calinda dancing and chanting

storeside At the store

sweetman Man supported financially by a woman in return for sexual favours

talcari Curry, usually of vegetables

tarantula Large black hairy spider with poisonous bite

ten cents worth of God help us Derogatory phrase which mocks the diminutive stature of the Chinese shopkeeper in "A Little Cargo"

Voodoo Polytheistic organized religion of coastal West Africa from Nigeria to Ghana, and Haiti; worship includes the use of talismans or fetishes, songs, rituals and animal sacrifices

wutless Worthless

BIBLIOGRAPHY

Works by Alfred H. Mendes

The Autobiography of Alfred H. Mendes. Edited by Michèle Levy. Kingston: University of the West Indies Press, 2002.

Black Fauns. London: Gerald Duckworth, 1935. Reprint, Millwood, NY: Kraus Reprints, 1970; London and Port of Spain: New Beacon Books, 1984.

The Man Who Ran Away and Other Stories of Trinidad in the 1920s and 1930s. Edited by Michèle Levy. Kingston: University of the West Indies Press, 2006.

Pablo's Fandango and Other Stories. Edited by Michèle Levy. London: Addison, Wesley and Longman, 1997.

Pitch Lake. London: Gerald Duckworth, 1934. Reprint, Millwood, NY: Kraus Reprints, 1970; London and Port of Spain: New Beacon Books, 1980.

The Poet's Quest. London: Heath Cranton, 1927.

Spare Moments. Port of Spain: Spack Printing Office, 1924.

Three Poems. Port of Spain: N.p., 1924.

The Wages of Sin and Other Poems. Port of Spain: Yuille's Printerie, 1925.

Secondary Sources

Ahye, Molly. *Cradle of Caribbean Dance. Beryl McBurnie and the Little Carib Theatre*. Port of Spain: Heritage Cultures, 1983.

Allsopp, Richard. *Dictionary of Caribbean English Usage*. Oxford: Oxford University Press, 1996.

Anthony, Michael. *The Making of Port-of-Spain*, vol. 1, *The History of Port-of-Spain, 1757–1939*. Cascade, Trinidad: Paria, 2007.

———. *The Making of Port-of-Spain*, vol. 2, *Port-of-Spain in a World at War, 1939–1945*. Cascade, Trinidad: Paria, 2008.

Baptiste, Rhona. *Trini Talk: A Dictionary of Words and Proverbs of Trinidad and Tobago.* Port of Spain: Caribbean Information Systems and Services, 1994.

Brereton, Bridget. *A History of Modern Trinidad 1783–1962.* Oxford: Heinemann International, 1989.

Mendes, John. *Cote ce, Cote la: Trinidad and Tobago Dictionary.* Arima, Trinidad: N.p., 1986.

Sander, Reinhard W., ed. *From Trinidad with Love: An Anthology of Early West Indian Writing.* London: Hodder and Stoughton; New York: Holmes and Meier, 1978.

———. *The Trinidad Awakening: West Indian Literature of the 1930s.* Westport, CT: Greenwood Press, 1988.

Stiling, P.D. *Butterflies and other Insects of the Eastern Caribbean.* London: Macmillan Education, 1986.

Winer, Lise. *Dictionary of the English Creole of Trinidad and Tobago.* Montreal: McGill-Queen's University Press, 2009.